VEHICULAR AD HOC NETWORK SECURITY AND PRIVACY

VEHICULAR AD HOC NETWORK SECURITY AND PRIVACY

Xiaodong Lin
Rongxing Lu

IEEE Press Series on
Information & Communication
Networks Security
Stamatios Kartalopoulos, Series Editor

IEEE PRESS

For general information on our other products and services or for technical support, please contact our
Customer Care Department within the United States at (800) 762-2974, outside the United States at
(317) 572-3993 or fax (317) 572-4002.

Wiley also publishes its books in a variety of electronic formats. Some content that appears in print may not
be available in electronic formats. For more information about Wiley products, visit our web site at
www.wiley.com.

Library of Congress Cataloging-in-Publication Data is available.

ISBN: 978-1-118-91390-1

Printed in the United States of America.

10 9 8 7 6 5 4 3 2 1

CONTENTS

LIST OF FIGURES

LIST OF TABLES

ACRONYMS

ABS	Antilock braking system
AES	Advanced Encryption Standard
AP	Access point; augmented packet
ASS	Anonymity set size
ATM	Automated teller machine
BLS	Boneh–Lynn–Shacham
CA	Certificate authority
CRL	Certificate revocation list
CRS	Certificate revocation system
CRT	Certificate revocation tree
CWBS	Collision warning with brake support
DoS	Denial of service
DRP	Distributed Revocation Protocol
DSA	Digital signature algorithm
DSRC	Dedicated short-range communication
EBL	Extended brake light
ECC	Elliptic curve cryptography
ECDSA	Elliptic curve digital signature algorithm
ECIES	Elliptic curve integrated encryption scheme
EMS	Emergency medical services
EMSS	Efficient multichained stream signature
ETC	Electronic toll collection
FCC	Federal Communications Commission
GPRS	General packet radio service
GPS	Global Positioning System
HIPAA	Health Insurance Portability and Accountability Act (of 1996)
IBC	Identity-based cryptography
ITS	Intelligent transportation systems
IVC	Intervehicle communication
KPSD	Key-insulated pseudonym self-delegation
LPR	License plate recognition
MAC	Message authentication code
MANET	Mobile ad hoc network
MM	Membership manager
MTO	Ministry of Transportation
OBU	Onboard unit
OCSP	Online Certificate Status Protocol
PCS	Pseudonyms changing at social spots

PD	Packet delay
PKI	Public key infrastructure
PLR	Packet loss ratio
QoP	Quality of privacy
RC2RL	Revocation using Compressed Certificate Revocation Lists
RFID	Radiofrequency identification
RL	Revocation list
RSU	Roadside unit
RTPD	Revocation of the Tamper-Proof Device
RVC	Roadside-to-vehicle (or RSU-to-vehicle) communication
SER	secure emergency report
SeVeCom	Secure vehicular communication
SUV	Sport utility vehicle
TA	Trusted authority
TCP	Transmission Control Protocol
TESLA	Timed efficient stream loss-tolerant authentication
TIGER	Topologically integrated geographic encoding and referencing
TLS	Transport layer security
TM	Tracing manager
TPD	Tamperproof device
TRC	Transportation regulation center
TTL	Time to live
USDOT	United States Department of Transportation
V2I	Vehicle-to-infrastructure
V2V	Vehicle-to-vehicle
VANET	Vehicular ad hoc network
VIN	Vehicle identification number
VLR	Verifier-local revocation
VSC	Vehicle safety communications
VSCC	Vehicle Safety Communications (VSC) Consortium
VSS	V2X Security Subsystem
WAVE	Wireless access in vehicular environment

PREFACE

Road safety has been drawing increasing public attention, and there has been extensive effort in both industry and academia to mitigate the impact of traffic accidents. Recent advances in wireless technology bring promising new ways to facilitate road safety and traffic management, in which each vehicle, equipped with wireless communication devices [referred to as *onboard units* (OBUs)], is allowed to communicate with vehicles, other as well as with *roadside units* (RSUs), which are located at critical sections of the road, such as traffic lights and stop signs.

With OBUs and RSUs, a self-organized network called a *vehicular ad hoc network* (VANET) can be formed. Recently, this has emerged as a promising approach toward increasing road safety and efficiency, as well as improving driving experience. These goals will be accomplished through a wide variety of vehicle applications enabled by communication between vehicles, such as emergency braking warning. While society experiences tremendous benefits from adopting the new technologies, we also continue to face challenges; the biggest challenge is always how to address security and privacy issues that may be caused by the adoption of a new technology. The attractive features of VANETs will inevitably incur higher risks for abuse, if we do not take security and privacy issues into consideration before the wide deployment of such networks.

Being a special implementation of wireless ad hoc networks or *mobile ad hoc networks* (MANETs), a VANET has many unique features and applications. First, the connectivity among nodes (vehicles and RSUs) can often be highly transient and a one-time event; two vehicles may remain within their transmission ranges, or within a few wireless hops, for only a very limited period of time. As a result, vehicular network topology is highly dynamic. Further, a VANET is a huge network, which can potentially consist of millions of nodes (on-road vehicles and RSUs). Such size makes it very challenging to guarantee security and privacy in VANETs, particularly regarding message authenticity and integrity, as well as protecting user-related privacy information, such as the driver's name and the car's license plate, model, and traveling route. Unfortunately, existing studies on (and solutions for) communication security and privacy preservation cannot work effectively in VANETs, since they do not take the scalability and communication overhead into consideration. Message authentication is a common tool for ensuring information reliability, but it faces a challenge in VANETs. Particularly when a vehicle receives a large number of messages, traditional authentication mechanisms may generate unaffordable computational overhead on the vehicles, and bring unacceptable delay to time-critical applications (e.g., accident warning). Another challenge is the privacy concerns of vehicular communication, where the identity, position, and movement track of a specific vehicle should not be obtained by an unauthorized third party. We will refer to the combined concepts of message authenticity and privacy as *anonymous message authentication*.

In this book, we focus on message authentication and privacy issues in VANETs. We first provide an overview of security and privacy issues in VANETs, as well as the challenges facing VANETs in addressing these issues.

Chapter 2 identifies the unique security and privacy requirements of communications between different types of communication devices, including OBUs and RSUs in VANETs. We determined the most suitable cryptographic primitives and designed a secure and privacy-preserving protocol, which utilizes a combination of group signature and identity (ID)-based signature techniques to addresses these unique security and privacy requirements for vehicular communications.

Chapter 3 further exploits the unique challenges in privacy-preserving VANETs, i.e., how to efficiently deal with the growing revocation list while achieving conditional traceability. Based on the on-the-fly short-term anonymous key generation between OBUs and RSUs, we proposed an efficient conditional privacy preservation protocol, which is characterized by providing the conditional privacy preservation, improving efficiency in terms of the minimized anonymous key storage at each OBU and fast verification on safety messages.

Chapter 4 discusses the pseudonym changing strategy for location privacy in VANETs, as even though an OBU holds a large number of pseudonyms in VANETs, if the pseudonym does not change at the right time and right place, location privacy could still be violated. To enable vehicles to achieve high-level location privacy, we proposed an efficient *pseudonym changing at social spots* (PCS) strategy, where the social spots are the places where many vehicles temporarily gather.

Afterward, we take a cooperative approach toward addressing the technology's challenges of complex anonymous message authentication. Cooperation on anonymous message authentication in VANETs can be defined as vehicles and RSUs working together to ensure the integrity of messages received by each individually, as well as verifying that messages are indeed from legitimate users. Cooperation can take many forms and occur in many ways in VANETs, for example, either between vehicles and RSUs, or only among vehicles. Cooperation can also occur in many different ways, based on the roles of vehicles and RSUs in groups. For example, the resource-rich RSUs are usually seen as trusted entities in VANETs, since RSUs are usually deployed by governments or service providers, and their locations are fixed. As a result, a straightforward approach for message authentication in VANETs is to leverage the vast resources of RSUs and take advantage of their fixed locations. RSUs can be used to assist vehicles to authenticate messages received by the vehicles, largely by allowing resource-rich and trustworthy RSUs take the lead processing role in message authentication. In the case of cooperation only among vehicles, which will be very common in the early stages of VANET adoption (due to a lack of RSUs), each vehicle can probabilistically validate a certain percentage of its received messages in accordance with its own computing capacity, and report any invalid message detected. When work all units together, redundant effort in message authentication and verification can be minimized, if not entirely eliminated. Further, cooperation can occur by taking into consideration the context of messages transmitted over the vehicular networks. For example, of all vehicle communication network applications, dissemination of emergency messages to the vehicles in a specific area is one of the most crucial. The fast propagation of emergency and local warning messages to the approaching vehicles will be helpful for preventing secondary accidents, especially in conditions where visibility is impeded, such as fog. In most cases, a VANET performs such an emergency message propagation in a multihop transmission manner, particularly in the suburban areas where fewer RSUs are installed. Given any emergency, it is expected that multiple sensing vehicles in the area could detect the same common event, and therefore, taking advantage of this property to cross-validate the emergency event could possibly serve as a promising approach toward enhancing the overall security level of VANETs. Such a method of cross-checking the emergency event by collecting the feedback of witnesses is defined as a voting mechanism, which was originally used to detect the misbehaving nodes in a distributed ad hoc network without any centralized security authority. This kind of cooperation is often applied to deal with special types of messages, such as emergency messages, and the mechanism can be migrated to VANETs to enhance the overall security of emergency events authentication.

We classify cooperative authentication mechanisms in VANETs into four categories: RSU-aided authentication (Chapter 5), TESLA-based authentication (Chapter 6), distributed cooperative authentication (Chapter 7), and context-aware cooperative authentication (Chapter 8). For each category, we introduce a corresponding protocol for message authentication, and will also analyze security, efficiency, and effectiveness of these proposed cooperative authentication protocols. Both theoretical analysis and simulation results show that cooperative authentication is a promising and effective way to achieve secure message authentication for vehicular communications.

Because of the movement of the vehicles, the vehicles can roam among RSUs deployed along the roadsides. The final chapter looks into the challenges in realizing seamless mobility in VANETs. By considering some intrinsic features of vehicular communication networking, such as predictable vehicle movement, we introduce a seamless authentication scheme based on mobility prediction to achieve fast authentication and reduce the authentication delay.

The book primarily presents our research results of anonymous message authentication in VANETs, but also provides a comprehensive survey of existing challenges and solutions in security and privacy in VANETs.

We wish to thank many people whose insightful comments and suggestions have helped us significantly improve our research work. In particular, we would like to acknowledge the following researchers who have collaborated with us on this exciting research topic described in the book: Prof. Xuemin (Sherman) Shen, Prof. Pin-Han Ho, Prof. Haojin Zhu, Dr. Chenxi Zhang, Xiaoting Sun, Dr. Xiaoyu Wang, Dr. Xiaohui Liang, Dr. Tom H. Luan, and Dr. Xu Li. Our discussions and collaboration with them provide a critical foundation for the current book. Also, we would like to thank the IEEE for allowing us to use our IEEE-copyrighted work.

XIAODONG LIN

University of Ontario Institute of Technology, Canada

RONGXING LU

Nanyang Technological University, Singapore

1

INTRODUCTION

1.1 BACKGROUND

Impaired driving, traffic congestion, and treacherous driving conditions have caused numerous accidents every year all over the world, leading to great suffering of people in different ways such as great anguish, fatal injuries, and horrendous loss of human lives. There were nearly 6,420,000 auto accidents in the United States in 2005, where 2.9 million people were injured and 42,636 people killed, which caused a financial loss of more than 230 billion dollars. Statistically, about five people die each hour in traffic accidents in the United States, that is, one death every 12 minutes [1]. Under such circumstances, how to improve the driving safety has been drawing increasing attention in the public and has been subject to extensive efforts from both industry and academia in mitigating the impact of traffic accidents and injuries. For example, car manufacturers have made great efforts to improve the safety of their vehicles by developing "passive" vehicle safety systems, such as seat belts, air bag systems, and crumple zones, to minimize postcrash driver and passenger injury, as well as by accommodating "active" vehicle safety systems that explore precollision accident avoidance, such as the antilock braking system (ABS), blind-spot safety, roll stability control, active steering systems, collision warning with brake support (CWBS), lane departure warning system, and Mazda precrash safety system [2]. Although the aforementioned safety technologies

Vehicular Ad Hoc Network Security and Privacy, First Edition. Xiaodong Lin and Rongxing Lu.
© 2015 The Institute of Electrical and Electronics Engineers, Inc. Published 2015 by John Wiley & Sons, Inc.

have led to enormous improvements on driving safety over the last few decades, we still witness tremendous loss on the roads. Hence, it is crucial to explore the new techniques to improve road safety.

Over the last 20 years, the miraculous evolution of wireless technology has imposed a major impact on the revolution of human lifestyle by providing the best-ever convenience and flexibility in accessing the Internet services and various types of personal communication applications. Recently, technologies built on IEEE 802.11p and IEEE 1609 standards, 5.9-GHz dedicated short-range communication (DSRC) protocols [3], are proposed to support advanced vehicle safety applications through effective, reliable, and secure vehicle-to-vehicle (V2V) [also known as *intervehicle communication* (IVC)] and vehicle-to-infrastructure (V2I) communications, which are also known as *vehicle safety communication* (VSC) technologies. The US Department of Transportation (USDOT) works with seven automotive manufacturers—BMW, DaimlerChrysler, Ford, GM, Nissan, Toyota, and VW—to form the Vehicle Safety Communications Consortium (VSCC) to establish the VSC project to evaluate vehicle safety applications enabled or enhanced by external vehicle communications [4]. For example, if a possible red-light violation is detected at an intersection, the potential violator will receive a warning to slow down to avoid unintentional red-light violations. Meanwhile, a warning on the running red-light event will be given to the other drivers at the intersection to minimize the possibility of collision.

1.2 DSRC AND VANET

1.2.1 DSRC

The Dedicated Short-Range Communications (DSRC) protocol is one of short-range wireless protocols, which is specifically designed for V2V and V2I communications to enhance the safety and productivity of the transportation system, which is also referred to as an *intelligent transportation system* (ITS). Originally, DSRC is proposed to work in the 915-MHz band, and US Federal Communications Commission (FCC) later allocates 75 MHz of spectrum at 5.9 GHz for DSRC in 1999. Similar activities also undergo in Japan and Europe, where the 5.8-GHz band is used for DSRC instead. The DSRC radio technology is a variant of the IEEE 802.11a technology [5], which provides high data transfer rates of up to 27 Mb/s over a range of 1 km while maintaining low overhead in the DSRC spectrum. Recently, both industry and academia have been extensively working on standardization of DSRC. One of the activities is done by the IEEE P1609 Working Group, which is currently working on the IEEE 802.11p standard for both PHY and MAC layers of DSRC, as well as applications and management services over DSRC, which are also known as *wireless access in vehicular environments* (WAVE). Furthermore, VSC adopts IEEE 1609 standards to develop many DSRC/WAVE applications, which can be categorized into the following two classes according to different aspects of their design premises and abilities.

- *Vehicle safety-related applications*, which are used to improve road safety. For example, currently, drivers can only see the brake light of vehicles ahead of them;

and the brake light system can only demonstrate whether the vehicle is braking, but cannot indicate the level of deceleration. When there is an emergency braking, drivers may not see the brake lights of any other vehicles but the one in front of them, especially when visibility is poor beyond the car in front of them (in fog), or in heavy traffic when everyone is so close or behind bigger vehicles like minivans, trucks, and sport utility vehicles (SUVs). Under such circumstances, rear-end collisions could occur much more often. To countermeasure this situation, V2V communication can serve to extend the range of brake light signals for drivers and also indicate the level of deceleration [or referred to as *extended brake lights* (EBL)] [4]. Through V2V communication, the hard braking information of a vehicle is disseminated in a timely fashion so that the other vehicles can be alerted.

- *Vehicle non-safety-related applications*, which are used to facilitate traffic management and infotainment dissemination for drivers and passengers. For example, in modern transportation systems, traffic lights play an important role in automatically performing traffic control and management in urban areas, which enhance driver safety and also facilitate smooth multiplexing at intersections. Hence, there has been increasing attention to making traffic light controllers more intelligent, where collecting traffic-related information plays an important role in traffic flow control. Currently, this has been done by equipping traffic lights with sensing devices such as electromagnetic wires (loops), which are embedded in street pavement. However, deploying sensors in pavement at an intersection could be very expensive and difficult to maintain. In addition, the sensors can become inaccurate and fail to function regularly as time goes by. Instead, V2I communication can be used to effectively collect traffic information. Through V2I communication, an RSU at an intersection can probe the traffic load in all directions of the intersection, and then intelligently control the corresponding traffic light according to the dynamic traffic load.

1.2.2 VANET

Nowadays, car manufactories and telecommunication industries gear up to equip each car with the technology that allows drivers and passengers to communicate with each other as well as with a roadside infrastructure, which is located in some critical sections of the road, such as at any traffic light or any intersection or any stop sign, in order to improve the driving experience and make driving safer. For example, Microsoft Corp.'s MSN TV and KVH Industries, Inc. have introduced an automotive vehicle Internet access system called *TracNet*, which can bring the Internet service to any in-car videoscreens. It also turns the entire vehicle into an IEEE 802.11-based Wi-Fi hotspot, so passengers can use their wireless-enabled laptops to access the Internet just like they are at home or in the office. Furthermore, by using those equipped communication devices, also known as *onboard units* (OBUs), vehicles can communicate with each other as well as with the roadside units (RSUs) located at the critical points of the road. As shown in Fig. 1.1, a self-organized network can be formed by connecting the vehicles and RSUs, which is called

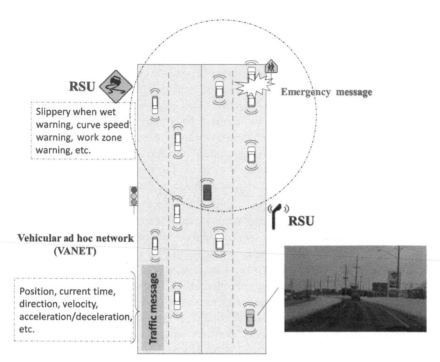

Figure 1.1. Vehicular ad hoc network.

vehicular ad hoc network (VANET), and the RSUs are further connected to the backbone network via the high-speed network connections. Recently there has been increasing interest in applications through V2V and V2I communications, aiming to improve the driving safety and traffic management while providing drivers and passengers with Internet access. It is estimated that the market for vehicular communications will reach the multi-billion-dollar range in the next few years.

In VANETs, RSUs can provide assistance in finding a facility such as a restaurant or gas station, and broadcast traffic-related messages such as "maximum curve turning speed" notifications to give drivers a heads-up. For example, a vehicle can communicate with a traffic light through V2I communications, and a traffic light can communicate wirelessly with a vehicle and tell the vehicle how many seconds are left before it turns to yellow or red. This can serve as an advance-warning sign to the drivers, and will be very helpful to those who are driving under winter weather conditions or in an unfamiliar area, especially when facing a wide angle of road curve ahead of a traffic light. This could prevent many drivers from running red lights, which could result in a disaster. Through V2V communications, on the other hand, the drivers can get a better idea of what's going on in their driving environment and take early actions to respond to an abnormal situation. For implementation, an OBU regularly broadcasts routine traffic-related messages with the information of position, current time, direction, speed, brake status, steering angle, turn signal, acceleration/deceleration, traffic conditions, and traffic events. In addition, emergency messages can be generated and sent by OBUs in case of

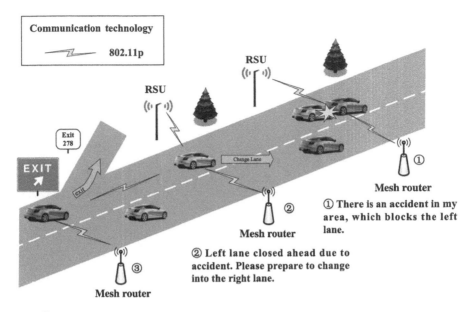

Figure 1.2. Example of a road emergency response operation under VANET.

emergent braking, traffic jam, or other accidents, etc. For example, as shown in Fig. 1.2, whenever there is an accident in highway, several lanes can be blocked. Drivers can experience a long delay. However, the delay can be mitigated if the drivers are informed in advance so that they can follow a detour route or change lanes to avoid traffic jams.

Another scenario where VANETs can be very useful is in school bus tracking, shown in Fig. 1.3. In addition to communication devices (or OBUs), there is now an increasing presence of GPS devices in modern cars including school buses. If the location of a school bus is constantly transmitted to a central database, either through V2V and V2I communications or traditional cellular data services [e.g., general packet radio service (GPRS)], a parent can track the bus's status and location. This is particularly useful in some areas where winter weather is harsh. This can make school bus schedules unpredictable. A parent can check the current location of a school bus before letting his/her child leave for a bus. This is a safer alternative to waiting in the cold. Furthermore, if school buses are equipped with personal tracking devices [e.g., radiofrequency identification (RFID) readers], parents can monitor where and when their children board or disembark buses. When boarding or disembarking the bus, students can scan special cards equipped with RFID chips to alert a central database of their presence. Parents can access the database to track their children's whereabouts.

Enabled by V2V and V2I communications, VANETs open up new avenues to create conveniences and safer lifestyles.

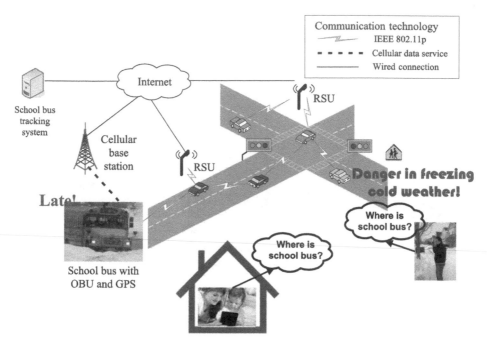

Figure 1.3. School bus tracking under VANET.

1.2.3 Characteristics of VANET

VANET is a special case of *mobile ad hoc network* (MANET), where the mobile nodes are instantiated with vehicles equipped with OBU communication devices, as shown in Fig. 1.4. Thus, VANET has some unique characteristics different from MANET [6, 7].

- *Rapid Change in Topology*. Since vehicles are moving at high speeds, the topology of VANETs is prone to frequent and rapid changes, and usually follows the real-world freeway and surface streets.

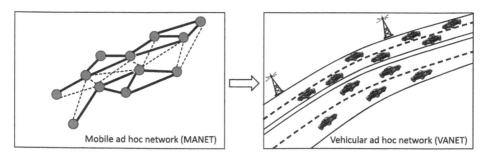

Figure 1.4. The relation between VANET and MANET.

TABLE 1.1. Comparisons between VANET and MANET

	VANET	MANET
Topology	Freeway and surface streets in real world	Random waypoint
Architecture	Vehicle-to-vehicle, vehicle-to-RSU	Node-to-node
Connectivity	Random and intermittent	Random
Resource	Almost unlimited	Limited hardware, power limited by battery
Scalability	Huge	50–100 nodes
Application	Safety, traffic, payment, electronic toll collection (daily life)	Military, disaster (specific)

- *No Power Constraint.* Since the batteries of the vehicles are self-charging, vehicles in VANETs do not have the conventional power constraints of the handheld devices in MANETs.
- *Large Scale.* VANETs constitute the largest instance of MANETs that the world has ever seen, where the order of the number of vehicles is around 10^7 in reality.
- *Variable Network Density.* The number of vehicles in one area of the road temporally fluctuates during the day; e.g., during rush hour roads are busier than at other times of the day.
- *High Predictable Mobility.* The velocity of vehicles in cities ranges from 0 to 60 km/h, and the average velocity can reach up to 100 km/h on a highway. Therefore, the road geometric topology regulates the mobility of vehicles.

In summary, in Table 1.1 we give brief comparisons between VANET and MANET in terms of topology, architecture, connectivity, resource, scalability, and application.

1.3 SECURITY AND PRIVACY THREATS

There are several possible security attacks in VANETs, which are listed as follows:

- *Bogus Information Attack.* The adversary may send fake messages to meet a specific purpose. For example, one may send a fake approaching emergency vehicle warning in order to push over the others such that it can manipulate to get a better traffic condition.
- *Unauthorized Preemption Attack.* An RSU could be used to control a traffic light when any emergent situation occurs. Similar to the bogus-information attack, the adversary may illegally interrupt a traffic light through the RSU in order to meet some specific purposes [8].
- *Message Replay Attack.* The adversary replays the valid messages previously sent by a legitimate source in order to disturb the traffic.

- *Message Modification Attack.* A message is altered during or after transmission. The adversary may wish to change the source or content of the message in terms of the position and/or time information that had been sent and saved in its device to escape from the consequence of a criminal or traffic accident event.
- *Impersonation Attack.* The adversary may pretend to be another vehicle or even an RSU to fool the others.
- *RSU Replication Attack.* An RSU may be compromised such that the adversary can relocate RSU to launch any malicious attack, such as broadcasting fake traffic information.
- *Denial-of-Service (DoS) Attack.* The adversary sends irrelevant bulk messages to take up the channels and consume the computational resources of the other nodes, such as RF interference, jamming, and layer 2 packet flooding [9].

Since a VANET is on an open shared medium, which facilitates the illegal collection and processing of information. After the adversary intercepts a significant number of messages in a certain region, the adversary may trace a vehicle in terms of its physical position and moving patterns simply through information analysis. Since drivers are concerned about leakage of the aforementioned sensitive information to the public, resolving such concerns becomes one of the major issues in the design of a modern VANET.

- *Personal Information Leakage.* If information transmitted over a VANET is not protected, an adversary can easily collect the information by sniffing the network and discover some user-related sensitive information, such as a driver's name, address, and license. The personal information leakage could result in identity theft, which could disrupt the victim's personal life.
- *Location Privacy.* After an adversary intercepts a significant amount of messages in a certain region, the adversary may be able to trace a vehicle in terms of its physical position and moving patterns simply through information analysis.

Since the topic on DoS attacks in wireless communication networks has been extensively investigated [10–13], we will not focus on the security and privacy issues related to the DoS attack here.

1.4 SECURITY AND PRIVACY REQUIREMENTS

In order to protect VANET against the threats mentioned above, the security mechanisms employed in VANETs should satisfy the following security requirements:

- *Authentication.* Authentication is the ability to ascertain that a thing is indeed the one that it claims to be. Message authentication is of vital importance in VANETs because it ensures that a received message is indeed sent from a legitimate and authorized vehicle in the networks.

- *Integrity*. Integrity is the ability to ensure that messages exchanged between vehicles have not been subject to modifications, additions, or deletions. Integrity ensures that all messages sent by vehicles should be delivered unaltered.
- *Nonrepudiation*. Nonrepudiation is the ability to prevent an authorized vehicle from denying the existence or contents of the message sent by itself. Nonrepudiation is a critical property for VANETs because it can prevent an attacker from denying the attacks that he/she have launched.
- *Access Control*. Access control is necessary to ensure reliable and secure operations of a system. In VANETs, any misbehaving entity should be revoked from the network to protect the safety of other legitimate entities in the network. Moreover, any action taken by that misbehaving entity should be canceled.
- *Privacy*. Privacy is the ability to protect private information from an unauthorized party. In VANETs, the real identity of any individual vehicle is blind only to other vehicles and roadside units, but should be transparent to a trusted authority (TA). This security requirement is also called *conditional privacy preservation*. Currently, IEEE 802.11p [14] and IEEE 1609.x are called *wireless access in vehicular environments* (WAVE) standards [15] since their goal, as a whole, is to facilitate the provision of wireless access in vehicular environments.

1.5 CHALLENGES AND PROSPECTS

1.5.1 Conditional Privacy Preservation in VANETs

Privacy preservation is a very important design requirement for VANETs, where the source privacy of safety messages is envisioned to emerge as a key security issue because some privacy-sensitive information, such as the driver's name and car license plate, position, and driving route, could be intentionally deprivatized so that the personal privacy of the driver is jeopardized. Therefore, safety message authentication with source privacy preservation is critical for a VANET to be considered for practical implementation and commercialization. In particular, the privacy preservation in VANETs should be conditional, where senders are anonymous to receivers while traceable by an authority, such as certificate authority (CA). With traceability, the CA can reveal the source identity of a message once a dispute occurs regarding the safety message.

In spite of its ultimate importance, conditional privacy preservation has not been well studied. Raya et al. [6] proposed a security protocol based on anonymous key pairs, hereafter referred to as *anonymous credentials*. With installation of a large number of short-lived anonymous credentials in a vehicle and random selection of one of them to sign each message, the vehicle's anonymity requirement can be met. Also, a unique electronic identity is devised and can be used by the police to associate the identities of vehicle owners with launched messages. However, this protocol may be inefficient when the CA would like to identify the sender of a malicious message since the CA needs to keep the anonymous credentials of all the vehicles in an administrative region (which could be a province or a whole country). Once a malicious message is detected, the CA has to exhaustively search a very large credential database to find the identity related to the compromised anonymous credential, which incurs tremendous complexity for identity and credential management. In addition, since compromised or expired vehicles have to be revoked, all credentials belonging to those revoked vehicles have to be released in the certificate revocation list (CRL), which tremendously increases the size of the CRL and makes the dissemination of the CRL intractable.

Besides, how to obtain a good tradeoff between authentication and privacy is another challenge for conditional privacy preservation. To ensure that one node does not impersonate another node, it is essential to authenticate all message transmissions. However, this leads to identification of vehicles from the message they send. This can enable tracking of vehicles, which most consumers would not like to enable in their systems. Privacy is a major issue in a VANET, because cars are highly personal devices. This has to be balanced with the need to establish accountability and liability of vehicles and their drivers. This requires an authentication system to be designed that enables messages to be anonymous for general nodes but also enables identification by central authorities in liability-related cases like car accidents.

1.5.2 Authentication with Efficient Revocation in VANETs

There are many cases when the certificate of a vehicle or an RSU needs to be revoked. For example, a private key specified in the certificate may be identified as compromised. In the traditional public key infrastructure (PKI) system, a commonly used revocation scheme is through the CRL, in which the revocation of a vehicle, issued by the trusted authority (TA), is stored, to be broadcast throughout the network. However, this could be a big challenge in VANETs, for several reasons: (1) the distribution of RSUs is sporadic, so when vehicles are traveling in rural areas where RSUs are sparse, they may not be able to update the CRL in time and (2) CRL distribution will suffer from a long delay due to the large scale of VANETs. Either problem could render the malicious behaviors even when the vehicles have already been revoked. Ensuring the fairness of revocation has also been a challenge when a vehicle misbehaves because of a fault in the system, and thus is unfairly added to the CRL. Problems that need to be addressed in the proposed certificate revocation system are (1) how to reduce the overhead of the distribution of CRL, (2) how to timely notify the revocation events, although they are rare and the vehicles are distributed in a wide area; (3) how to solve the storage problem even though the storage of a specific RSU could be very small and the CRL is very large; and (4) how to expedite the spread of warning information in the network.

There are a few solutions based on the centralized architecture; alternative solutions to CRL could be by way of a certificate revocation system (CRS), certificate revocation tree (CRT), the *Online Certificate Status Protocol* (OCSP) [16], and other methods. There is a common requirement for these schemes: high availability of the centralized CAs where frequent data transmission with OBUs to obtain timely revocation information may cause significant overhead. Thus, with the high-speed mobility and extremely large amount of network entities in VANETs, the centralized CRL architecture may be far from realistic.

Raya et al. [6] proposed three certificate revocation protocols to be applied in VANETs: Revocation Using Compressed Certificate-Revocation Lists (RC2RL), Revocation of the Tamper-Proof Device (RTPD), and Distributed Revocation Protocol (DRP). The compression technique is used to reduce the overhead of CRL distribution. RTPD removes revoked certificates from corresponding vehicles from the CRL, rather than checking the status of a certificate by introducing a tamperproof device as a vehicle's key and certificate management tool. The owner of the vehicle possessing the revoked certificates is informed of the revocation in cases where the tamperproof device automatically removes those revoked certificates. Distinct from RC2RL and RTPD, a distributed certificate revocation mechanism is implemented in DRP to determine the status of a certificate. In DRP each vehicle is equipped with an attack detection system, which enables a vehicle to identify any compromised peer. When a compromised or malicious vehicle is detected and located, its neighbors can work together to temporarily revoke the compromised one.

1.6 STANDARDIZATION AND RELATED ACTIVITIES

Securing V2V and V2I communications is mandatory in VANETs, and has drawn tremendous attention from both industry and academia. Over the past a few years, a number of initiatives have been launched. The Vehicle Safety Communications (VSC) project [4], which was initiated by USDOT in 2002, aims to evaluate the feasibility of supporting vehicle safety/non-safety-related applications through telecommunication technologics, such as the DSRC standard [3]. The VSC project investigates the security issues associated with VSC and identifies four major security goals for a VSC system: message integrity/origin authentication, correctness, privacy, and robustness under attack. In addition, the project discusses possible solutions for the aforementioned security goals. The VSC project proposes a dual authentication structure in which a list of short-lived anonymous certificates is taken to guarantee the privacy of OBUs and ensure the security, where the short-lived certificates are discarded once after use. It is worth noting that a pseudonym is used in any anonymous certificate instead of the real identity of the vehicle, which protects the privacy of the vehicle. In addition, the classic hierarchical PKI is presented for the purpose of ensuring the security of RSUs and public safety OBUs since RSUs and public safety OBUs do not have any privacy issue. The scheme can provide a higher level of privacy preservation and security assurance because the certificates are blindly signed by the certificate authority (CA) in order to deal with any possible insider attack. An insider attack could be simply launched by the CA, which abuses its authority by mishandling driver information. In order to achieve traceability, a linkage is devised for the escrow authorities to associate each blindly signed anonymous certificate with a single vehicle. All the compromised and expired vehicles have to be revoked by storing anonymous certificates belonging to those vehicles in the CRL. The disadvantage of this scheme is that the CRL may grow quickly such that it takes a long time to check through the whole CRL to see if a given certificate is valid. Another disadvantage is that, to achieve traceability, a unique electronic identity is assigned to each vehicle that enables the police and other authorities to inspect the identity of the vehicle owner in case of any dispute. Although this scheme can effectively meet the conditional anonymity requirement, it is far from efficient and can hardly become a scalable and reliable approach because the ID management authority has to keep all the anonymous certificates for the vehicles in the administrative region. Once a malicious message is identified, the authority has to exhaustedly search in a very large database to find the identity related to the compromised anonymous certificate.

Similar activities are underway in Europe. The European Car-2-Car Communication Consortium [17], which is backed by General Motors, Audi, BMW, Fiat, Honda, Renault, etc., was formed to work on V2V technologies to help to make driving safer and improve driving experience. A prerequisite for the successful deployment of vehicular communications is to ensure that the vehicular communication is secure and that driver privacy is protected. The secure vehicular communication (SeVeCom) project [18], which is part of the eSafety initiative [19], the Information Society and Media Initiative [20], and the Sixth Framework Programme of the European Commission [21], has been funded in Europe to identify the variety of security and privacy threats facing vehicular communications, define security requirements for vehicular communications, and investigate the cryptographic primitives that are suitable for the VC environment. In 2011, the Preparing Secure Vehicle-to-X Communication Systems (PRESERVE) project was funded under the Seventh Framework Programme of the European Commission [22], and its goal is to design and develop a secure and scalable security system for V2X (V2V and V2I) communication, which can be readily applied in realistic deployment scenarios. The developed V2X Security Subsystem (VSS) is publicly available on the project website.

Meanwhile, international standardizing bodies have addressed the issue of standardizing V2V communication technologies. The IEEE 1609 WAVE communication standards, which are also known as *dedicated short-range communication* (DSRC) protocols, have emerged recently to enhance the 802.11 to support the wireless communications among vehicles for the roadside infrastructure [5]. The IEEE 1609.2 standard addresses the issues of securing WAVE messages against eavesdropping, spoofing, and other attacks. The components of the IEEE Std. 1609.2 security infrastructure are shown in Fig. 1.5, which are based on industry standards for PKI, including the support for elliptic curve cryptography (ECC) [23], WAVE certificate formats, and hybrid encryption methods, in order to provide secure services for WAVE communications. The security infrastructure is also responsible for the administrative functions necessary to support the core security functions, such as certificate revocation. Note that, for some unexplained reason, for example, if a private key corresponding to a public key specified in the certificate is identified as compromised, certificate revocation is essential to any security system based on PKI. This issue has not been addressed in the current IEEE Std. 1609.2 by considering the unique features of vehicular networks; IEEE 1609.2 also, does not define driver identification and privacy protection, and has left many open issues.

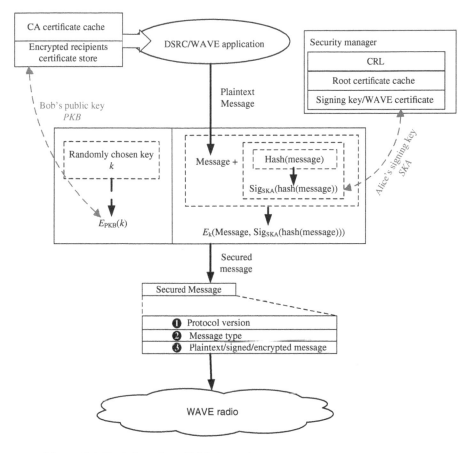

* Assume that Alice is the sender and Bob is the receiver.

<u>Figure 1.5.</u> IEEE Std. 1609.2 security services framework for creating and exchanging WAVE messages between WAVE devices.

1.7 SECURITY PRIMITIVES

In order to secure VANET, the following security primitives will be considered and specific to VANET settings.

- *Primitives for Confidentiality.* In order to achieve the confidentiality against the attacks in VANETs, encryption techniques can be adopted. Encryption is an important cryptographic technique, which can transform a data in plaintext into a ciphertext before data transmission to resist eavesdropping attacks. In general, according to different key materials used in encryption, the encryption

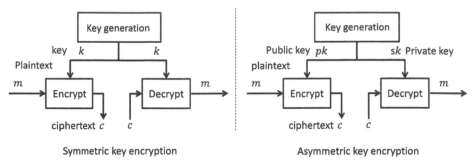

Figure 1.6. Symmetric key encryption and asymmetric key encryption.

technique can be categorized into symmetric key encryption, e.g., AES and the Data Encryption Standard (DES) [24], where the same key is used in both encryption and decryption, and asymmetric key encryption, e.g., Rivest–Shamir–Adleman (RSA) [25] and El Gamal [26] algorithms, where the public key, for encryption and the private key is used for decryption, as shown in Fig. 1.6. Therefore, in VANETs, if two vehicles or one vehicle and one RSU have already shared a key, they can efficiently use the symmetric key encryption to achieve the confidentiality; if each vehicle (or RSU) has a public–private key pair, public key encryption can be used to achieve the confidentiality. However, compared with the symmetric key encryption, the efficiency is much lower.

Hence, a hybrid concept encryption was introduced, also known as *hybrid encryption*, as shown in Fig. 1.7, which is a method of encrypting data that combines both symmetric and asymmetric key encryption. The basic idea of the hybrid encryption approach is that secure data transmission is divided into two phases. Initial exchange of a shared secret key is done using asymmetric key cryptography, and it works by encrypting a randomly chosen secret key with the receiver's public key and sending it to the receiver. The receiver will

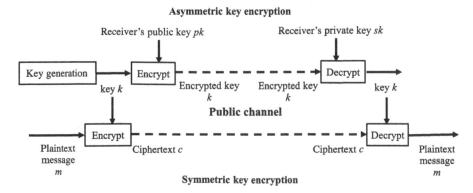

Figure 1.7. Hybrid encryption.

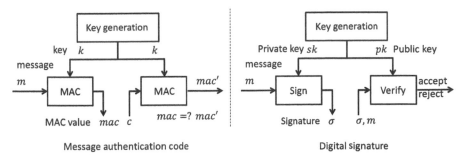

Figure 1.8. Message authentication code and digital signature.

decrypt the secret key with its own private key. Then, the secret key is used for symmetric key encryption to ensure data confidentiality between sender and receiver. It combines the best features of two different encryption systems, solving the problem of key management from asymmetric key encryption and gaining the speed of encryption and decryption from symmetric key encryption.

- *Primitives for Data Integrity and Authentication.* In order to achieve the data integrity and authentication, message authentication code (MAC) and digital signature are suggested to be against the attacks in VANETs, as shown in Fig. 1.8. If two vehicles share a key, the two vehicles can use MAC to achieve the data integrity and source authentication. However, if a group of vehicles share the same key, only data integrity can be ensured, while the source cannot be authenticated, since any vehicle which holds the key can generate the same MAC value. If each vehicle has a public–private key pair, digital signature can be used to achieve the data integrity and authentication, where the private key is used for signature generation and the public key is used for signature verification. Further, in order to compensate for inefficiency of public key cryptosystems, especially when dealing with large messages, the hash value of the original message is calculated before being digitally signed by the sender. Note that, in order to resist the replay attack in VANETs, a timestamp is required to be embedded in the transmitted message.

- *Primitives for Nonrepudiation.* Nonrepudiation can guarantee that the sender of a message cannot later deny having sent the message and that the recipient cannot deny having received the message. In order to achieve the nonrepudiation in VANETs, digital signature provides an effective solution.

- *Primitives for Privacy.* The privacy challenges in VANETs include the content-oriented privacy and contextual privacy. The content oriented privacy, also called *confidentiality*, can be achieved by the encryption techniques, as discussed above. The contextual privacy means an attacker has the ability to link the source and the destination of a message [27] or reveal the real identity of a vehicle. In order to achieve the contextual privacy in VANETs, some anonymity techniques, such as mixing network [28], aggregate encryption [29], or group signature [30] can be adopted.

The recently approved IEEE Standard 1609.2 - 2013, *Advanced Encryption Standard* (AES), and the *elliptic curve integrated encryption scheme* (ECIES) are suggested for symmetric key encryption and asymmetric key encryption in VANETs, respectively. In addition, the *elliptic curve digital signature algorithm* (ECDSA) is also recommended as the digital signature algorithm in VANETs. However, because of the unique characteristics and particular challenges of VANET, those algorithms recommended in the standards cannot fully address all security and privacy challenges. Therefore, in the following chapters, we will introduce several security mechanisms to address the security and privacy challenges in VANETs. Since most of security mechanisms in this book are built on the bilinear pairings, a brief introduction to bilinear pairings is also given in the following.

Bilinear Groups of Prime Order. Bilinear pairing is an important cryptographic primitive and has been widely adopted in many positive applications in cryptography [31]. Let G be a cyclic additive group and G_T be a cyclic multiplicative group of the same prime order q. We assume that the discrete logarithm problems in both G and G_T are hard. A bilinear pairing is a mapping $e : G \times G \to G_T$ that satisfies the following properties:

1. *Bilinearity.* For any $P, Q \in G$ and $a, b \in \mathbb{Z}_q^*$, we have $e(aP, bQ) = e(P, Q)^{ab}$.
2. *Nondegeneracy.* There exists $P \in G$ and $Q \in G$ such that $e(P, Q) \neq 1_{G_T}$.
3. *Computability.* There exists an efficient algorithm to compute $e(P, Q)$ for all $P, Q \in G$.

From Reference 31, we note that such a bilinear pairing may be realized using the modified Weil pairing associated with a supersingular elliptic curve. Note that we also frequently write G as a multiplicative group in this book, i.e., for any $g, h \in G$ and $a, b \in \mathbb{Z}_q^*$, we have $e(g^a, h^b) = e(g, h)^{ab}$.

Definition 1 (Bilinear Generator) *A bilinear parameter generator $\mathcal{G}en$ is a probability algorithm that takes a security parameter κ as input and outputs a 5-tuple (q, P, G, G_T, e), where q is a κ-bit prime number, $(G, +)$ and $(G_T, \times)$ are two groups with the same order q, $P \in G$ is a generator, and $e : G \times G \to G_T$ is an admissible bilinear map.*

Asymmetric Bilinear Groups of Prime Order. Let G, G', and G_T be three cyclic multiplicative groups of the same prime order q, i.e., $|G| = |G'| = |G_T| = q$. Let P be a generator of G, P' be a generator of G', and ψ be an isomorphism from G' to G, with $\psi(P') = P$. An efficient admissible bilinear map $e : G \times G' \to G_T$ holds the following properties:

1. *Bilinearity.* For all $P_1 \in G$, $P_2 \in G'$ and $a, b \in \mathbb{Z}_q^*$, $e(aP_1, bP_2) = e(P_1, P_2)^{ab}$.
2. *Nondegeneracy.* There exist $P_1 \in G$ and $P_2 \in G'$ such that $e(P_1, P_2) \neq 1_{G_T}$.
3. *Computability.* There exists an efficient algorithm to compute $e(P_1, P_2) \in G_T$ for any $P_1 \in G$, $P_2 \in G'$.

Such an admissible asymmetric bilinear map e can be constructed by the modified Weil or Tate pairings on the elliptic curves. As Boneh et al. [32] mention the Tate pairing on MNT curves gives the efficient implementation, where $G \neq G'$, the *one-way* isomorphism ψ, can be implemented by the trace map, and the representations of G can be expressed in 171 bits when the order q is a 170-bit prime. By this construction, the discrete logarithm problem in G can reach as hard as the discrete logarithm in $\mathbb{Z}_p^*$ where p is 1020 bits. Note that, we sometimes also write G, G' as multiplicative groups in this book, i.e., for all $g_1 \in G$, $g_2 \in G'$ and $a, b \in \mathbb{Z}_q^*$, $e(g_1^a, g_2^b) = e(g_1, g_2)^{ab}$.

Definition 2 (Asymmetric Bilinear Generator)   *An asymmetric bilinear parameter generator $\mathcal{AGen}$ is a probabilistic algorithm that takes a security parameter k as input and outputs a 7-tuple $(q, G, G', G_T, e, g, g')$ as the bilinear parameters, including a prime number q with $|q| = k$, three cyclic groups G, G', G_T of the same order q, an admissible bilinear map $e : G \times G' \to G_T$, and generators g, g' of G, G', respectively.*

1.8   OUTLINE OF THE BOOK

The organization of the remainder of the book is as follows. Chapter 2 presents a secure and privacy-preserving protocol GSIS for VANET, which is based on a combination of group signature and identity (ID)-based signature techniques. An efficient and conditional privacy preservation protocol ECPP for VANET is presented in Chapter 3. An effective pseudonym changing at social spots (PCS) strategy for facilitating vehicles to achieve high-level location privacy in VANETs is given in Chapter 4. An RSU-aided message authentication scheme for VANET is shown in Chapter 5. A TESLA-based broadcast authentication for VANET is illustrated in Chapter 6. A distributed cooperative message authentication for VANET and a context-aware cooperative authentication for VANET are presented in Chapter 7 and Chapter 8, respecively. Finally, a seamless authentication scheme based on the combination of mobility prediction and one-way hash chain is proposed in Chapter 9.

REFERENCES

1. "State traffic safety information for year 2006, National Highway Traffic Safety Administration," http://www-nrd.nhtsa.dot.gov/Pubs/810791.pdf.
2. "Increased driving safety through auto accident avoidance technologies, Ford Motor Company," http://www.ford.com/innovation/car-safety/helping-avoid-accidents/accident-avoidance-technologies/avoid-accidents-349p.
3. "Dedicated Short-Range Communications (DSRC) Protocol," http://grouper.ieee.org/groups/scc32/dsrc/index.html.
4. "Vehicle safety communications (VSC) project," http://www-nrd.nhtsa.dot.gov/pdf/nrd-12/060419-0843/PDFTOC.htm.

5. Intelligent Transportation Systems Committee, IEEE Vehicular Technology Society, "Ieee trial-use standard for wireless access in vehicular environments—security services for applications and management messages," *IEEE Std. 1609.2*, 2006.

6. M. Raya and J.-P. Hubaux, "Securing vehicular ad hoc networks," *Journal of Computer Security*, vol. 15, no. 1, pp. 39–68, 2007.

7. X. Lin, X. Sun, P.-H. Ho, and X. Shen, "GSIS: A secure and privacy-preserving protocol for vehicular communications," *IEEE Transactions on Vehicular Technology*, vol. 56, no. 6, pp. 3442–3456, 2007.

8. "Traffic light," http://en.wikipedia.org/wiki/Traffic_light.

9. C. Liu and J. T. Yu, "An analysis of DoS attacks on wireless LAN," *Proc.* (in *Proceedings of the 6th International Association of Science and Technology Development (IASTED) International Multi-Conference on Wireless and Optical Communications: Conference on Communication Systems and Applications, Conference on Optical Communication Systems and Networks, Conference on Wireless Networks and Emerging Technologies, Conference on Wireless SENSOR Networks*, Banff, Alberta: IASTED, July 3–5, 2006.

10. I. Aad, J. Hubaux, and E. W. Knightly, "Denial of service resilience in ad hoc networks," *Proc. 10th Annual International Conference on Mobile Computing and Networking (MOBI-COM'04), Philadelphia*, ACM, Sept. 26–Oct. 1, 2004, pp. 202–215. (Available online at http://doi.acm.org/10.1145/1023720.1023741

11. S. Ranjan, R. Swaminathan, M. Uysal, and E. W. Knightly, "DoS-resilient scheduling to counter application layer attacks under imperfect detection," *Proc. INFOCOM 2006, 25th IEEE International Conference on Computer Communications, Joint Conference of the IEEE Computer and Communications Societies*, Barcelona, Catalunya: IEEE, April 23–29 2006. (Available online at http://dx.doi.org/10.1109/INFOCOM.2006.127.)

12. J. Mölsä, "Increasing the DoS attack resiliency in military ad hoc networks," *Proc. Military Communications Conference, 2005 (MILCOM'05). IEEE*, Oct. 2005, vol. 4, pp. 2282–2288.

13. J. V. E. Mölsä, "Cross-layer designs for mitigating range attacks in ad hoc networks," *Proc. 24th IASTED International Conference on Parallel and Distributed Computing and Networks*, ser. PDCN'06. Anaheim, CA: ACTA Press, 2006, pp. 64–69. (Available online at http://dl.acm.org/citation.cfm?id=1168920.1168931.)

14. "Draft amendment to standard for information technology-telecommunications and information exchange between systems-local and metropolitan area networks-specific requirements 1 part 11: Wireless LAN medium access control (MAC) and physical layer (phy) specifications-amendment 7: Wireless access in vehicular environment," IEEE P802.11p/D3.0, Technical Report, 2007.

15. "IEEE 1609—family of standards for wireless access in vehicular environments (wave)," http://www.standards.its.dot.gov/fact_sheet.asp?f=80.

16. P. Wohlmacher, "Digital certificates: A survey of revocation methods," *Proc. 2000 Association for Computing Machinery (ACM) Workshops on Multimedia*. ACM, 2000, pp. 111–114.

17. "Car 2 car communication consortium," http://www.car-to-car.org/index.php?id=130.

18. "Secure vehicular communication (sevecom) project," http://www.sevecom.org/.

19. "esafety," http://ec.europa.eu/information_society/activities/esafety/index_en.htm.

20. "Information society and media directorate-general," http://ec.europa.eu/dgs/information_society/index_en.htm.

21. "Sixth framework programme of the European Commission," http://cordis.europa.eu/fp6/dc/index.cfm?fuseaction=UserSite.FP6HomePage.

22. "Preparing Secure Vehicle-to-X communication Systems (PRESERVE) project," http://www.preserve-project.eu/.

23. N. Koblitz, "Elliptic curve cryptosystems," *Mathematics of Computation*, vol. 48, no. 177, pp. 203–209, 1987.

24. W. Mao, *Modern Cryptography: Theory and Practice*, Prentice-Hall Professional Technical Reference, 2003.

25. R. L. Rivest, A. Shamir, and L. Adleman, "A method for obtaining digital signatures and public-key cryptosystems," *Communications of the ACM*, vol. 21, no. 2, pp. 120–126, Feb. 1978. (Available online at http://doi.acm.org/10.1145/359340.359342.)

26. T. El Gamal, "A public key cryptosystem and a signature scheme based on discrete logarithms," *Proc. CRYPTO 84 on Advances in Cryptology*. New York: Springer-Verlag, 1985, pp. 10–18. (Available online at http://dl.acm.org/citation.cfm?id=19478.19480.)

27. X. Lin, R. Lu, X. Shen, Y. Nemoto, and N. Kato, "SAGE: A strong privacy-preserving scheme against global eavesdropping for ehealth systems," *IEEE Journal on Selected Areas in Communications*, vol. 27, no. 4, pp. 365–378, 2009.

28. J. Freudiger, M. Raya, M. Félegyházi, P. Papadimitratos, et al., "Mix-zones for location privacy in vehicular networks," *Proceed. 1st International Workshop on Wireless Networking for Intelligent Transportation Systems (Win-ITS)*, ICST, 2007.

29. R. Lu, X. Liang, X. Li, X. Lin, and X. Shen, "EPPA: An efficient and privacy-preserving aggregation scheme for secure smart grid communications," *IEEE Transactions on Parallel Distribution Systems*, vol. 23, no. 9, pp. 1621–1631, 2012.

30. J. Camenisch and M. Stadler, "Efficient group signature schemes for large groups," *Proc. 17th Annual International Cryptology Conference on Advances in Cryptology*, ser. CRYPTO '97. London: Springer-Verlag, 1997, pp. 410–424. (Available online at http://dl.acm.org/citation.cfm?id=646762.706305.)

31. D. Boneh and M. K. Franklin, "Identity-based encryption from the weil pairing," *Proc. Advances in Cryptology—CRYPTO 2001, 21st Annual International Cryptology Conference*, Santa Barbara, CA, Aug. 19–23, 2001, ser. Lecture Notes in Computer Science, vol. 2139. Springer, 2001, pp. 213–229.

32. D. Boneh, X. Boyen, and H. Shacham, "Short group signatures," *Proc. Advances in Cryptology—CRYPTO 2004, 24th Annual International Cryptology Conference*, Santa Barbara, CA: Springer, Aug. 15–19, 2004, pp. 41–55. (Available online at http://dx.doi.org/10.1007/978-3-540-28628-8_3.)

2

GSIS: GROUP SIGNATURE AND ID-BASED SIGNATURE-BASED SECURE AND PRIVACY-PRESERVING PROTOCOL

2.1 INTRODUCTION

The progress and wide deployment of wireless communication technologies have revolutionized human lifestyle by providing the best-ever convenience and flexibility in accessing the Internet services and various types of personal communication applications. Recently, car manufactories and telecommunication industries have geared up to equip each car with a technology that allows drivers and passengers from different cars to communicate with each other in order to improve the driving experience. For example, KVH [1] and Microsoft's MSN TV [2] introduced an automotive vehicle Internet access system called *TracNet*, which can bring the Internet services to in-car videoscreens and turn the entire vehicle into IEEE 802.1-based Wi-Fi hotspots. The passengers can then use their wireless-enabled laptops to access the Internet. Furthermore, by using those communication devices equipped on vehicles [also known as *on-board units* (OBUs)], the vehicles can communicate with each other as well as with the *roadside units* (RSUs) located in the critical points of the road, such as a traffic light at a road intersection. With the OBUs and RSUs, a self-organized network can be formed, which is called a *vehicular ad hoc network* (VANET). Because of low cost and easy

Vehicular Ad Hoc Network Security and Privacy, First Edition. Xiaodong Lin and Rongxing Lu.
© 2015 The Institute of Electrical and Electronics Engineers, Inc. Published 2015 by John Wiley & Sons, Inc.

deployment of wireless access points, it is expected that the roadside will be densely covered with a variety of RSUs like traffic lights, traffic signs, and wireless routers, which may provide wireless access to vehicles on the road. In addition, the RSUs could be connected to the Internet backbone to support diversified services such as TCP and real-time multimedia streaming applications. Thus, an increasing interest has been raised by both industry and academia in the applications of *roadside-to-vehicle communications* (RVC) and *Intervehicle communications* (IVC), aiming to improve the driving safety and traffic management while providing drivers and passengers with Internet access at the same time.

The creation of VANET is important to traffic management and roadside safety. Unfortunately, a VANET also comes with its own set of challenges, especially in the aspects of security and privacy. As a special implementation of *mobile ad hoc networks* (MANETs), a VANET could be subject to many security threats that may lead to increasing malicious attacks and service abuses. It is obvious that any malicious behavior of users, such as a modification and replay attack on the disseminated messages, could be fatal to the other users. Furthermore, *conditional privacy preservation* must be achieved in the sense that the user-related private information, including the driver's name and the license plate, speed, position, make, model, and *vehicle identification number* (VIN) of the vehicle, and traveling routes as well as their relationships, has to be protected. The authorities should be able to reveal the identities of message senders in the case of a traffic-related dispute such as a crime or accident scene investigation, which can be used to look for witnesses. Therefore, it is critical to develop a suite of elaborate and carefully designed security mechanisms for achieving security and conditional privacy preservation in VANETs before they can be practically launched. However, only a very limited number of previously reported studies have tackled the security and privacy issues of VANETs despite its ultimate importance.

In this chapter, we are committed to tackling the problem of security assurance and conditional privacy preservation in vehicular communication applications. We introduce a novel security and privacy preserving protocol for VANETs, called GSIS [3], by integrating the techniques of group signature [4] and identity-based signature [5]. The security problems are divided into the following two aspects: security and privacy preservation among multiple OBUs, as well as that between OBUs and RSUs, in light of their different design requirements. In the first aspect, group signature is used to secure communication inter-OBU, where messages can be securely and anonymously signed by the senders while the identities of the senders can be recovered by the authorities (or group managers in group signature schemes). In the second aspect, a signature scheme using *identity-based cryptography* (IBC) is adopted at RSUs to digitally sign each message launched by RSUs to ensure its authenticity, where the signature overhead can be greatly reduced. OBUs installed in emergency vehicles will be treated the same as RSUs since it is unnecessary to protect the privacy of both RSUs and OBUs installed in emergency vehicles. Note that with IBC, any string can serve as a valid public key for an RSU or an emergency vehicle, such as the location of the RSU, the unique number and the code of the RSU, or emergency vehicle license plate number [6]. By adopting any publicly known identity of an RSU or an emergency vehicle, such as the location of the RSU or emergency vehicle license plate number, as the public keys, the certificate management in the VANETs can be greatly simplified compared with that in the traditional *public key infrastructure* (PKI).

The remainder of the chapter is organized as follows. Preliminaries and background of the proposed security protocol are presented in Section 2.2. In Section 2.3, the proposed security protocol is presented along with the enabling signaling initiations and transactions in detail. Section 2.4 evaluates the performance of the proposed protocol through extensive simulation. Finally, we conclude the chapter in Section 2.5.

2.2 PRELIMINARIES AND BACKGROUND

2.2.1 Group Signature

The concept of group signature was first introduced in 1991 [4]. As a variation of the standard digital signature, it allows a member of a group to digitally sign a message on behalf of the group while the signer's identity remains unknown. On receiving a group signature, anyone can check its validity, but doesn't know which member signs the message. Further, as to a group signature scheme, it is essential that there be a group manager who is in charge of managing the group members and has the ability to reveal the real identity of the message signer in the event of dispute.

It can be observed that group signature perfectly matches the security and privacy requirements in VANETs, especially conditional privacy issue for vehicle-to-vehicle communications.

2.2.2 Bilinear Pairing and ID-Based Cryptography

We already discussed bilinear pairing in Section 1.7, and bilinear pairing can solve some previously well-recognized unsolvable problems, such as *ID-based cryptography* (IBC) [6]. IBC is a public key cryptosystem where any string can be used to derive a valid public key such as user names, email addresses, IP addresses, and host or node names. Compared with conventional public key cryptosystems, IBC simplifies the certificate management since the public key of a user could be any of its publicly known identity. Another advantage is that they can save communication bandwidth compared with traditional schemes such as RSA [7] and El Gamal [8] because pairing-based schemes feature a relatively small signature overhead, due to the usage of bilinear pairing in the design of signature schemes and/or security protocols. The promising features of IBC make it a good candidate approach to protect the communication from RSUs.

2.2.3 Threat Model

There are several possible attacks in VANETs, which are listed as follows:

- *Bogus-Information Attack.* The adversary may send fake messages to meet a specific purpose. For example, one may send a fake traffic jam message to others such that it can manipulate to get a better traffic condition.

- *Unauthorized Preemption Attack.* In many places, an RSU, especially a traffic light, can be controlled to provide special traffic priority for emergency vehicles, such as ambulance, police, and fire vehicles. As in a bogus-information attack, the adversary may illegally interrupt traffic lights by manipulating the traffic light preemptive system in order to get a better traffic condition [9].
- *Message Replay Attack.* The adversary replays the valid messages previously sent in order to disturb the traffic.
- *Message Modification Attack.* The message is altered during or after transmission. The adversary may wish to change the source or content of the message in terms of the position or time that it was sent and saved in its device to escape the consequences of a traffic-related dispute.
- *Impersonation Attack.* The adversary may pretend to be another vehicle or even an RSU to fool the others.
- *RSU Replication Attack.* Because of the high number of RSUs, cost considerations prevent the RSUs from being sufficiently protected from malicious attacks, which results in RSU compromise. Afterward, an adversary can relocate the captured RSU to launch any malicious attack, such as broadcasting fake traffic information.
- *Denial-of-Service (DoS) Attack.* The adversary sends irrelevant bulk messages to occupy the channel and consume the computational resources of the other nodes. Such attacks include RF interference or jamming or layer 2 packet flooding [10].
- *Movement Tracking.* Since wireless communication is based on an open shared medium, an adversary can easily eavesdrop on any traffic. After the adversary intercepts a significant number of messages in a certain region, the adversary may trace a vehicle in terms of its physical position and moving patterns simply through information analysis.

Since DoS attack in wireless communication networks has been extensively investigated in the past [10–14], in this study, we will focus on the security and privacy issues that are not related to the DoS attack.

2.2.4 Desired Requirements

To countermeasure and mitigate the potential threats in the security models described above, a well-developed security protocol should meet the following requirements:

1. *Data Origin Authentication and Integrity.* All the messages should be unaltered in delivery, and can be authenticated by the receiver, regardless of whether the messages are sent by an RSU or an OBU.
2. *Anonymous User Authentication.* Anonymous user authentication is the process of attempting to verify that a user is authentic and legitimate but doesn't reveal the real identity of the user.
3. *Vehicle Anonymity.* The identity of a vehicle should be transparent to any normal message receiver to support the sender anonymity while providing information on their position.

4. *RSU ID Exposure*. The RSUs or any other roadside infrastructure are not subject to any privacy issue; instead, they should evidently present their identities, including the physical locations and the services that can be provided.

5. *Prevention of RSU Replication*. It is very likely that a RSU may be compromised and/or relocated to any other place by an adversary, thereby enabling the adversary to launch various attacks through the compromised/relocated RSU, possibly causing disruption of the whole VANET. Effective countermeasures to RSU replication attack must be provided to maintain the security of VANETs.

6. *Vehicle ID Traceability*. The authorities should be able to reveal the real identities of the message senders in order to guard the truth when there is any dispute.

7. *Efficiency*. The communication overhead of each packet and processing latency at each vehicle must be as small as possible.

2.3 PROPOSED SECURE AND PRIVACY-PRESERVING PROTOCOL

2.3.1 Problem Formulation

Each vehicle is equipped with a reliable positioning device [e.g., a *global positioning system* [GPS]] and can get accurate time information. To explore the highest security level, we assume a very critical scenario where the adversaries can intercept any message they desire in the VANET. Furthermore, because it is unnecessary to maintain confidentiality of each message in IVC applications (since everybody has the right to know the content of the message), we choose to use the digital signature technique to sign every message sent by the OBUs and RSUs. Therefore, each receiver can verify the received messages and ensure the integrity and authenticity of the messages with the nonrepudiation property. The security design is divided into the following two categories: (1) the security mechanisms between two OBUs and (2) those between an RSU and an OBU. With this, the security solutions are considered separately in these two categories, due to the different design requirements, which are discussed below.

2.3.1.1 Communications Between OBUs. The main challenge of the communications between OBUs lies in the contradiction between the design requirements for vehicle anonymity from regular users while for traceability by the authorities.[1] For this sake, the traditional public key encryption scheme is not suitable in signing the safety messages because the identity information is included in the public key certificates. One solution is to use a list of anonymous certificates for message authentication, where the relationships of these anonymous certificates with their owners are kept in the *transportation regulation center* (TRC) such that the real ID of a message sender can be traced. This method can achieve the conditional privacy in a straightforward manner while at the expense of possibly huge efforts paid to maintain and manage a global

---

[1] In this chapter, we term the coexisting privacy and identity traceability as *conditional privacy*.

certificate list by the authorities. It could also be a time-consuming task in tracing back to the real identity of a vehicle when there is any dispute. Thus, we propose a security protocol by using the group signature scheme [4] to sign the messages sent by the vehicles. The main feature of the group signature scheme is that it provides anonymity of the signers. A verifier can judge whether the signer belongs to a group without knowing who the signer is in the group. However, in an exceptional situation, the certificate authority, which serves as a group manager, can reveal the unique identity of the signature's originator. Therefore, the group signature technique brings up a better way to meet the anonymity and traceability requirements rather than storing all the certificates in the terminal devices. The group signature technique also reduces the workload of the public key verification and certificate path verification operations. Besides, the group signature scheme can satisfy other basic security requirements such as message integrity and data origin authentication.

A secure group signature must be correct, anonymous, unlinkable, while traceable under some circumstances. More details on these properties can be found in Refs. [15 and 16]. In addition to the properties mentioned above, some other features are also preferred in the IVC application, which are listed as follows:

- *Role Separation*. In the real world, it is more preferred if the role of the group manager can be divided into a *membership manager* (MM) and a *tracing manager* (TM). The TRC can serve as the MM for assigning private keys and group public keys to the vehicles, whereas the law authorities could serve as a TM for possibly revealing the real IDs of the message senders if necessary.
- *Group Membership Revocation*. It is indispensable in the IVC system to have the ability to selectively revoke the group membership of a compromised vehicle either by updating keys or releasing *revocation lists* (RLs).
- *High Efficiency*. The computational cost and the length of the signatures should be small in order to meet the stringent communication requirement in the IVC system.

Dozens of group signature schemes have been proposed since 1991. However, some proposed group signature schemes are questionable in the security and anonymity assurance. For instance, many identity-based group signature schemes [15,17–19] failed to meet the unlinkability requirement. In addition, some schemes such as [15,20] were proved forgeable and traceable. Also, because most of the reported group signature schemes involve very long and nonrevocable signatures, and/or the role of the group manager may be indivisible, they fail to meet the requirements in the application scenario of interest. Thus, after a thorough evaluation, we choose the short group signature scheme that was introduced by Boneh et al. [21], which is secure and considered to be best suited to the IVC application.

2.3.1.2 *Communications between RSU and OBU.* The main feature with respect to security requirements between RSUs and OBUs is that the messages sent by RSUs are not subject to the privacy requirement. Thus, the identifier string of each

TABLE 2.1. Notations and Descriptions

Notations	Descriptions
TRC	Transportation regulation center
MM	Membership manager
TM	Tracing manager
$gpk = (g_1, g_2, g, w)$	Group public key
$gmsk_t = (\xi_1, \xi_2)$	The TM's private key
$gmsk_m = \gamma$	The MM's private key
$gsk[i]$	Vehicle i's private key
$\gamma \leftarrow^R \mathbb{Z}$	Randomly select a number γ from set $\mathbb{Z}$
RL	Revocation list
1_G, $1_{G'}$ and 1_{G_T}	The identity elements of G, G', and G_T, respectively

RSU is used as the public key to sign messages launched from the RSUs. For OBUs installed in emergency vehicles, the license plate numbers are used as their public keys. With the identity-based signature scheme, the workload of certificate management can be significantly reduced, and the public key update and revocation operations can be largely simplified. Among all the known identity-based signature schemes, the provably-secure identity-based signature scheme given in Ref. 22 is adopted in the study as the length of the signature is significantly reduced with the use of bilinear pairing. The scheme is also among the most efficient ones in terms of complexity of the verification operation, which takes only one pairing computation.

For ease of presentation, the notations throughout this chapter for describing our security protocol are listed in Table 2.1.

2.3.2 System Setup

For the considered system, there are three types of network entities: the TM, the MM, and the mobile OBUs supplied on the moving vehicles,[2] while their relationship is shown in Fig. 2.1. All vehicles need to be registered with the MM and preloaded with public system parameters and their own private keys before the vehicles can join the VANET. When the vehicles are on the road, they regularly broadcast routine traffic-related messages such as position, current time, direction, speed, brake status, steering angle, acceleration/deceleration, traffic conditions, and traffic events, to help drivers get a better idea of conditions in their driving environments and take early actions to respond to abnormal situations [23]. Whenever there is a situation where the involved vehicles' IDs need to be revealed, for example, police officers look for someone who may be able to provide valuable information about an accident, and the evidence, such as signed traffic messages, can be submitted to the TM, who authorizes the revelation of the real

---

[2] For simplicity, we assume that a vehicle is equipped with an OBU. Without loss of generality, we use the terms *vehicle* and *OBU* interchangeably in this text.

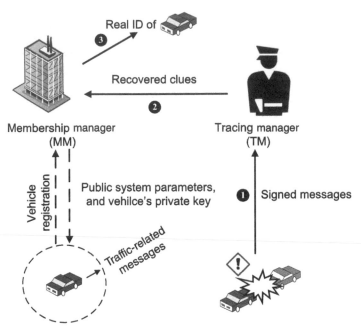

Figure 2.1. Secure communication system between OBUs.

IDs of the involved vehicles. The TM then forwards the recovered clues and evidence to the MM, who finally finds the real IDs from its membership database.

First, the law authority who serves as a TM generates the required bilinear groups as the system parameters [6], which are described as follows.

Let $\mathbb{G}$ and $\mathbb{G}'$ denote two multiplicative cyclic groups with a generator g_1 and g_2 of the same prime order p, respectively. Let ψ be a computable isomorphism from $\mathbb{G}'$ to $\mathbb{G}$, with $\psi(g_2) = g_1$; and let $\hat{e}$ be a computable map $\hat{e} : \mathbb{G} \times \mathbb{G}' \to \mathbb{G}_T$ with the following properties:

- Bilinearity: for all $u \in \mathbb{G}$, $v \in \mathbb{G}'$ and $a, b \in \mathbb{Z}_p^*$, $\hat{e}(u^a, v^b) = \hat{e}(u, v)^{ab}$.
- Nondegeneracy: $\hat{e}(g_1, g_2) = g \neq 1_{\mathbb{G}_T}$.

Further, we assume that the strong Diffie–Hellman (SDH) assumption holds on $(\mathbb{G}, \mathbb{G}')$ and the linear Diffie–Hellman assumption holds on $\mathbb{G}$ [24].

Then, the TM randomly selects two elements $h \overset{R}{\leftarrow} \mathbb{G} \setminus \{1_\mathbb{G}\}$, $h_0 \overset{R}{\leftarrow} \mathbb{G}' \setminus \{1_{\mathbb{G}'}\}$ along with two random numbers $\xi_1, \xi_2 \overset{R}{\leftarrow} \mathbb{Z}_p^*$, and sets $u, v \in \mathbb{G}$ such that $u^{\xi_1} = v^{\xi_2} = h$, and $h_1, h_2 \in \mathbb{G}'$ such that $h_1 = h_0^{\xi_1}, h_2 = h_0^{\xi_2}$. In the end, the TM keeps the TM's private key $gmsk_t = (\xi_1, \xi_2)$ secretly, and sends the system parameters

$$(\mathbb{G}, \mathbb{G}', \mathbb{G}_T, g_1, g_2, g, p, \psi, \hat{e}, u, v, h, h_0, h_1, h_2)$$

to the TRC which works as the MM.

TABLE 2.2. Message Format for OBU

Group ID	Message ID	Payload	Timestamp	Signature	TTL
2 bytes	2 bytes	100 bytes	4 bytes	192 bytes	1 byte

Finally, the TRC randomly selects $\gamma \xleftarrow{R} \mathbb{Z}_p^*$ as the MM's private key $gmsk_m$, and sets $w = P_{pub} = g_2^{\gamma}$ as a system parameter. The TRC also chooses two secure cryptographic hash functions $H : \{0, 1\}^* \rightarrow \mathbb{Z}_p^*, H_1 : \{0, 1\}^* \times \mathbb{G}_T \rightarrow \mathbb{Z}_p^*$. In the end, the TRC publishes the system parameters *param* and group public key *gpk* as follows:

$$
\begin{cases}
param = \begin{pmatrix} \mathbb{G}, \mathbb{G}', \mathbb{G}_T, g_1, g_2, g, p, \psi, \hat{e}, \\ H, H_1, P_{pub}, u, v, h, h_0, h_1, h_2 \end{pmatrix} \\
gpk = (g_1, g_2, g, w)
\end{cases}
$$

In this way, the security system is initialized.

2.3.3 Security Protocol between OBUs

2.3.3.1 Message Format. The format of the safety messages sent by the OBU is defined as in Table 2.2, where "Group ID" is used to identify which group does the vehicle belong to. The message payload may include information about the vehicle's position, message sending time, direction, speed, acceleration/deceleartion, and traffic events. According to Ref. 23, the payload of a message is 100 bytes. A timestamp is used to prevent message replay attack. The last second field is the OBU's signature of the first four parts of the message. The last field is *time to live* (TTL), which records a timer that controls how long the message is allowed to remain in VANETs. This prevents the VANET from becoming swamped by messages.

2.3.3.2 Security Protocol for OBU and OBU Communication. The proposed security protocol is an elaboration of the short group signature scheme [21] in order to support the proposed hybrid membership revocation scheme, described below. Specifically, the proposed security protocol contains five phases.

1. *Membership Registration.* During the vehicle registration process, the MM generates a tuple (A_i, x_i) for each vehicle i with identity ID_i, which is the vehicle's private key $gsk[i]$ shown as follows: by using γ, the MM first computes

$$
x_i \leftarrow H(\gamma, ID_i) \in \mathbb{Z}_p^*
$$

and then sets $A_i \leftarrow g_1^{1/(\gamma + x_i)} \in \mathbb{G}$. In the end, the MM stores the pair (A_i, ID_i) in its record, which completes the membership registration.

Note that since the value x_i can be computed by γ and ID_i, the MM does not need to store x_i in order to save the storage space.

2. *Signing.* Given message M, vehicle i signs on M before sending it out. With the group public key *gpk* and the private key pair (A_i, x_i), the signing procedure is composed of the following computations:

Select the exponents $\alpha, \beta \overset{R}{\leftarrow} \mathbb{Z}_p^*$.

Compute an encryption of A_i and (T_1, T_2, T_3), where

$$T_1 \leftarrow u^\alpha, \quad T_2 \leftarrow v^\beta, \quad T_3 \leftarrow A_i h^{\alpha+\beta}. \tag{2.1}$$

Compute $\delta_1 \leftarrow x_i\alpha$ and $\delta_2 \leftarrow x_i\beta$.

Randomly pick up blinding values $r_\alpha, r_\beta, r_{x_i}, r_{\delta_1}, r_{\delta_2}$ from $\mathbb{Z}_p^*$.

Compute R_1, R_2, R_3, R_4, R_5 as below:

$$\begin{cases} R_1 \leftarrow u^{r_\alpha} \\ R_2 \leftarrow v^{r_\beta} \\ R_3 \leftarrow \hat{e}(T_3, g_2)^{r_{x_i}} \cdot \hat{e}(h, w)^{-r_\alpha - r_\beta} \cdot \hat{e}(h, g_2)^{-r_{\delta_1} - r_{\delta_2}} \\ R_4 \leftarrow T_1^{r_{x_i}} \cdot u^{-r_{\delta_1}} \\ R_5 \leftarrow T_2^{r_{x_i}} \cdot v^{-r_{\delta_2}} \end{cases}$$

Obtain the challenger c using the above values and M:

$$c \leftarrow H(M, T_1, T_2, T_3, R_1, R_2, R_3, R_4, R_5) \in \mathbb{Z}_p^*$$

Compute $s_\alpha, s_\beta, s_{x_i}, s_{\delta_1}, s_{\delta_2}$, where

$$\begin{cases} s_\alpha = r_\alpha + c\alpha \\ s_\beta = r_\beta + c\beta \\ s_{x_i} = r_{x_i} + cx_i \\ s_{\delta_1} = r_{\delta_1} + c\delta_1 \\ s_{\delta_2} = r_{\delta_2} + c\delta_2 \end{cases} \tag{2.2}$$

Finally, combine the values of Eq. (2.1) and Eq. (2.2) to form the message signature σ

$$\sigma \leftarrow (T_1, T_2, T_3, c, s_\alpha, s_\beta, s_{x_i}, s_{\delta_1}, s_{\delta_2})$$

Formulate the message according to Table 2.2 and send it out.

3. *Verification.* Once receiving a message, the receiver first checks whether the time information in the message payload is in the allowable time window. If so, the receiving vehicle will perform signature verification by first recomputing

the challenger $\tilde{c}$ followed by reconstructing $(\tilde{R}_1, \tilde{R}_2, \tilde{R}_3, \tilde{R}_4, \tilde{R}_5)$ according to the following formula:

$$
\begin{cases}
\tilde{R}_1 \leftarrow u^{s_\alpha}/T_1^c \\
\tilde{R}_2 \leftarrow v^{s_\beta}/T_2^c \\
\tilde{R}_3 \leftarrow \hat{e}(T_3, g_2)^{s_{x_i}} \cdot \hat{e}(h, w)^{-s_\alpha - s_\beta} \cdot \hat{e}(h, g_2)^{-s_{\delta_1} - s_{\delta_2}} \\
\qquad \cdot (\hat{e}(T_3, w)/\hat{e}(g_1, g_2))^c \\
\tilde{R}_4 \leftarrow T_1^{s_{x_i}} \cdot u^{-s_{\delta_1}} \\
\tilde{R}_5 \leftarrow T_2^{s_{x_i}} \cdot v^{-s_{\delta_2}}
\end{cases}
$$

Then, $\tilde{c}$ is recomputed from

$$
\tilde{c} = H(M, T_1, T_2, T_3, \tilde{R}_1, \tilde{R}_2, \tilde{R}_3, \tilde{R}_4, \tilde{R}_5)
$$

The receiver finally checks whether this value is the same as c in signature σ. If so, the receiver considers the message to be valid and unaltered from a trusted group member. If not, the receiver neglects the message.

4. *Membership Traceability.* A membership tracing operation is performed when solving a dispute, where the real identity of the signature generator is desired. The TM first checks the validity of the signature, and then computes A_i by using the following equation:

$$
A_i \leftarrow T_3/(T_1^{\xi_1} \cdot T_2^{\xi_2})
$$

Once the MM gets element A_i from the TM, it can look up the record (A_i, ID_i) to find the corresponding identity ID_i.

5. *Membership Revocation.* Once a vehicle is found to be compromised, it will be excluded from the system. Currently there are two approaches of revoking a compromised vehicle. One is through updating the group public key and private key at all unrevoked vehicles. Given the released private key pairs of the revoked vehicles in a *revocation list* (RL), unrevoked vehicles can locally update their private key pair $gsk[i]$ and the group public key gpk, whereas those revoked vehicles cannot update their keying materials [21]. Obviously, this scheme may introduce a significant amount of overhead since it needs to change the group public and private keys of each vehicle from time to time. The other revoking mechanism is similar to the traditional CRL-based revocation scheme, called *verifier-local revocation* (VLR) [25–27], by which only verifiers are involved in the revocation checkup operation. The VLR scheme is efficient when the revoked vehicles are few. However, since the signature verification time grows linearly with the number of revoked vehicles, the vehicle revocation verification procedure becomes very time-consuming and inefficient when a large number of revoked vehicles exist in the RL. Therefore, to initiate a graceful tradeoff, we propose a hybrid membership revocation mechanism. The basic idea of

the proposed mechanism is that when the number of revoked vehicles in the revocation list (denoted as $|RL|$) is less than some predefined threshold T_r, the VLR mechanism is adopted; otherwise, the first approach through updating the corresponding public keys and private key pairs is employed. The proposed mechanism is further described as follows:

Algorithm 1: Revocation Verification Algorithm

Data: Input $(param, RL, \sigma)$
Result: Output valid or invalid
for $i \leftarrow 1$ **to** $|RL|$ **do**
    get one A_i from RL
    if $\hat{e}(T_3/A_i, h_0) = \hat{e}(T_1, h_1)\hat{e}(T_2, h_2)$ **then**
        return invalid
    end
end
return valid

Case 1. When $|RL| < T_r$, the MM publishes the revocation list $RL = \{A_1, \ldots, A_b\}$, where $b < T_r$.

For a given group signature σ, any verifier first executes the signature verification operation, and then executes the revocation check, which is shown in Algorithm 1, where $param$ is $(\mathbb{G}, \mathbb{G}', \mathbb{G}_T, g_1, g_2, g, p, \psi, \hat{e}, H, H_1, P_{pub}, u, v, h, h_0, h_1, h_2)$. If the returned value is valid, no element of RL is encoded in (T_1, T_2, T_3) of σ, the signer of the group signature σ has not been revoked. However, if the returned value is invalid, then there exists some A_i being encoded in (T_1, T_2, T_3), which can be checked by $\hat{e}(T_3/A_i, h_0) = \hat{e}(T_1, h_1)\hat{e}(T_2, h_2)$, since

$$
\begin{aligned}
&\hat{e}(T_3/A_i, h_0) \\
&= \hat{e}(A_i h^{\alpha+\beta}/A_i, h_0) \\
&= \hat{e}(h^{\alpha+\beta}, h_0) = \hat{e}(h^\alpha, h_0)\hat{e}(h^\beta, h_0) \\
&= \hat{e}(u^{\alpha\xi_1}, h_0)\hat{e}(v^{\beta\xi_2}, h_0) \\
&= \hat{e}(u^\alpha, h_0^{\xi_1})\hat{e}(v^\beta, h_0^{\xi_2}) \\
&= \hat{e}(T_1, h_1)\hat{e}(T_2, h_2)
\end{aligned}
$$

Case 2. When $|RL| \geq T_r$, the MM sends all signers and verifiers in the system revocation list $RL = \{(A_1^*, x_1), \ldots, (A_b^*, x_b)\}$, where $b \geq T_r$. For each private key (A_i^*, x_i), $x_i \leftarrow H(\gamma, ID_i) \in \mathbb{Z}_p^*$ and $A_i^* \leftarrow g_2^{1/(\gamma+x_i)} \in \mathbb{G}'$. It is worth noting that $A_i = \psi(A_i^*)$.

After receiving the revocation list RL, group public key gpk can be easily updated. The following lemma demonstrates how to use a given group public key and all the revoked private keys to construct a new group public key.

Lemma 1 *Given group key gpk = (g_1, g_2, g, w) and all revoked private keys $\{(A_1^*, x_1), \dots, (A_b^*, x_b)\} \in RL$, the new group public key can be constructed as*

$$gpk_{new} = (\hat{g}_1, \hat{g}_2, \hat{g}, \hat{w})$$

where $\hat{g}_1 = g_1^{1/y}$, $\hat{g}_2 = g_2^{1/y}$, $\hat{g} = e(\hat{g}_1, \hat{g}_2)$ and $\hat{w} = \hat{g}_2^{\gamma}$ with $y = \prod_{i=1}^{b}(\gamma + x_i) \in \mathbb{Z}_p^*$.

Proof.

* Since $\hat{g}_2 = g_2^{1/y}$ should be derived from $(A_1^*, x_1), \dots, (A_b^*, x_b)$, we first construct the following equation

$$
\begin{aligned}
g_2^{1/y} &= \prod_{i=1}^{b} \left(A_i^*\right)^{y_i} \\
&= \left(A_1^*\right)^{y_1} \cdot \left(A_2^*\right)^{y_2} \cdots \left(A_b^*\right)^{y_b} \\
&= g_2^{y_1/(\gamma+x_1)} \cdot g_2^{y_2/(\gamma+x_2)} \cdots g_2^{y_b/(\gamma+x_b)} \\
&= g_2^{\sum_{i=1}^{b} y_i/(\gamma+x_i)}
\end{aligned}
\tag{2.3}
$$

with b unknown values $y_1, y_2, \dots, y_b$.
We raise (2.3) to an exponent equation as

$$
\begin{aligned}
\frac{1}{y} &= \sum_{i=1}^{b} \frac{y_i}{\gamma+x_i} \\
&= \frac{y_1}{\gamma+x_1} + \cdots + \frac{y_b}{\gamma+x_b}
\end{aligned}
$$

Then, we have

$$
\begin{aligned}
1 &= y \left(\frac{y_1}{\gamma+x_1} + \cdots + \frac{y_b}{\gamma+x_b} \right) \\
&= \prod_{i=1}^{b}(\gamma + x_i) \cdot \left(\frac{y_1}{\gamma+x_1} + \cdots + \frac{y_b}{\gamma+x_b} \right) \\
&= \prod_{i=2}^{b}(\gamma + x_i) \cdot y_1 + \prod_{i=1, i\neq 2}^{b}(\gamma + x_i) \cdot y_2 \\
&\quad + \cdots + \prod_{i=1, i\neq b}^{b}(\gamma + x_i) \cdot y_b
\end{aligned}
\tag{2.4}
$$

Without loss of generality, we assume $b = 2$, which leads to

$$
\begin{aligned}
1 &= y_1(\gamma + x_2) + y_2(\gamma + x_1) \\
&= (y_1 + y_2)\gamma + y_1 x_2 + y_2 x_1
\end{aligned}
\tag{2.5}
$$

Then, we have the following two equations:

$$
\begin{cases}
y_1 + y_2 = 0 \\
y_1 x_2 + y_2 x_1 = 1
\end{cases}
\tag{2.6}
$$

Solving (2.6), we obtain

$$\begin{cases} y_1 = \frac{1}{x_2 - x_1} \\ y_2 = \frac{1}{x_1 - x_2} \end{cases} \tag{2.7}$$

Substituting (2.7) in (2.3) gives

$$\hat{g}_2 = \left(A_1^*\right)^{y_1} \cdot \left(A_2^*\right)^{y_2}$$
$$= g_2^{1/(\gamma+x_1)(x_2-x_1)} \cdot g_2^{1/(\gamma+x_2)(x_1-x_2)}$$
$$= g_2^{1/(\gamma+x_1)(\gamma+x_2)}$$
$$\hat{g}_1 = \psi(\hat{g}_2) = g_1^{1/(\gamma+x_1)(\gamma+x_2)}$$

and

$$\hat{g} = e(\hat{g}_1, \hat{g}_2)$$

* To compute $\hat{w} = \hat{g}_2^\gamma = g_2^{\gamma/y}$, we construct the following equation

$$g_2^{\gamma/y} = g_2^{y_0} \cdot \prod_{i=1}^{b} (A_i^*)^{y_i}$$
$$= g_2^{y_0} \cdot (A_1^*)^{y_1} \cdots (A_b^*)^{y_b}$$
$$= g_2^{y_0} \cdot g_2^{y_1/(\gamma+x_1)} \cdots g_2^{y_b/(\gamma+x_b)} \tag{2.8}$$
$$= g_2^{y_0 + \sum_{i=1}^{b} y_i/(\gamma+x_i)}$$

with $b + 1$ unknown values $y_0, y_1, y_2, \ldots, y_b$.
We raise (2.8) to an exponent equation as follows:

$$\frac{\gamma}{y} = y_0 + \sum_{i=1}^{b} \frac{y_i}{\gamma + x_i}$$
$$= y_0 + \frac{y_1}{\gamma + x_1} + \cdots + \frac{y_b}{\gamma + x_b}$$

Then, we have

$$\gamma = y \left(y_0 + \frac{y_1}{\gamma + x_1} + \cdots + \frac{y_b}{\gamma + x_b} \right)$$
$$= \prod_{i=1}^{b} (\gamma + x_i) \cdot \left(y_0 + \frac{y_1}{\gamma + x_1} + \cdots + \frac{y_b}{\gamma + x_b} \right)$$
$$= \prod_{i=1}^{b} (\gamma + x_i) \cdot y_0 + \prod_{i=2}^{b} (\gamma + x_i) \cdot y_1$$
$$+ \cdots + \prod_{i=1, i \neq b}^{b} (\gamma + x_i) \cdot y_b$$

Similarly, assuming $b = 2$, we have

$$\begin{aligned}
\gamma &= y_0(\gamma + x_1)(\gamma + x_2) \\
&\quad + y_1(\gamma + x_2) + y_2(\gamma + x_1) \\
&= y_0\gamma^2 + (y_0(x_1 + x_2) + y_1 + y_2)\gamma \\
&\quad + y_0 x_1 x_2 + y_1 x_2 + y_2 x_1
\end{aligned}$$

which leads to the following three equations:

$$\begin{cases}
y_0 = 0 \\
y_0(x_1 + x_2) + y_1 + y_2 = 1 \\
y_0 x_1 x_2 + y_1 x_2 + y_2 x_1 = 0
\end{cases} \tag{2.9}$$

Solving (2.9), we obtain

$$\begin{cases}
y_0 = 0 \\
y_1 = \dfrac{x_1}{x_1 - x_2} \\
y_2 = \dfrac{x_2}{x_2 - x_1}
\end{cases} \tag{2.10}$$

Substituting (2.10) in $\hat{w} = g_2^{\gamma/y}$ gives

$$\begin{aligned}
\hat{w} = \hat{g}_2^{\gamma} &= g_2^{\gamma/y} \\
&= g_2^{y_0} \cdot \left(A_1^*\right)^{y_1} \cdot \left(A_2^*\right)^{y_2} \\
&= \left(A_1^*\right)^{x_1/x_1 - x_2} \cdot \left(A_2^*\right)^{x_2/x_2 - x_1} \\
&= g_2^{x_1/(\gamma + x_1)(x_1 - x_2)} g_2^{x_2/(\gamma + x_2)(x_2 - x_1)} \\
&= g_2^{\gamma/(\gamma + x_1)(\gamma + x_2)}
\end{aligned}$$

As a result, we proved that the group public key can be constructed as: $gpk_{new} = (\hat{g}_1, \hat{g}_2, \hat{g}, \hat{w})$.

Next, we show how an unrevoked vehicle updates its private key, $(A = g_1^{1/(\gamma + x_0)}, x_0)$, for a new one denoted as $(\hat{A}, x_0)$, where $\hat{A} = A^{1/y} \in \mathbb{G}_1$.

Lemma 2 *Given all revoked private keys* $\{(A_1^*, x_1), \ldots, (A_b^*, x_b)\} \in RL$, *the new private key for an unrevoked vehicle* $i = 0$ *can be constructed as*

$$(\hat{A}, x_0)$$

where $x_0 = H(\gamma, ID_0) \in \mathbb{Z}_p^*$, $\hat{A} = A^{1/y} \in \mathbb{G}$ *with* $y = \prod_{i=1}^b (\gamma + x_i) \in \mathbb{Z}_p^*$.

Proof.

* Since $\hat{A} = A^{1/y}$ should be derived from (A, x_0) and $(A_1^*, x_1), \ldots, (A_b^*, x_b)$. we first construct the equation

$$
\begin{aligned}
A^{1/y} &= A^{y_0} \cdot \prod_{i=1}^{b} (\psi(A_i^*))^{y_i} \\
&= A^{y_0} \cdot \left(\psi\left(A_1^*\right)\right)^{y_1} \cdots \left(\psi\left(A_b^*\right)\right)^{y_b} \\
&= g_1^{y_0/(\gamma+x_0)} \cdot g_1^{y_1/(\gamma+x_1)} \cdots g_b^{y_b/(\gamma+x_b)} \\
&= g_1^{\sum_{i=0}^{b} y_i/(\gamma+x_i)}
\end{aligned}
\tag{2.11}
$$

with $b + 1$ unknown values $y_0, y_1, \ldots, y_b$. We raise (2.11) to an exponent equation as

$$
\begin{aligned}
\frac{1}{y(\gamma+x_0)} &= \sum_{i=0}^{b} \frac{y_i}{\gamma+x_i} \\
&= \frac{y_0}{\gamma+x_0} + \frac{y_1}{\gamma+x_1} + \cdots + \frac{y_b}{\gamma+x_b}
\end{aligned}
$$

Then, we have

$$
\begin{aligned}
1 &= y(\gamma + x_0)\left(\frac{y_0}{\gamma+x_0} + \cdots + \frac{y_b}{\gamma+x_b}\right) \\
&= \prod_{i=0}^{b}(\gamma + x_i) \cdot \left(\frac{y_0}{\gamma+x_0} + \cdots + \frac{y_b}{\gamma+x_b}\right) \\
&= \prod_{i=1}^{b}(\gamma + x_i) \cdot y_0 + \prod_{i=0, i\neq 1}^{b}(\gamma + x_i) \cdot y_1 \\
&\quad + \cdots + \prod_{i=0, i\neq b}^{b}(\gamma + x_i) \cdot y_b
\end{aligned}
$$

Without loss of generality, we assume that $b = 2$. Thus, we have

$$
\begin{aligned}
1 &= y_0(\gamma + x_1)(\gamma + x_2) + y_1(\gamma + x_0)(\gamma + x_2) \\
&\quad + y_2(\gamma + x_0)(\gamma + x_1) \\
&= (y_0 + y_1 + y_2)\gamma^2 + [y_0(x_1 + x_2) \\
&\quad + y_1(x_0 + x_2) + y_2(x_0 + x_1)]\gamma \\
&\quad + y_0 x_1 x_2 + y_1 x_0 x_2 + y_2 x_0 x_1
\end{aligned}
$$

which leads to the following three equations:

$$
\begin{cases}
y_0 + y_1 + y_2 = 0 \\
y_0(x_1 + x_2) + y_1(x_0 + x_2) + y_2(x_0 + x_1) = 0 \\
y_0 x_1 x_2 + y_1 x_0 x_2 + y_2 x_0 x_1 = 1
\end{cases}
\tag{2.12}
$$

Solving (2.12), we obtain

$$
\begin{cases}
y_0 = \frac{1}{(x_1-x_0)(x_2-x_0)} \\
y_1 = \frac{1}{(x_0-x_1)(x_2-x_1)} \\
y_2 = \frac{1}{(x_0-x_2)(x_1-x_2)}
\end{cases}
\tag{2.13}
$$

Substituting (2.13) in (2.11) gives

$$
\begin{aligned}
\hat{A} &= A^{1/y} \\
&= A^{y_0} \cdot \left(\psi\left(A_1^*\right)\right)^{y_1} \cdot \left(\psi\left(A_2^*\right)\right)^{y_2} \\
&= g_1^{1/(\gamma+x_0)(x_1-x_0)(x_2-x_0)} \\
&\quad \cdot g_1^{1/(\gamma+x_1)(x_0-x_1)(x_2-x_1)} \\
&\quad \cdot g_1^{1/(\gamma+x_2)(x_0-x_2)(x_1-x_2)} \\
&= g_1^{1/(\gamma+x_0)(\gamma+x_1)(\gamma+x_2)}
\end{aligned}
$$

Thus, $(\hat{A}, x)$ is a valid private key with respect to the group public key $gpk_{new} = (\hat{g}_1, \hat{g}_2, \hat{g}, \hat{w})$.

2.3.3.3 Message Length.
The length of the OBU message can be expressed as

$$
\begin{aligned}
L_{msg\_OBU} = &\; L_{groupID} + L_{msgID} + L_{payload} \\
&+ L_{timestamp} + L_{sig} + L_{TTL}.
\end{aligned}
$$

We have p as a prime with 170 bits long [6]. Each element in $\mathbb{G}$ is 171 bits long, and $L_{sig} = 192$ bytes long. Thus, $L_{msg\_OBU} = 2 + 2 + 100 + 4 + 192 + 1 = 301$ bytes.

2.3.3.4 Security Analysis.
Using group signatures allows any member in the group to anonymously sign an arbitrary number of messages on behalf of the group. The security requirements of a group signature scheme include correctness, unforgeability, anonymity, unlinkability, traceability, and revocation [16], which will be discussed as follows.

- *Correctness.* With the proposed security protocol, a group signature σ generated by a valid group member can be surely identified by the above verification procedure.
- *Unforgeability.* Only a valid group member can sign a message on behalf of the group. A valid group signature cannot be forged, otherwise the strong Diffie–Hellman (SDH) assumption will be in contradiction.
- *Anonymity.* Given a valid group signature σ of some messages, it is computationally difficult to identify the actual signer by anyone but the group manager.

TABLE 2.3. Message Format for RSU

Type ID	Message ID	Payload	Timestamp	Signature	ID	TTL
2 bytes	2 bytes	100 bytes	4 bytes	43 bytes	40 bytes	1 byte

According to the linear Diffie–Hellman assumption, the interactive protocol underlying the group signature scheme is zero knowledge such that no information is revealed by σ.

- *Unlinkability*. According to the verification procedure, it is computationally hard to decide whether two valid signatures of different groups are computed by the same group member.
- *Traceability*. The group manager can always create a valid signature and identify the actual signer by the membership recovery procedure. Let the group signature $\sigma = (T_1, T_2, T_3, c, s_\alpha, s_\beta, s_{x_i}, s_{\delta_1}, s_{\delta_2})$ be valid. The group manager can thus first derive

$$A_i \leftarrow T_3 / \left(T_1^{\xi_1} \cdot T_2^{\xi_2} \right)$$

by which the signer's identity can be traced.
- *Revocation*. Membership revocation can be fulfilled by the abovementioned two revocation schemes.

Boneh et al. [21] give a more comprehensive description of security analysis.

2.3.4   Security Protocol between RSUs and OBUs

2.3.4.1   Message Format. We define the format of safety messages between RSUs and OBUs as shown in Table 2.3.

The first four fields are signed by the RSU, by which the "Signature" field can be derived. The "ID" is 40 bytes long and serves as the public key of the sender. Note that the ID may also include the name of the RSU, the authorized geographic region in which to operate, and the authorized message type. As mentioned earlier, OBUs installed in emergency vehicles are treated the same as RSUs. Thus, the ID can also be the emergency vehicle license plate number, the types of emergency vehicles, for example police, fire or *emergency medical services* (EMS); and the name of municipality where emergency services are provided. The last field is TTL, which records a timer that controls how long the message is allowed to remain in VANETs. In this case, the situation in which a VANET becomes swamped by messages can be avoided. Without loss of generality, we

TABLE 2.4. The Format of RSU's Identity

Serial No.	Physical Location Information	Type ID

use RSU as an example to illustrate the proposed protocol. The length of the signature will be discussed later.

2.3.4.2 Security Protocol for RSU–OBU Communication. The proposed security protocol between RSU and OBU contains the following three phases:

1. *Private Key Generation.* A unique identifier string is obtained for each RSU as its ID according to its property, whose format is shown in Table 2.4, where the first field records a unique serial number, the second field records its physical location information, and the third field indicates the attribute of the message, such as a traffic-sign-related message and a warning message. The TRC computes the private key for each RSU by

$$S_{ID_i} \leftarrow g_1^{1/(\gamma + H(ID_i))}$$

   and sends it to each RSU through a secure channel.

2. *Signing.* Before sending each safety message M, RSU signs the message M by first picking up a random value $x \xleftarrow{R} \mathbb{Z}_p^*$ and computing

$$r \leftarrow g^x \in \mathbb{G}_T$$

   With r, we can set

$$h_\sigma \leftarrow H_1(M, r) \in \mathbb{Z}_p^*$$

   and compute

$$S_\sigma \leftarrow S_{ID_i}^{x + h_\sigma} \in \mathbb{G}_1$$

   The signature σ is simply the pair $(h_\sigma, S_\sigma) \in \mathbb{Z}_p^* \times \mathbb{G}$. Finally, the message is formatted according to Table 2.3 and is sent out by RSU.

3. *Verification.* Any vehicle receiving a message from a RSU will first guarantee that the sender is working under the authorized domain. The vehicle compares the physical location of the message sender with the location information in the RSU's identifier string in order to prevent any attacker from taking the device down from one RSU and putting it elsewhere. Then, the receiver compares the type ID in the received message with the property stated in the identifier string. If the type ID cannot match with the property, the message will be ignored. For example, the messages with a property of curve speed warning will not be acceptable in case the content of the message is "road under construction ahead." The receiver should also check the time information in the payload to make sure

the message is in the allowable time window. Finally, the receiver checks the validity of the message signature by computing

$$\tilde{h}_\sigma \leftarrow H_1\left(M, e\left(S_\sigma, g_2^{H(ID_i)} \cdot P_{pub}\right)g^{-h_\sigma}\right)$$

This check is to see whether $\tilde{h}_\sigma = h_\sigma$, where h_σ is from σ. If the equation holds, the vehicle accepts the message, otherwise the message is dropped.

2.3.4.3 Message Length. The length of an RSU message can be evaluated in the following expression:

$$L_{msg\_RSU} = L_{typeID} + L_{msgID} + L_{payload}$$
$$+ L_{timestamp} + L_{sig} + L_{ID} + L_{TTL}$$

Similarly, since p is a prime with 170 bits long, and each element in $\mathbb{G}_1$ is 171 bits long, we get the size of the signature σ as 43 bytes. Therefore, $L_{msg\_RSU} = 2 + 2 + 100 + 4 + 43 + 40 + 1 = 192$ bytes.

2.3.4.4 Security Analysis. Using the provably-secure identity-based signature [22] allows RSU to sign an arbitrary number of messages by guaranteeing unforgeability, authentication, data integrity, and nonrepudiation. Barreto et al. [22] give a more comprehensive description of security analysis. In this section, we analyze the proposed protocol, especially the aspects of RSU replication attack prevention and replay attack prevention, discussed below.

- *Prevention of RSU Replication Attack.* The message from a RSU has an "ID" field keeping the RSU's original physical location as well as its type indicating the type of traffic management offered by the RSU. On receipt of the message, the OBU compares the physical location of the OBU with the location information in the RSU's ID string. If the distance is farther than RSU's transmission range, the OBU ignores the message. Therefore, the RSU replication attack can be defeated. Furthermore, the OBU compares the type ID in the received message with the property specified in the ID string of the RSU. If the type ID cannot match with the property, the message will be ignored. For example, the messages with a property of curve speed warning will not be acceptable in case the content of the message is "road under construction ahead."
- *Prevention of Replay Attack.* With a replay attack, an adversary replays the intercepted message from a RSU in order to impersonate as a legitimate RSU. Obviously, it cannot work in the proposed protocol because of the time interval checked in verification procedure. On receiving the message, the OBU checks the time information in the timestamp to ensure that the message is in the allowable time window. If the time information included in the timestamp of the message is not reasonable, the OBU will simply drop the message.

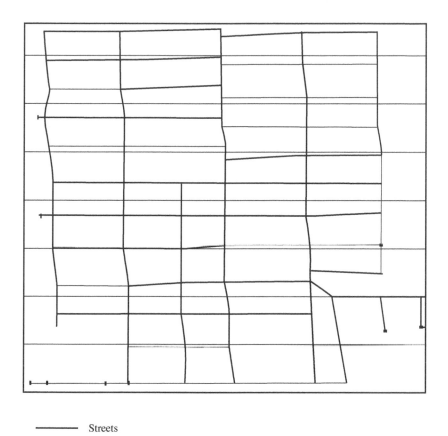

——— Streets

Figure 2.2. A city street scenario corresponding to a square area of size 1000 m × 1000 m.

2.4 PERFORMANCE EVALUATION

In this section, simulation is conducted to verify the efficiency of the proposed secure protocol for IVC applications with the network simulator ns-2 [28]. To properly estimate the real-world road environment and vehicular traffic, two different road systems are considered. The first real-world environment is by way of the mobility model generation tool introduced in 2004 [29], which is specialized to generate realistic city traffic scenario files for vehicles under ns-2. This tool makes use of the publicly available TIGER (topologically integrated geographic encoding and referencing) database from the US Census Bureau, where detailed street maps of each city/town in the United States of America are given. The map adopted in the study is a real-world city traffic environment shown in Fig. 2.2, which corresponds to the Afton Oaks area in Houston, TX. Each vehicle is first randomly scattered on one intersection of the roads and repeatedly moves toward another randomly selected intersection along the paths in the map. Each vehicle is driving with a randomly fluctuating speed in a range of ±5 mi/h centered at the road speed limit that ranges from 35 to 75 mi/h along different streets. The

TABLE 2.5. Simulation Configuration

Simulation Scenario	City Environment
City simulation area	1000 m × 1000 m
Communication range	300 m
Simulation time	100 s
Channel bandwidth	6 Mb/s
Pause time	0 s
Packet size for OBU message	301 bytes
Packet size for RSU message	200 bytes
Highway simulation area	2500 m × 30 m

second type of road system considered in the study is the traffic scenario on a straight bidirectional six-lane highway, where the vehicles are driving with the speed within the range of 100 ± 10 mi/h. In both cases, the RSU is allocated every 500 m along each road, which sends messages every 300 ms. Other simulation parameters are listed in Table 2.5.

The performance metrics considered are the average message delay and average message loss ratio, which are denoted as $avgD_{Msg}$ and $avgLR$, respectively, and are expressed as follows:

$$avgD_{Msg} = \frac{1}{N_D \cdot M_{sent\_n} \cdot K_n} \sum_{n \in D} \sum_{m=1}^{M_{sent\_n}} \sum_{k=1}^{K_n}$$
$$\left(T_{sign}^{n\_m} + T_{transmission}^{n\_m\_k} + T_{verify}^{n\_m\_k} \cdot \left(L_{n\_m\_k} + 1 \right) \right)$$

where D is the sample district in the simulation, N_D is the number of vehicles in D, M_{sent_n} is the number of messages sent by vehicle n, K_n is the number of vehicles within the one-hop communication range of vehicle n, $T_{Sign}^{n\_m}$ is the time taken by vehicle n for signing message m, n_m_k represents the message m sent by vehicle n and received by vehicle k, and $L_{n\_m\_k}$ is the length of the queue in vehicle k when message m send by vehicle n is received. Thus

$$avgLR = \frac{1}{N_D} \sum_{n=1}^{N_D} \frac{M_{consumed}^n}{\sum_{k=1}^{K_n} M_{arrived}^n}$$

where $M_{consumed}^n$ represents the number of messages consumed by vehicle n in the application layer; $M_{arrived}^n$ represents the number of messages that are received by vehicle n in the MAC layer. Here we only consider the message loss caused by the security protocol rather than the wireless transmission channel. Note that the message will be lost if the queue is full when the message arrival rate is higher than the message verification rate. In the following, two sets of experiments are conducted to analyze the impacts of having different traffic loads and cryptographic algorithm processing speeds.

2.4.1 Impact of Traffic Load

The density of the vehicles on the road is the main factor that has a major impact on the system performance since it is related to the total number of messages received by each vehicle. Previous studies considered the effect brought by the actual vehicle density on the road such as vehicles/km or vehicles/km^2, which failed to capture the varying relationship between the communication range and the actual vehicle density. Raya and Hubaux [23] observed that the denser the traffic is, the shorter the communication range (or a smaller radiation power) that should be adopted in order to achieve a satisfied packet loss ratio. Therefore, the number of messages received by a certain vehicle within a dissemination period should be considered as a factor for evaluating system performance instead of taking only the actual traffic density into consideration. Thus, this study takes the average number of neighboring vehicles within the communication range of each vehicle as the traffic load, which serves as the upper bound on the number of packets that a vehicle could receive within a dissemination cycle. Furthermore, the delay induced by any cryptographic operation is considered in the ns-2 simulation through the measurement of cryptographic library MIRACL [30]. In this study, the group signature signing delay and verification delay are 3.6 ms and 7.2 ms,[3] respectively, while the delay of an identity-based signature verification is 3.6 ms.

Simulation results are shown in Fig. 2.3 and Fig. 2.4. It can be seen that with the increase of traffic load (i.e., the number of vehicles within the communication range), the message end-to-end delay does not vary much (around 22 ms), which is smaller than the maximum allowable message end-to-end transmission latency of 100 ms defined in Ref. 23. However, the message loss ratio increases when the traffic load is increased. It is notable that the loss ratio reaches as high as 68% when the traffic load is up to 150. However, such a traffic load can be experienced only when the road is in a severe traffic jam according to the relationship between the communication range and the intervehicle distance [23]. In this situation, it is acceptable if a large number of messages are lost because most of the messages are repeatedly sent by each vehicle. Normal traffic load occurs when the traffic load is below 50, where 20% loss ratio is achieved.

2.4.2 Impact of Cryptographic Signature Verification Delay

Another important factor that determines the performance of a security protocol is the latency utilized by the cryptographic operations in the protocol. However, the speed of implementing a cryptographic algorithm is determined largely by the adopted hardware facility. In this study, we assume that a powerful processor is installed in each vehicle, which can achieve a very high processing speed. By referring to the parameter in given in Ref. 22, where one pairing operation takes 3.6 ms and that in MIRACL library as 8.5 ms, it is a reasonable assumption that the group signature verification latency ranges

---

[3] The computation bottleneck for the signing process of the group signature is one pairing operation and two pairing operations for verification. Based on the measurement, the time to do one pairing is 3.6 ms, so we use 7.2 ms as the verification delay. Similarly, the bottleneck for identity-based signature is one pairing operation during verification, so we use 3.6 ms as the verification delay.

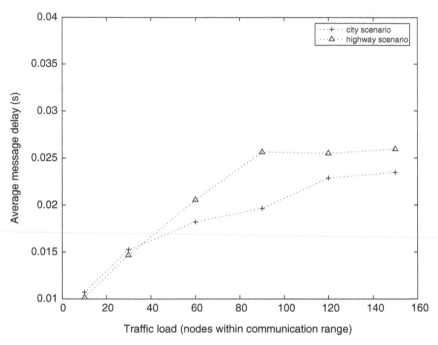

Figure 2.3. Impact of traffic load on the message end-to-end delay.

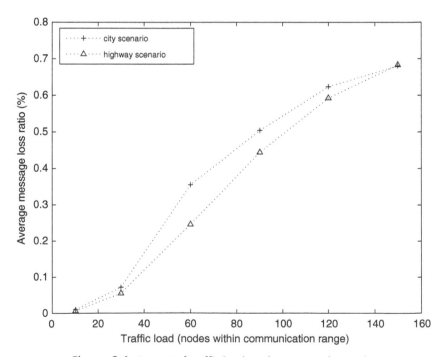

Figure 2.4. Impact of traffic load on the message loss ratio.

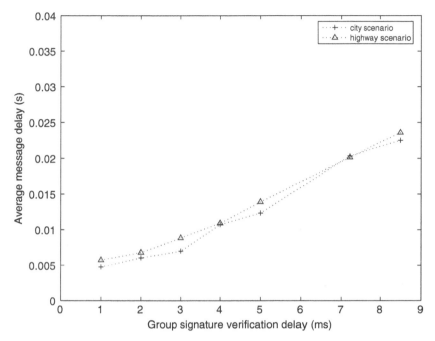

Figure 2.5. Impact of signature verification latency on the message end-to-end delay.

from 1 to 8.5 ms. In the simulation, a normal traffic load in a city is assumed, where in average 60 vehicles are within the communication range of a vehicle. Simulation results are shown in Fig. 2.5 and Fig. 2.6.

It can be seen that the message end-to-end delay and loss ratio increase when the cryptographic operation cost increases. Also, the message loss ratio is significantly increased after the signature verification latency reaches a certain value. Furthermore, the performances under various road systems are very close. This demonstrates the stability and insensitivity of the proposed security protocol to different road systems and traffic loads.

2.4.3 Membership Revocation and Tracing Efficiency

Next, we evaluate the efficiency of membership revocation and tracing schemes in the proposed protocol. We give an efficiency comparison with the schemes in Ref. 31. The efficiency of the membership revocation and tracing schemes is a key requirement to the success of any vehicular application since a user is exposed to a serious risk if a malicious user conducts any dangerous activity or an adversary impersonates a compromised legitimate group member, which is very popular in our daily life. Thus, we need to improve the performance of membership revocation and tracing schemes as much as possible.

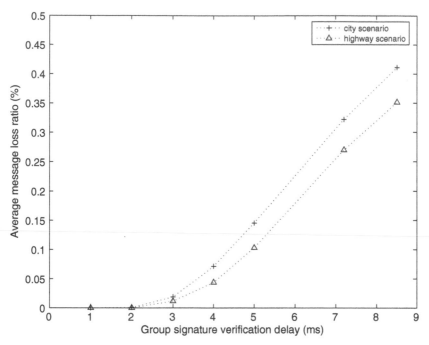

Figure 2.6. Impact of signature verification delay on the average message loss ratio.

When a vehicle is compromised, its certificates need to be revoked, to eliminate potential safety hazards. In the Raya–Hubaux study [31], 43,800 anonymous certificates have to be put in the CRL. The storage cost of the CRL is 43,800 kB.[4] For the proposed membership revocation scheme, only an A_i needs to be put on the CRL, where i represents vehicle i. The storage cost of the CRL is only 171 bits. It can easily be seen that the size of the CRL is considerably reduced. The more revoked vehicles are in the CRL, the more saving the proposed membership revocation scheme can have. This is extremely important since the CRL can be distributed to any individual OBU and RSU, to avoid contacting a centralized CRL when performing membership revocation verification.

Furthermore, in the case of a dispute such as a crime or accident scene investigation, where one needs to look for witnesses, the authorities should be able to trace the message senders by revealing the identity of the message sender. In the Raya–Hubaux study [31], the authority keeps all the anonymous certificates for each vehicle in the administrative region, results in a huge database with a storage cost of 43,800 kB $* n$, where n is the total number of vehicles (probably millions of cars). Similarly, the proposed membership tracing scheme also needs to maintain a table containing an A_i and its corresponding real identity of the vehicle for each vehicle, which is only 307 bits if the identity of the vehicle is 136 bits (The VIN of a vehicle is a 17-character number containing both

---

[4] The size of a X.509 public key certificate is about 1 kB [32].

alpha and numeric characters.) Thus, the storage cost for the proposed scheme is only 307 bits $* n$, and this is a very significant storage saving.

2.5 CONCLUDING REMARKS

A novel security protocol has been proposed for the *intervehicle communication* (IVC) applications based on group signature and identity-based signature schemes. With group signature, security, privacy, and efficient traceability can be achieved without inducing the overhead of managing a huge number of stored certificates at the *membership manager* (MM) and *tracing manager* (TM) sides. With the identity-based signature, the management complexity on public key and certificate can be further reduced. Extensive simulation has been conducted on both surface (city) roads and highway systems to demonstrate that the message delay and loss ratio can be kept quite low even in the presence of a large computational latency due to the cryptographic operations.

REFERENCES

1. "KVH industries," http://www.kvh.com/.
2. "MSN TV," http://www.msntv.com/.
3. X. Lin, X. Sun, P.-H. Ho, and X. Shen, "GSIS: A secure and privacy-preserving protocol for vehicular communications," *IEEE Transactions on Vehicular Technology*, vol. 56, no. 6, pp. 3442–3456, 2007.
4. D. Chaum and E. Van Heyst, "Group signatures," in *Proc. 10th Annual International Conference on Theory and Application of Cryptographic Techniques*, ser. EURO-CRYPT'91. Berlin, Heidelberg: Springer-Verlag, 1991, pp. 257–265. (Available online at http://dl.acm.org/citation.cfm?id=1754868.1754897.)
5. A. Shamir, "Identity-based cryptosystems and signature schemes," *Proc. Advances in Cryptology, (CRYPTO'84)*, Santa Barbara, CA, USA, Aug. 19–22, 1984, ser. Lecture Notes in Computer Science, vol. 196. Springer, 1984, pp. 47–53.
6. D. Boneh and M. K. Franklin, "Identity-based encryption from the weil pairing," in *Advances in Cryptology—CRYPTO 2001, 21st Annual International Cryptology Conference*, Santa Barbara, CA, Aug. 19–23, 2001, ser. Lecture Notes in Computer Science, vol. 2139. Springer, 2001, pp. 213–229.
7. R. L. Rivest, A. Shamir, and L. Adleman, "A method for obtaining digital signatures and public-key cryptosystems," *Communications of the ACM*, vol. 21, no. 2, pp. 120–126, Feb. 1978. (Available online at http://doi.acm.org/10.1145/359340.359342.)
8. T. El Gamal, "A public key cryptosystem and a signature scheme based on discrete logarithms," *Proc. of CRYPTO 84 on Advances in Cryptology*. New York: Springer-Verlag, 1985, pp. 10–18. (Available online at http://dl.acm.org/citation.cfm?id=19478.19480.)
9. "Traffic light," http://en.wikipedia.org/wiki/Traffic_light.
10. C. Liu and J. T. Yu, "An analysis of dos attacks on wireless LAN," *Proc. 6th IASTED International Multi-Conference on Wireless and Optical Communications: Conference on Communication Systems and Applications, Conference on Optical Communication Systems*

and Networks, Conference on Wireless Networks and Emerging Technologies, Conference on Wireless SENSOR Networks, Banff, Alberta: IASTED, July 3–5, 2006, 2006.

11. I. Aad, J. Hubaux, and E. W. Knightly, "Denial of service resilience in ad hoc networks," Proc. 10th Annual International Conference on Mobile Computing and Networking, MOBI-COM 2004, Philadelphia: ACM, Sept. 26–Oct. 1, 2004, pp. 202–215. (Available online at http://doi.acm.org/10.1145/1023720.1023741.)

12. S. Ranjan, R. Swaminathan, M. Uysal, and E. W. Knightly, "DoS-resilient scheduling to counter application layer attacks under imperfect detection," Proc. INFOCOM 2006. 25th IEEE International Conference on Computer Communications, Joint Conference of the IEEE Computer and Communications Societies, Barcelona, Catalunya: IEEE, April 23–29, 2006. (Available online at http://dx.doi.org/10.1109/INFOCOM.2006.127.)

13. J. Mölsä, "Increasing the DoS attack resiliency in military ad hoc networks," Proc. Military Communications Conference, 2005. MILCOM 2005. IEEE, Oct. 2005, vol. 4, pp. 2282–2288.

14. J. V. E. Mölsä, "Cross-layer designs for mitigating range attacks in ad hoc networks," Proc. 24th IASTED International Conference on Parallel and Distributed Computing and Networks, ser. PDCN'06. Anaheim, CA: ACTA Press, 2006, pp. 64–69. (Available online at http://dl.acm.org/citation.cfm?id=1168920.1168931.)

15. G. Wang, "Security analysis of several group signature schemes," Proc. Progress in Cryptology—INDOCRYPT 2003, 4th International Conference on Cryptology in India, New Delhi: Springer, Dec. 8–10, 2003, pp. 252–265. (Available online at http://dx.doi.org/10.1007/978-3-540-24582-7_19.)

16. G. Ateniese, J. Camenisch, M. Joye, and G. Tsudik, "A practical and provably secure coalition-resistant group signature scheme," Proc. Advances in Cryptology—CRYPTO 2000, 20th Annual International Cryptology Conference, Santa Barbara, CA: Springer, Aug. 20–24, 2000. pp. 255–270. (Available online at http://dx.doi.org/10.1007/3-540-44598-6_16.)

17. S. Han, J. Wang, and W. Liu, "An efficient identity-based group signature scheme over elliptic curves," Proc. European Conference on Universal Multiservice Networks (ECUMN'04), IEEE, 2004, pp. 417–429.

18. C. Popescu, "An efficient id-based group signature scheme," Studia Univ. Babes-Bolyai, Informatica, vol. 47, no. 2, pp. 29–38, 2002.

19. A. Miyaji and K. Umeda, "A fully-functional group signature scheme over only known-order group," Proc. 2nd International Conference on Applied Cryptography and Network Security, 2004 (ACNS'04), Yellow Mountain, China, June 8–11, 2004, Springer, pp. 164–179. (Available online at http://dx.doi.org/10.1007/978-3-540-24852-1_12.)

20. J. Zhang, Q. Wu, and Y. Wang, "A novel efficient group signature scheme with forward security," Proc. Information and Communications Security, 5th International Conference, ICICS 2003, Huhehaote, China: Springer, Oct. 10–13, 2003, pp. 292–300. (Available online at http://dx.doi.org/10.1007/978-3-540-39927-8_27.)

21. D. Boneh, X. Boyen, and H. Shacham, "Short group signatures," Proc. Advances in Cryptology—CRYPTO 2004, 24th Annual International Cryptology Conference, Santa Barbara, CA: Springer, Aug. 15–19, 2004, pp. 41–55. (Available online at http://dx.doi.org/10.1007/978-3-540-28628-8_3.)

22. P. S. L. M. Barreto, B. Libert, N. McCullagh, and J.-J. Quisquater, "Efficient and provably-secure identity-based signatures and signcryption from bilinear maps," Proc. 11th International Conference on Theory and Application of Cryptology and Information Security, ser. ASIACRYPT'05. Berlin, Heidelberg: Springer-Verlag, 2005, pp. 515–532. (Available online at http://dx.doi.org/10.1007/11593447_28.)

23. "Vehicle Safety Communications (VSC) project," http://www-nrd.nhtsa.dot.gov/pdf/nrd-12/060419-0843/PDFTOC.htm.

24. D. Boneh and X. Boyen, "Short signatures without random oracles," *Proc. Advances in Cryptology—EUROCRYPT 2004, International Conference on the Theory and Applications of Cryptographic Techniques*, Interlaken, Switzerland: Springer, May 2–6, 2004, pp. 56–73. (Available online at http://dx.doi.org/10.1007/978-3-540-24676-3_4.)

25. G. Ateniese, D. X. Song, and G. Tsudik, "Quasi-efficient revocation in group signatures," *Proc. Financial Cryptography, 6th International Conference, FC 2002*, Southampton, Bermuda: Springer, March 11–14, 2002, revised papers, pp. 183–197. (Available online at http://dx.doi.org/10.1007/3-540-36504-4_1.)

26. D. Boneh and H. Shacham, "Group signatures with verifier-local revocation," *Proc. 11th ACM Conference on Computer and Communications Security, CCS 2004*, Washington, DC: Springer, Oct. 25–29, 2004, pp. 168–177. (Available online at http://doi.acm.org/10.1145/1030083.1030106.)

27. A. Kiayias, Y. Tsiounis, and M. Yung, "Traceable signatures," *Proc. Advances in Cryptology—EUROCRYPT 2004, International Conference on the Theory and Applications of Cryptographic Techniques*, Interlaken, Switzerland, Springer, May 2–6, 2004, pp. 571–589. (Available online at http://dx.doi.org/10.1007/978-3-540-24676-3_34.)

28. "The network simulator," http://nsnam.isi.edu/nsnam/index.php/User_Information.

29. A. K. Saha and D. B. Johnson, "Modeling mobility for vehicular ad-hoc networks," *Proc. 1st ACM International Workshop on Vehicular Ad Hoc Networks*, ser. VANET '04. New York: ACM, 2004, pp. 91–92. (Available online at http://doi.acm.org/10.1145/1023875.1023892.)

30. "Multiprecision integer and rational arithmetic C/C++ library," http://indigo.ie/ mscott/.

31. M. Raya and J.-P. Hubaux, "The security of vehicular ad hoc networks," *Proc. 3rd ACM Workshop on Security of Ad Hoc and Sensor Networks*, ser. SASN '05. New York: ACM, 2005, pp. 11–21. Available online at http://doi.acm.org/10.1145/1102219.1102223.)

32. "X.509," http://en.wikipedia.org/wiki/ X.509.

3

ECPP: EFFICIENT CONDITIONAL PRIVACY PRESERVATION PROTOCOL

3.1 INTRODUCTION

The increasing demand for improving road safety and optimizing road traffic has generated wide interest in vehicular ad hoc networks (VANETs) [1]. As a special instantiation of mobile ad hoc networks (MANETs), VANETs have been positioned to serve as a general platform for the future development of vehicle-centered applications, which requires local data collection and generation via local information, data floating, and information distribution through both point-to-multipoint and peer-to-peer fashions. A VANET consists mainly of onboard units (OBUs) and roadside units (RSUs) [2], where OBUs are installed on vehicles to provide wireless communication capability, while RSUs are deployed to provide wireless interfaces to vehicles within their radio coverage.

Extensive research has been conducted by both industry and academia to investigate some key issues in vehicular networks [3–7], where security assurance and privacy preservation are two primary concerns [8–11]. Without the security and privacy guarantee, serious attacks may jeopardize the benefits brought by the improved driving safety since an attacker could track the locations of the interested OBUs and obtain their moving patterns. Therefore, how to provide anonymous safety message authentication has become a fundamental design requirement in secure vehicular networks. However,

Vehicular Ad Hoc Network Security and Privacy, First Edition. Xiaodong Lin and Rongxing Lu.
© 2015 The Institute of Electrical and Electronics Engineers, Inc. Published 2015 by John Wiley & Sons, Inc.

anonymous message authentication in vehicular networks is a double-edged sword. A well-behaved OBU, due to the privacy protection mechanism, is willing to offer as much local information as possible to its neighboring OBUs and RSUs to create a safer and more efficient driving environment. However, a maliciously behaving OBU may abuse the privacy protection mechanism by damaging the regular driving environment. This usually occurs when a driver who is involved in a dispute regarding safety messages attempts to escape from the investigation and responsibility. Therefore, anonymous message authentication in vehicular networks should be conditional, such that a trusted authority can find a way to track a targeted OBU and collect the safety messages that it has disseminated, even though the OBU is not traceable by the public.

Most of the existing security proposals [12, 13] for secure vehicular networks were intended simply for authentication with privacy preservation but lacked an effective and efficient conditional tracking mechanism. To the best of our knowledge, only two reported schemes, which are based on a huge number of anonymous keys (denoted as HAB in the following text) [1] and a pure group signature technique (denoted as GSB in the following text) [14], respectively, have targeted the design of conditional privacy preservation. Although both HAB and GSB can provide an efficient tracking mechanism, they require a huge storage space for anonymous keys and safety message anonymous authentication. This problem can become fatal when the revocation list, which keeps all the revoked anonymous keys, is large and unwieldy. Note that when a signature is being verified, the validity of the public key should also be authenticated; however, this task is not as easy in vehicular networks as in wired networks.

In this chapter, we propose the use of the novel Efficient Conditional Privacy Preservation (ECPP) protocol for secure vehicular communications [15]. The ECPP protocol can efficiently deal with the growing revocation list while achieving conditional traceability by the authorities. Instead of relying on a huge storage space at each OBU, as did most of the previously reported schemes, the proposed protocol can keep the minimal anonymous key storage without losing the security level. Meanwhile, the proposed protocol gains merits in the rapid verification of safety messages and provides an efficient conditional privacy-tracking mechanism, which can serve as an excellent candidate for the future VANETs.

The remainder of this chapter is organized as follows. Security model and problem formulation are introduced in Section 3.2. Section 3.3 presents the proposed ECPP protocol in detail. Conditional privacy preservation analysis and performance analysis are given in Section 3.4 and Section 3.5, respectively. Finally, we draw our conclusions in Section 3.6.

3.2 SYSTEM MODEL AND PROBLEM FORMULATION

3.2.1 System Model

3.2.1.1 System Roles. Figure 3.1 illustrates the network architecture, which consists of three network entities: the top trusted authority (TA), the immobile RSUs at the roadside, and the mobile OBUs equipped on the running vehicles.

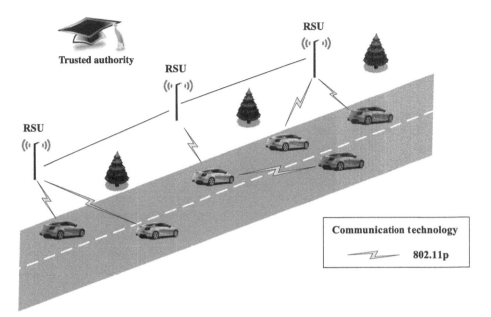

Figure 3.1. System model.

- *TA*. TA is in charge of the registration of immobile RSUs at the roadside and mobile OBUs equipped on the vehicles, and can reveal the real OBU identity of a safety message by incorporating its subordinate RSUs. The TA is assumed to be empowered with sufficient computation and storage capability.

- *RSU*. Subordinate to the TA, the RSUs hold storage units for storing information coming from the TA and the OBUs. The main tasks of RSUs are (1) issuing a short-time anonymous public key certificate to each OBU when the OBU requests it, and (2) assisting the TA to efficiently track the real OBU identity of any safety message.

- *OBU*. Installed on the running vehicles, the OBUs communicate mainly with each other for sharing local traffic information to improve the whole safety driving conditions, and with RSUs for requesting the short-time anonymous public key certificate.

3.2.1.2 Channels. Since the secure vehicular communications serve mainly for civilian applications, in most highway scenarios, RSUs are assumed to connect with the TA by wired links or any other links with high bandwidth, low delay, and low bit error rates [2]. RSUs also talk to each other either via the TA or through a secure and reliable peer-to-peer channel. The medium used for communications between neighboring OBUs and between OBUs and RSUs is 5.9 GHz dedicated short-range communication (DSRC) by IEEE 802.11p [16].

3.2.1.3 Assumptions.

- The TA is fully trusted by all parties in the system, and it is infeasible for any attacker to compromise.
- RSUs are immobile and subordinate to the TA in most scenarios. Without authorization of the TA, most RSUs will not disclose any inside information. However, we do not exclude that a fraction of RSUs at roadside may be compromised by an attacker and in collusion with each other. Nevertheless, since the application scenarios considered in the study are civilian, the TA can inspect all the RSUs at a high level. Once an RSU is compromised in one time slot, the TA can detect and take action to recover it in the next time slot.
- OBUs are mobile and move in most of the time, and could be easily compromised by a malicious attacker. Compared with that of the RSUs, the population of the OBUs in the system could be in the millions, whereas the number of RSUs is at most tens of thousands, based on the national infrastructure construction.

3.2.2 Design Objectives

We focus on conditional privacy preservation, where the following two security issues will be addressed.

3.2.2.1 Efficient Safety Message Anonymous Authentication. First, the proposed protocol employs an efficient safety message anonymous authentication mechanism in secure vehicle communications in order to resist the bogus-message spoofing attack. *Bogus-message spoofing* is a basic attack in VANETs, in which an adversary diffuses bogus messages in the network to maliciously affect the behavior of others to achieve specific purpose. For example, adversaries may send fake traffic jam messages to other vehicles in order to obtain the best traffic condition for themselves. Meanwhile, from the perspective of the OBUs, it may not be acceptable to leak their personal privacy, including identity and location, while the safety messages are being authenticated. Therefore, providing a secure yet anonymous safety message authentication in secure vehicular communications is critical to the applicability of VANETs. In addition, the proposed protocol should be efficient in terms of (1) minimal anonymous key storage at OBUs and (2) rapid verification on the safety messages. The two requirements are of ultimate importance to the scalability in the task of updating the revocation list.

3.2.2.2 Efficient Tracking on the Source of a Disputed Safety Message.
An important and challenging issue for safety message authentication with anonymity is to maintain traceability for all the safety messages in the presence of the anonymous authentication. Without the tracking mechanism, the above message anonymous authentication can only prevent an outside attack, but cannot deal with an inside one. For example, an inside attacker could launch a *bogus-message spoofing* attack, *denial-of-service* (DoS) attack, or an *impersonation* attack, provided with no traceability by the authorities. In a DoS attack, the adversary sends massive irrelevant messages to jam

TABLE 3.1. Definitions of Conditional Privacy Level

	Authentication	Anonymity	Unlinkability
Level 1 privacy	✓	✗	✗
Level 2 privacy	✓	✓	✗
Level 3 privacy	✓	✓	✓

the channel or to consume the rare computational resources of the other OBUs; while in an *impersonation* attack, the adversary actively pretends to be another OBU to send false messages. Because both the attacks jeopardize the whole vehicular communication system, the traceability for safety messages must be provided to prevent the inside attack.

To subtly capture the safety message authentication with conditional privacy preservation, we essentially define three levels of user privacy, which is required for achieving authentication, anonymity, and unlinkability, respectively, as shown in Table 3.1.

Level 1. This privacy level is anticipated by the TA, and is most likely to be required by the TA that can track the real OBU identity from an authenticated safety message. From the perspective of users, no privacy has been defined in this level.

Level 2. This privacy level indicates that although each safety message is anonymously authenticated, an adversary can track an individual OBU by collecting a number of safety messages launched by the OBU. This level of privacy is not sufficient to resist a movement tracking attack.

Level 3. This privacy level is the most desirable for OBUs, since the safety messages are anonymously authenticated, and even though an adversary has collected several safety messages from an OBU, the OBU is still not traceable.

3.3 PROPOSED ECPP PROTOCOL

The proposed ECPP protocol consists of four parts: system initialization, OBU short-time anonymous key generation, OBU safety message generation and sending, and OBU fast tracking algorithm.

3.3.1 System Initialization

Given the security parameter k, the TA first generates the bilinear parameters $(q, \mathbb{G}, \mathbb{G}', \mathbb{G}_T, e, P, P')$ by running $\mathcal{G}en(k)$. Then, the TA chooses two random numbers $u, v \in \mathbb{Z}_q^*$ as the *master key*, and computes $U' = uP' \in \mathbb{G}'$, and $U = uP, V = vP \in \mathbb{G}$. The TA also chooses two cryptographic hash functions: f and g, where $f, g : \{0, 1\}^* \to \mathbb{Z}_q^*$, and a secure symmetric encryption algorithm $Enc_k()$ with secret key k [17]. After that, the system parameters will be published, which include $(q, \mathbb{G}, \mathbb{G}', \mathbb{G}_T, e, P, P', U, V, U', f, g, Enc_k())$.

Algorithm 1: [A1] InitialRegister

Data: With system parameters and *master-key* (u, v), the TA inputs an identity ID_i for private key extraction.

Result: Generate a valid private key sk_i corresponding to ID_i, or do nothing if $\perp$.

begin

    Check the validity of the identity ID_i

    if ID_i *is invalid* **then**

        return $\perp$

    end

    if ID_i *is an RSU* **then**

        Choose a random number $x_i \in \mathbb{Z}_q^*$ such that $x_i + u \neq 0 \bmod q$, and a location

        information L_i

        Set $A_i = \frac{1}{x_i+u}P, B_i = \frac{1}{h(L_i)+u}P \in \mathbb{G}$

        Store the duplet (ID_i, uA_i) into the trace list

        return $sk_i = (x_i, A_i, B_i)$

    else if ID_i *is an OBU* **then**

        Compute the pseudo-id $RID_i = Enc_v(ID_i)$

        Set $S_i = \frac{1}{h(RID_i)+u}P \in \mathbb{G}$

        return $sk_i = (RID_i, S_i)$

    end

end

When an RSU or OBU submits its identity ID_i for registering itself to the system, the TA invokes Algorithm A1 to obtain the private key $sk_i = $ InitialRegister(ID_i), then returns the system parameters and private key sk_i to the requester. If the requester is an RSU, the RSU with the private key $sk_i = (x_i, A_i, B_i)$ can normally work at location L_i, where (x_i, A_i) is the anonymous signing key, and B_i is the location-awareness key. On the other hand, if the requester is an OBU, the OBU can use the private key $sk_i = (RID_i, S_i)$ to anonymously authenticate itself when requesting the short-time anonymous public key certificates, where RID_i is the pseudo-id computed from the real identity ID_i, and S_i is the identity-based private key corresponding to the RID_i. Note that even though several OBUs and RSUs are compromised, due to the q-SDH hardness assumption, it is still computationally infeasible to deduce other OBUs and RSUs' private keys from the compromised private keys.

3.3.2 OBU Short-Time Anonymous Key Generation

Instead of having each OBU to prepare a large storage for the huge revocation list (which was done by all the previously reported studies), the proposed protocol avoids the disadvantage by having each OBU to issue a request for a short-time anonymous key certificate from an RSU when the OBU is passing by the RSU. In addition, to tackle the revocation issue, when the OBU requests a short-time anonymous key certificate, the RSU will check whether the OBU is in the newly updated revocation list (retrieved from the TA). If it is, the RSU will not take any action for updating the certificate revocation

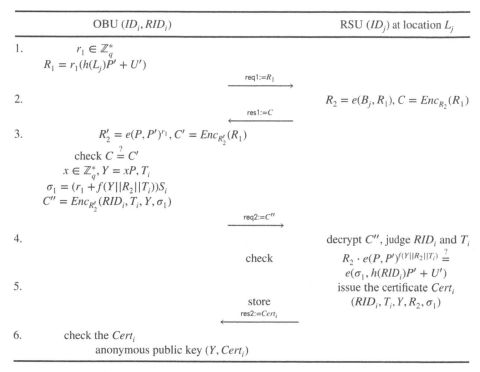

Figure 3.2. OBU short-time anonymous key generation.

list. In this subsection, we will mainly describe how the OBU short-time anonymous key certificate can be generated. Figure 3.2 shows the OBU short-time anonymous key generation, and the detailed protocol steps are described as follows.

An OBU with identity ID_i and pseudo-id RID_i requests for a short-time anonymous key pair from an RSU at the location L_j through the following request–response protocol:

Step 1. When the OBU moves into location L_j, it should first authenticate the RSU to determine whether the OBU should send its pseudo-id RID_i to the RSU for the short-time anonymous key request. If the OBU does not authenticate the RSU, it subjects to a risk in disclosing its pseudo-id RID_i to an attacker, which could launch a collusive tracking attack through multiple compromised RSUs. Therefore, the OBU chooses a random number $r_1 \in \mathbb{Z}_q^*$, uses the location information L_j to compute $R_1 = r_1(h(L_j)P' + U') \in \mathbb{G}'$, and sends req1 := R_1 to the RSU located at L_j.

Step 2. After receiving req1 := R_1, the RSU uses its location-awareness private key $B_j = \frac{1}{h(L_j)+u}P$ to compute $R_2 = e(B_j, R_1)$, encrypts R_1 as $C = Enc_{R_2}(R_1)$ with the secret key R_2, and sends res1 := C back to the OBU.

Step 3. The OBU computes $R_2' = e(P, P')^{r_1}$, $C' = Enc_{R_2'}(R_1)$ and checks the relation $C \overset{?}{=} C'$. If it holds, the RSU is authenticated, and the OBU can send its pseudo-id RID_i for the short-time anonymous key request; otherwise, the RSU fails to pass the authentication since $R_2 = e(B_j, R_1) = e(\frac{1}{h(L_j)+u}P, r_1(h(L_j)P' + U')) = e(\frac{1}{h(L_j)+u}P, r_1(h(L_j) + u)P') = e(P, P')^{r_1} = R_2'$.

The OBU then chooses a short-time valid period T_i, with a random number $x \in \mathbb{Z}_q^*$ as its short-time anonymous private key, and computes the corresponding public key $Y = xP \in \mathbb{G}$ in period T_i. Also, the OBU uses its private key $S_i = \frac{1}{h(RID_i)+u}P \in \mathbb{G}$ to compute $\sigma_1 = (r_1 + f(Y||R_2||T_i))S_i$, computes $C'' = Enc_{R_2'}(RID_i, T_i, Y, \sigma_1)$, and then sends the request req2 $:= C''$ to the RSU.

Step 4. When receiving req2 $:= C''$, the RSU first decrypts $(RID_i, T_i, Y, \sigma_1)$ from C'' with R_2, and then looks up the newly updated revocation list retrieved from the TA to check the validity of the pseudo-id RID_i. If the RID_i is in the revocation list, the RSU refuses to issue the certificate on short-time anonymous public key Y and terminates the protocol. Otherwise, the RSU checks the valid period T_i, because a long valid period T_i will result in the risk of continued circulation of an invalid certificate or being tracked by attackers. Therefore, if T_i is not reasonable, the RSU should also refuse to issue the certificate. Otherwise, the OBU checks the equation $R_2 \cdot e(P, P')^{f(Y||R_2||T_i)} = e(\sigma_1, h(RID_i)P' + U')$. If it holds, the OBU is authenticated; otherwise, the OBU cannot pass the authentication since

$$
\begin{aligned}
&e(\sigma_1, h(RID_i)P' + U') \\
=\ &e((r_1 + f(Y||R_2||T_i))S_i, h(RID_i)P' + uP') \\
=\ &e((r_1 + f(Y||R_2||T_i))\frac{1}{h(RID_i) + u}P, (h(RID_i) + u)P') \\
=\ &e((r_1 + f(Y||R_2||T_i))P, P') \\
=\ &e(P, P')^{r_1 + f(Y||R_2||T_i)} = R_2 \cdot e(P, P')^{f(Y||R_2||T_i)}.
\end{aligned}
$$

Step 5. Once the OBU is authenticated, the RSU issues the certificate $Cert_i$ on the short-time anonymous public key Y to the OBU. First, the RSU chooses four random numbers $\alpha, r_\alpha, r_x, r_\delta \in \mathbb{Z}_q^*$ and computes $T_U, T_V, \delta, \delta_1, \delta_2, \delta_3$, where

$$
\begin{cases}
T_U = \alpha U, T_V = A_j + \alpha V, \delta = \alpha \cdot x_j \bmod q, \\
\delta_1 = r_\alpha U, \delta_2 = r_x T_U - r_\delta U, \\
\delta_3 = e(T_V, r_x P')/e(V, r_\alpha U' + r_\delta P').
\end{cases}
$$

Then, the RSU computes $c, s_\alpha, s_x, s_\delta \in \mathbb{Z}_q^*$, where

$$
\begin{cases}
c = f(U||V||Y||T_i||T_U||T_V||\delta_1||\delta_2||\delta_3), \\
s_\alpha = r_\alpha + c \cdot \alpha \bmod q, s_x = r_x + c \cdot x_j \bmod q, \\
s_\delta = r_\delta + c \cdot \delta \bmod q.
\end{cases}
$$

In the end, the RSU sets the certificate as $Cert_i = (T_U, T_V, c, s_\alpha, s_x, s_\delta)$ and sends $\text{res2} := Cert_i$ back to the OBU. In addition, the RSU also stores $(RID_i, T_i, Y, R_2, \sigma_1)$ in its local certificate list for maintaining traceability.

Step 6. To check the validity of certificate $Cert_i$, the OBU computes $\delta'_1, \delta'_2, \delta'_3$, where

$$\begin{cases} \delta'_1 = s_\alpha U - cT_U, \delta'_2 = s_x T_U - s_\delta U, \\ \delta'_3 = \dfrac{e(T_V, s_x P' + cU')}{e(V, s_\alpha U' + s_\delta P')e(P, cP')} \end{cases}$$

Check $c = f(U||V||Y||T_i||T_U||T_V||\delta'_1||\delta'_2||\delta'_3)$. If it holds, the $Cert_i$ is valid; otherwise it is invalid. In the end, the OBU holds the short-time private key x at the valid period T_i and the corresponding anonymous public key $(Y, Cert_i)$.

3.3.2.1 Correction.
Because of the bilinear pairing property, the correction will hold, on the basis of the following three relations:

$$\delta'_1 = s_\alpha U - cT_U = (r_\alpha + c \cdot \alpha)U - c \cdot \alpha U = r_\alpha U = \delta_1$$
$$\delta'_2 = s_x T_U - s_\delta U = (r_x + cx_j)T_U - (r_\delta + c\delta)U = \delta_2$$
$$\begin{aligned} \delta'_3 &= \frac{e(T_V, s_x P' + cU')}{e(V, s_\alpha U' + s_\delta P')e(P, cP')} \\ &= \frac{e(T_V, (r_x + c \cdot x_j)P' + cU')}{e(V, (r_\alpha + c \cdot \alpha)U' + (r_\delta + c \cdot \delta)P')e(P, cP')} \\ &= \frac{e(T_V, r_x P')e(T_V, c \cdot x_j P' + cU')}{e(V, r_\alpha U' + r_\delta P')e(V, c \cdot \alpha U' + c \cdot \delta P')e(P, cP')} \\ &= \frac{e(T_V, r_x P')e(V, c \cdot \delta P' + \alpha cU')}{e(V, r_\alpha U' + r_\delta P')e(V, \alpha cU' + c \cdot \delta P')} \\ &= \frac{e(T_V, r_x P')}{e(V, r_\alpha U' + r_\delta P')} = \delta_3 \end{aligned}$$

3.3.2.2 Security.
The OBU short-time anonymous key generation is accomplished by the request–response protocol between the OBU and the RSU. In the following paragraphs, we examine its security in terms of mutual authentication and anonymity of the short-time certificate.

- *The OBU can quickly authenticate the RSU at location L_j.* In step 2, if the RSU returns $C = Enc_{R_2}(R_1)$, where $R_2 = e(P, P')^{r_1}$, the OBU can authenticate the RSU because without knowing the corresponding location-aware key $B_j = \frac{1}{h(L_j)+u}P$, it is infeasible for an adversary to compute the correct $R_2 = e(P, P')^{r_1}$ from $R_1 = r_1(h(L_j) + u)P'$.

- *The RSU can also efficiently authenticate the OBU with pseudo-id RID_i.* In step 4, if the verification equation $R_2 \cdot e(P, P')^{f(Y||R_2||T_i)} = e(\sigma_1, h(RID_i)P' + U')$ holds, the RSU can authenticate the OBU. Since (R_2, σ_1) is actually the *identity-based signature* with respect to RID_i, which is provably secure under the adaptively chosen message and ID attacks, therefore, no adversary can launch an impersonations attack on the RSU.

- *The short-time certificate $Cert_i$ is anonymous.* Since the group signature technique can achieve anonymous authentication, the employed group signature in step 6 for constructing short-time certificate $Cert_i$ can be regarded as a variant of Boneh et al.'s VLR group signature [18], which not only inherits the original version's property of anonymous authentication but also provides the authority tracking capability as the short group signature [19]. Therefore, the short-time certificate $Cert_i$ can achieve the property of anonymity, which guarantees the location privacy preservation of the OBU since no one can judge the location that the OBU had stayed by way of $Cert_i$.

3.3.2.3 Discussions. Since steps 1–5 must be executed within the RSU's valid coverage, the short-time anonymous key has to be generated on the wheel with a stringent time limitation. Thus, there could be constraints on the vehicle moving speed and vehicle density on the road. To examine the performance, we first calculate the time overhead (denoted as T_k) in these steps. Since the point multiplication in G and pairing computations dominates each party's computation overhead, only these operations are counted in the calculation.

Table 3.2 gives the measured processing time (in milliseconds) for an MNT curve [20] of embedding degree $k = 6$ and 160-bit q. The implementation was executed on an Intel Pentium IV 3.0-GHz machine [21]. From the execution time results, we have

$$T_k = 13T_{pmul} + 6T_{pair}$$
$$= 13 \times 0.6 + 6 \times 4.5 = 34.8 \text{ ms}$$

The following assumptions are also made to simulate a rather practical scenario:

- The average speed of vehicles (denoted as v) varies from 10 m/s $\sim$ 40 m/s (or 36 km/h $\sim$ 144 km/hr). The valid coverage range of an RSU (denoted as R_{range}) is 300 m.
- The vehicle's density (denoted as d) varies from 100 to 400 when four-lane two-way highways are considered.

TABLE 3.2. Cryptographic Operation Execution Time

Descriptions		Execution Time (ms)
T_{pmul}:	The time for one point multiplication in G	0.6
T_{pair}:	The time for one pairing operation	4.5

- Within the valid coverage range of an RSU, each OBU independently requests a short-time anonymous public key certificate from the RSU. Let ρ be the probability for each OBU to issue a request, and let X be a random variable denoting the number of requesting OBUs among total d OBUs. Then, X follows the Binomial distribution $\mathcal{B}(d, \rho)$, and we have

$$P\{X = x\} = \binom{d}{x} \rho^x (1 - \rho)^{d-x}, \quad x = 0, 1, 2, \ldots, d$$

and the mathematical expectation

$$E(X) = \sum_{x=0}^{d} \binom{d}{x} \rho^x (1 - \rho)^{d-x} = d \cdot \rho$$

Here the expectation $E(X)$ stands for the average number of requests for a short-time anonymous public key certificate, which is denoted as

$$S_{req} = E(X) = d \cdot \rho$$

To measure the RSU valid serving capability, we first estimate the number of maximal anonymous keys (denoted as S_{max}) that the RSU can process. With the average speed of vehicles v, the valid coverage range of RSU R_{range}, and the time overhead T_k, we have

$$S_{max} = \frac{R_{range}}{v \cdot T_k}$$

Then we calculate the number of actual processed anonymous keys (denoted as S_{proc}) as

$$S_{proc} = \begin{cases} S_{req}, & \text{if } S_{req} \leq S_{max} \\ S_{max}, & \text{otherwise} \end{cases}$$

We define the RSU valid serving ratio (denoted as S_{ratio}) as

$$S_{ratio} = \frac{S_{proc}}{S_{req}}$$

Then, S_{ratio} can be measured by

$$S_{ratio} = \begin{cases} 1, & \text{if } \dfrac{R_{range}}{T_k \rho} \cdot \dfrac{1}{vd} \geq 1 \\ \dfrac{R_{range}}{T_k \rho} \cdot \dfrac{1}{vd}, & \text{otherwise} \end{cases}$$

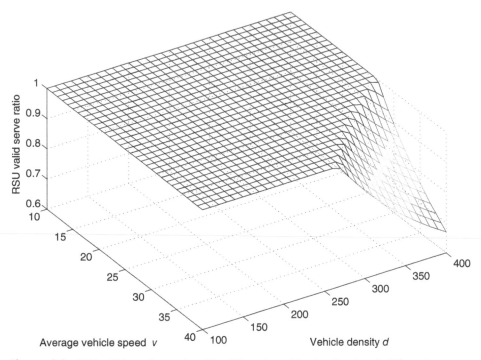

Figure 3.3. RSU valid serving ratio with different vehicle density d and different average vehicle speed v, when $R_{range} = 300$ m, $T_k = 34.8$ ms, $\rho = 0.8$.

When $R_{range} = 300$ m, $T_k = 34.8$ ms, $\rho = 0.8$, the RSU valid serving ratio varies with vehicle density d and speed v, where $100 \leq d \leq 400$ and $10 \leq v \leq 40$, as illustrated in Figure 3.3. Also, we observed that the RSU can efficiently process the OBUs' short-time anonymous public key certificate requests in most cases, and is inversely proportional to the average vehicle speed v and the vehicle density d. Therefore, we conclude that the proposed OBU short-time anonymous key generation protocol is feasible.

3.3.3 OBU Safety Message Sending

After requesting one short-time anonymous key pair (x, Y) within certificate $Cert_i$, the OBU can send the safety message within the short-time valid period T_i. The format of the safety messages in our ECPP protocol is defined in Table 3.3. Group ID is used to identify which group the vehicle is in, which is the identity of TA in our case. Message

TABLE 3.3. Safety Message Format

Group ID	Payload	Signature	Anonymous Key	Short-Time Certificate
2 bytes	100 bytes	40 bytes	26 bytes	121 bytes

payload may include position, current time, direction, speed, acceleration/deceleration, and current traffic events of the OBU. The payload M of a safety message is 100 bytes [22]. The third part is the 40-byte OBU signature σ_M on the message payload. The fourth part is the OBU short-time anonymous key (Y, T_i), and the last part is the certificate $Cert_i$ of the short-time anonymous key.

With the proposed ECPP protocol, an OBU that intends to send a safety message M with privacy preservation can run the following steps.

Step 1. Choose a random number $r \in \mathbb{Z}_q^*$, compute $R = rP \in \mathbb{G}$ and $s_r = r + x \cdot h(M, R) \bmod q$. Set $\sigma_M = (R, s_r)$.

Step 2. According to the format described in Table 3.3, format the message Msg as $[\mathrm{ID_{TA}}||M||\sigma_M||(Y, T_i)||Cert_i]$ and send it out. Once receiving the safety message, the receiver does the following steps to verify the validity.

- Check the valid period T_i. If it is overdue, stop the verification process.
- Use the same verification operations in *step 6* in Section 3.3.1 to check the anonymous key (Y, T_i) and the certificate $Cert_i$. If it is invalid, terminate the verification.
- Verify the signature $\sigma_M = (R, s_r)$ by checking the equation $s_r P = R + h(M, R)Y$. If it holds, the safety message can be accepted; otherwise neglected.

3.3.3.1 Correction. The correction of the protocol follows because of the relation $s_r P = (r + x \cdot h(M, R))P = R + h(M, R)Y$.

3.3.3.2 Security. The signature $\sigma_M = (R, s_r)$ is secure against existential forgery under an adaptively chosen message attack in the random oracle model. The brief security analysis is shown as follows. Suppose that there is an adversary $\mathcal{A}$ that takes M and Y as input, and outputs an existential forgery with a nonnegligible probability in polynomial time. We assume that h behaves as a random oracle. Then according to the *forking lemma* [23], $\mathcal{A}$ may obtain two forgeries for the same message M. Let the two signature forgeries for M be $\sigma_M = (R, s_r')$ and $\sigma_M' = (R, s_r')$, respectively, where $R = rP$, $s_r = r + x \cdot h(M, R) \bmod q$ and $s_r' = r + x \cdot h'(M, R) \bmod q$. It then follows that $s_r - s_r' = x(h(M, R) - h'(M, R)) \bmod q$. Hence $x = (s_r - s_r')(h(M, R) - h'(M, R))^{-1} \bmod q$. However, the result contradicts the discrete logarithm assumption. Therefore, the signature σ_M is unforgeable, which means the ECPP protocol can resist the bogus-message spoofing attack and the impersonation attack.

3.3.4 OBU Fast Tracking Algorithm

Once a dispute occurs regarding a safety message $Msg = [\mathrm{ID_{TA}}||M||\sigma_M||(Y, T_i)||Cert_i]$, the ECPP protocol is equipped with a fast algorithm for tracking the corresponding OBU of the disputed safety message. Expressed succinctly, the TA first uses the *master key* to fast-position the RSU that issued the certificate $Cert_i$ in the disputed safety message Msg. According to the TA's demand, the RSU then retrieves the pseudo-id of the source of the disputed safety message Msg by searching the local certificate list and returns pseudo-id to the TA, and then the TA recovers the real identity from the returned pseudo-id. The detailed steps are as follows.

Step 1. TA first obtains the (T_U, T_V) from the certificate $Cert_i$, then uses the *master key* (u, v) to recover uA_j as

$$uT_V - vT_U = uA_j + u\alpha V - v\alpha U$$
$$= uA_j + \alpha uvP - \alpha uvP = uA_j$$

By searching the entry (ID_j, uA_j) in the trace list with search condition uA_j, TA can fast-find the identity ID_j of the RSU that issued the certificate $Cert_i$. The TA then sends the demand to the specified RSU.

Step 2. The RSU first gets the anonymous public key (Y, T_i) from the safety message *Msg*, then retrieves the entry $(RID_i, T_i, Y, R_2, \sigma_1)$ by searching the local certificate list with condition (Y, T_i), and sends the OBU pseudo-id RID_i and signature (R_2, σ_1) on (Y, T_i) back to the TA.

Step 3. The TA recovers the real identity ID_i by decrypting $RID_i = Enc_v(ID_i)$ with *master key* v, and verifies the signature (R_2, σ_1) on (Y, T_i), which can provide the nonrepudiation proof on the OBU's anonymous key request. The TA then broadcasts the pseudo-id RID_i to all RSUs, and each RSU adds the pseudo-id RID_i into the local revocation list. Since the RID_i is in the revocation list, the OBU can no longer get its short-time anonymous key from the RSU, which subsequently resolves the certificate revocation issues in secure vehicular communications.

3.4 ANALYSIS ON CONDITIONAL PRIVACY PRESERVATION

In this section, we analyze the conditional privacy preservation of the ECPP protocol. First, since no OBU can reveal the real identity or launch the moving track attack through safety messages, the ECPP is level 3 privacy secure to the OBUs. Second, from the OBU tracking algorithm, which is illustrated in section 3.3.4, the TA can reveal the real OBU identity of a safety message. Thus, the safety message in the ECPP protocol is level 1 privacy secure to the TA.

Since the RSUs issue the short-time certificates to OBUs, the privacy level for these RSUs is also of interest. Clearly, when the OBU requests its short-time anonymous key, only the pseudo-id is sent to the RSUs, where the anonymity can obviously be achieved. Therefore, we focus mainly on the unlinkability, i.e., the moving tracking attack on OBUs' location. Here we develop a probabilistic model to characterize the risk that some RSUs will be compromised and used to track a victim OBU based on the following assumptions:

- Since the RSUs are relatively robust, we assume that at most of 0.2% RSUs can be compromised by an attacker at some period and can be quickly rescued in the next period. When the number of RSUs N_{rsu} is assumed to be 10^4, the number of compromised RSUs N_c is $N_{rsu} \times 0.2\% = 10^4 \times 0.2\% = 20$.

- The number of anonymous keys that an OBU requests at some period is N_k. Then, only at least two among N_k anonymous keys are requested from different compromised RSUs. The location of the victim OBU thus can be tracked.

Let $\Pr\{i\}$ represent the probability that exactly i among N_k anonymous keys are requested from different compromised RSUs, we have $\Pr\{i\} = \dfrac{\binom{N_{rsu}-N_c}{N_k-i}\binom{N_c}{i}}{\binom{N_{rsu}}{N_k}}$. Then the probability that the OBU can be tracked by at least two compromised RSUs is as follows:

$$\Pr\{\geq 2\} = 1 - \Pr\{0\} - \Pr\{1\}$$
$$= 1 - \frac{\binom{N_{rsu}-N_c}{N_k}\binom{N_c}{0} + \binom{N_{rsu}-N_c}{N_k-1}\binom{N_c}{1}}{\binom{N_{rsu}}{N_k}}$$

In Fig. 3.4, we show how the location tracking of an OBU is affected as the number of compromised RSUs increases. It can be seen that the tracking probability increases very slowly with the increase of the number of compromised RSUs and the number of

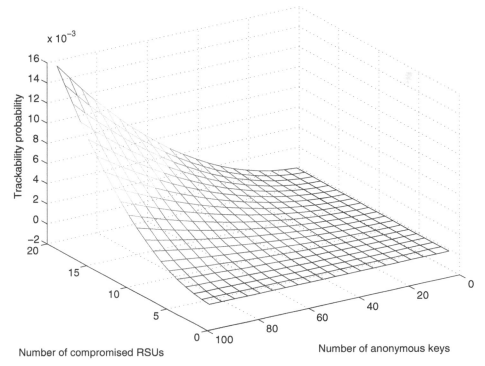

Figure 3.4. Tracking probability in ECPP under different N_k and different N_c, where $1 \leq N_k \leq 100$, $1 \leq N_c \leq 20$.

requests for a anonymous key. For example, when $N_c = 20$ and $N_k = 100$, the tracking probability is still less than 1.6% in some period. This observation implies that the the proposed ECPP protocol can achieve level 3 privacy secure to the RSUs in most cases, and level 2 privacy secure to the compromised RSUs in some rare cases.

3.5 PERFORMANCE ANALYSIS

In this section, we evaluate the performance of the proposed ECPP protocol in terms of the OBU anonymous key storage and computation overhead for an OBU to verify a valid safety message, and the computation complexity of the TA for tracking a safety message.

3.5.1 OBU Storage Overhead

In this section we compare the OBU storage overhead of ECPP with two previously reported protocols: HAB [1] and GSB [14]. In the ECPP protocol, each OBU stores one unique private key issued by the TA, and a short-time key pair together with its anonymous certificate issued by the RSU. Let each key (with its certificate) occupy one storage unit. Then, since the OBU does not need to store the revocation list, the storage overhead in ECPP is only two units, denoted as $S_{ECPP} = 2$. In HAB, on the other hand, each OBU should store not only its own N_{okey} anonymous key pairs, but also all the anonymous public keys and their certificates in the revocation list. Assume that there are n OBUs being revoked; then the scale of revoked anonymous public keys is $n \cdot N_{okey}$. Thus, the total storage overhead in HAB (denoted as S_{HAB}) is $S_{HAB} = (n + 1) \cdot N_{okey}$. By assuming that $N_{okey} = 10^4$, we have $S_{HAB} = (n + 1) \cdot 10^4$.

In GSB, each OBU stores one unique private key issued by the TA, and n revoked public keys in the revocation list. Let S_{GSB} denote the total storage unit. Thus, $S_{GSB} = n + 1$.

Figure 3.5 shows the storage units of ECPP, GSB, and HAB as n increases. We can observe that the storage overhead in HAB linearly increases with n, and is much larger than that in the other two protocols. The storage overhead of GSB is still small in spite of its linear increase with n, while the storage overhead in the proposed ECPP is the most efficient, which always occupies only two storage units in an OBU and does not increase with n. The more the revoked OBUs are, the larger the revocation list is. Therefore, this also implies that the OBUs in GSB and HAB would take a long time to update their local revocation lists, which, nonetheless, is not the case in the proposed ECPP protocol.

3.5.2 OBU Computation Overhead on Verification

This subsection compares the OBU computation overhead of the proposed ECPP and GSB. In the proposed ECPP protocol, to verify a safety message, it requires

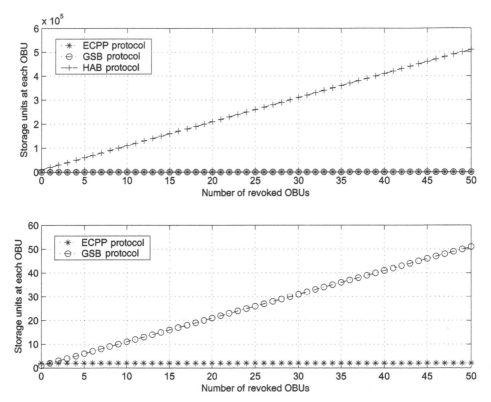

Figure 3.5. Each OBU storage overhead of ECPP, GSB, and HAB in different n revoked OBUs, with n varying from 1 to 50.

$11T_{pmul} + 3T_{pair}$, as shown in Section 3.3.3. Let T_{ECPP} be the required time cost in ECPP, then we have

$$T_{ECPP} = 11T_{pmul} + 3T_{pair} = 11 \times 0.86 + 3 \times 4.14 = 21.88 \text{ ms}$$

In GSB, the time cost of verifying a safety message is related to the revoked OBUs in the revocation list. Let T_{GSB} be the required time cost in GSB. Assuming that there are n revoked OBUs, according to [14], we have

$$\begin{aligned}T_{GSB} &= 6T_{pmul} + (3 + 2n)T_{pair} \\ &= 6 \times 0.86 + (3 + 2n) \times 4.14 = 17.58 + n \times 8.28 \text{ ms}\end{aligned}$$

Let

$$T_{EG} = \frac{T_{ECPP}}{T_{GSB}} = \frac{21.88}{17.58 + n \times 8.28}$$

be the time cost ratio between the proposed ECPP and GSB. Figure 3.6 plots the time cost ratio T_{EG} when n OBUs are revoked, where n ranges from 0 to 50. Then, we can

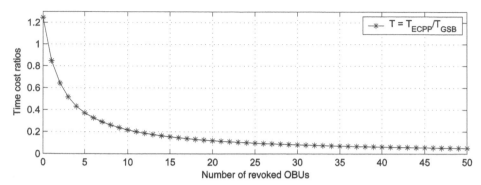

Figure 3.6. Time efficiency ratio $T_{EG} = T_{ECPP}/T_{GBS}$ with a number of n revoked OBUs, where n ranges from 1 to 50.

TABLE 3.4. Notations and Rough Scale

	Descriptions	Scale
N_{rsu}:	Number of RSUs in the system	10^4
N_{rkey}:	Number of anonymous keys processed by one RSU during a time slot	10^3
N_{obu}:	Number of OBUs in the system	10^7
N_{okey}:	Number of anonymous keys owned by one OBU	10^4

observe that the time cost ratio T_{EG} decreases as n increases, which demonstrates the much better efficiency of the proposed ECPP protocol than the other two, especially when the revocation list is huge.

3.5.3 TA Computation Complexity on OBU Tracking

In this subsection, we evaluate the TA computation complexity on OBU tracking in GSB, HAB, and the proposed ECPP protocol. For fair comparison, we use the same linear and binary search algorithms in these three protocols. The notations adopted in the description are listed in Table 3.4, and Table 3.5 shows the comparison results on the computation complexity for the three protocols. It is observed that the TA tracking algorithm in the proposed ECPP protocol outperforms the other two protocols with the

TABLE 3.5. Comparison of Computation Complexity

Protocol	Linear search	Binary search
ECPP	$O(N_{rsu} + N_{rkey})$	$O(\log(N_{rsu} \cdot N_{rkey}))$
HAB	$O(N_{obu} \cdot N_{okey})$	$O(\log(N_{obu} \cdot N_{okey}))$
GSB	$O(N_{obu})$	$O(\log N_{obu})$

linear search algorithm, and it has almost the same computation complexity as the binary search algorithm.

3.6 CONCLUDING REMARKS

In this chapter, we have presented a novel conditional privacy preservation (ECPP) protocol for secure vehicular communications. Based on the on-the-fly short-time anonymous key generation between an OBU and an RSU, the proposed ECPP protocol has been identified to be capable of not only providing the conditional privacy preservation that is critically demanded in the VANET applications but also improving efficiency in terms of the minimized anonymous keys storage at each OBU, fast verification on safety messages, and an efficient conditional privacy tracking mechanism. Through extensive performance evaluation, we have demonstrated that the proposed ECPP protocol can achieve much better efficiency than the two previously reported counterparts GSB and HAB.

REFERENCES

1. M. Raya and J.-P. Hubaux, "Securing vehicular ad hoc networks," *Journal of Computer Security*, vol. 15, no. 1, pp. 39–68, 2007.

2. Y. Peng, Z. Abichar, and J. M. Chang, "Roadside-aided routing (rar) in vehicular networks," *Proc. IEEE International Conference on Communications*, IEEE, 2006, vol. 8, pp. 3602–3607.

3. P. Golle, D. Greene, and J. Staddon, "Detecting and correcting malicious data in vanets," *Proc. 1st ACM International Workshop on Vehicular Ad Hoc Networks*. ACM, 2004, pp. 29–37.

4. J.-P. Hubaux, S. Capkun, and J. Luo, "The security and privacy of smart vehicles," *IEEE Security and Privacy*, vol. 2, no. 3, pp. 49–55, 2004.

5. C. Zhang, X. Lin, R. Lu, and P.-H. Ho, "RAISE: An efficient RSU-aided message authentication scheme in vehicular communication networks," *Proc. International Conference on Communications 2008 (ICC'08)*, IEEE, pp. 1451–1457.

6. M. Lott, R. Halfmann, E. Schultz, and M. Radimirsch, "Medium access and radio resource management for ad hoc networks based on ultra TDD," *Proc. 2nd ACM International Symposium on Mobile Ad Hoc Networking & Computing*. ACM, 2001, pp. 76–86.

7. Q. Xu, T. Mak, J. Ko, and R. Sengupta, "Medium access control protocol design for vehicle–vehicle safety messages," *IEEE Transactions on Vehicular Technology*, vol. 56, no. 2, pp. 499–518, 2007.

8. B. Parno and A. Perrig, "Challenges in securing vehicular networks," *Proc. Workshop on Hot Topics in Networks (HotNets-IV)*, ACM, 2005, pp. 1–6.

9. M. Raya and J.-P. Hubaux, "The security of vehicular ad hoc networks," *Proc. 3rd ACM Workshop on Security of Ad Hoc and Sensor Networks*, ser. SASN '05. New York: ACM, 2005, pp. 11–21. (Available online at http://doi.acm.org/10.1145/1102219.1102223.)

10. K. Ren, W. Lou, K. Kim, and R. H. Deng, "A novel privacy preserving authentication and access control scheme for pervasive computing environments," *IEEE Transactions on Vehicular Technology*, vol. 55, no. 4, pp. 1373–1384, 2006.

11. X. Lin, R. Lu, C. Zhang, H. Zhu, P.-H. Ho, and X. Shen, "Security in vehicular ad hoc networks," *IEEE Communications Magazine*, vol. 46, no. 4, pp. 88–95, 2008.

12. K. Sha, Y. Xi, W. Shi, L. Schwiebert, and T. Zhang, "Adaptive privacy-preserving authentication in vehicular networks," *Proc. 1st International Conference on Communications and Networking in China, 2006. (ChinaCom '06)*, ICST, Oct. 2006, pp. 1–8.

13. Y. Xi, K. Sha, W. Shi, L. Schwiebert, and T. Zhang, "Enforcing privacy using symmetric random key-set in vehicular networks," *Proc. 8th International Symposium on Autonomous Decentralized Systems, 2007 (ISADS'07)*. IEEE, 2007, pp. 344–351.

14. X. Lin, X. Sun, P.-H. Ho, and X. Shen, "GSIS: A secure and privacy-preserving protocol for vehicular communications," *IEEE Transactions on Vehicular Technology*, vol. 56, no. 6, pp. 3442–3456, 2007.

15. R. Lu, X. Lin, H. Zhu, P. Ho, and X. Shen, "ECPP: Efficient conditional privacy preservation protocol for secure vehicular communications," *Proc. 27th IEEE International Conference on Computer Communications, Joint Conference of the IEEE Computer and Communications Societies (INFOCOM' 08)*, Phoenix: IEEE, April 13–18, 2008, pp. 1229–1237. (Available online at http://dx.doi.org/10.1109/INFOCOM.2008.179.)

16. "Dedicated short-range communications (DSRC) protocol," http://grouper.ieee.org/groups/scc32/dsrc/index.html.

17. B. Schneier, *Applied Cryptography: Protocols, Algorithms, and Source Code in C*, 2nd ed. New York: Wiley, 1995.

18. D. Boneh and H. Shacham, "Group signatures with verifier-local revocation," *Proc. 11th ACM Conference on Computer and Communications Security, CCS 2004*, Washington, DC: ACM, Oct. 25–29, 2004, pp. 168–177. (Available online at http://doi.acm.org/10.1145/1030083.1030106.)

19. D. Boneh, X. Boyen, and H. Shacham, "Short group signatures," *Proc. Advances in Cryptology—CRYPTO 2004, 24th Annual International Cryptology Conference*, Santa Barbara, CA: Springer, Aug. 15–19, 2004, pp. 41–55. (Available online at http://dx.doi.org/10.1007/978-3-540-28628-8_3.)

20. A. Miyaji, M. Nakabayashi, and S. Takano, "New explicit conditions of elliptic curve traces for fr-reduction," *IEICE Transactions on Fundamentals of Electronics, Communications and Computer Sciences*, vol. 84, no. 5, pp. 1234–1243, 2001.

21. M. Scott, "Efficient implementation of cryptographic pairings," http://www.pairing-conference.org/2007/invited/Scott slide. pdf, 2007.

22. CVSC. Consortium et al., *Vehicle Safety Communications Project: Task 3 Final Report: Identify Intelligent Vehicle Safety Applications Enabled by DSRC*, National Highway Traffic Safety Administration, US Department of Transportation, Washington DC, 2005.

23. D. Pointcheval and J. Stern, "Security arguments for digital signatures and blind signatures," *Journal of Cryptology*, vol. 13, no. 3, pp. 361–396, 2000.

PSEUDONYM-CHANGING STRATEGY FOR LOCATION PRIVACY

4.1 INTRODUCTION

In previous chapters, we discussed GSIS and ECPP for authentication and conditional privacy preservation in VANETs. In this chapter, we propose an effective pseudonym changing at social spots strategy to facilitate a vehicle to achieve high-level location privacy.

It is well known that, to achieve location privacy, a popular approach recommended in VANETs is that vehicles periodically change their pseudonyms when they are broadcasting *safety messages* (where each *safety message* is a 4-tuple including `Time`, `Location`, `Velocity`, `Content`, and is authenticated with a `Signature` with respect to a `Pseudonym`) [1–3]. Because a vehicle uses different pseudonyms on the road, the *unlinkability* of pseudonyms can guarantee a vehicle's location privacy. However, if a vehicle changes its pseudonym in an improper occasion, changing pseudonyms has no use to protect location privacy, since an adversary could still link a new pseudonym with the old one [4]. As an example shown in Fig. 4.1, when three vehicles are running on the road, if only one vehicle changes its pseudonyms during Δt, an adversary can still monitor the pseudonyms' link. Even though all three vehicles change their pseudonyms simultaneously, the `Location` and `Velocity` information embedded in *safety messages* could still provide a clue to the adversary to link the pseudonyms, making the

Vehicular Ad Hoc Network Security and Privacy, First Edition. Xiaodong Lin and Rongxing Lu.
© 2015 The Institute of Electrical and Electronics Engineers, Inc. Published 2015 by John Wiley & Sons, Inc.

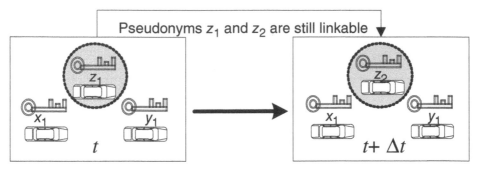

Figure 4.1. Pseudonyms link when they are changed at an inappropriate occasion.

privacy protection fail. Therefore, it is imperative for us to exploit the accuracy of location privacy achieved by frequent changing pseudonyms in VANETs [5–10]. Formally, we let $\vec{F} = \{F_1, F_2, F_3, \dots\}$ be the multidimensional character factors associated with a pseudonym-changing process. For example, the vector $\vec{F} = \{F_1, F_2, F_3, \dots\}$ can represent factors {Time, Location, Velocity, ...}. In some specific scenarios, an adversary has the ability to monitor a subset $\vec{F}_n = \{F_1, F_2, \dots, F_n\} \subset \vec{F}$ and use it for identifying a vehicle pseudonym-changing process. Let $\vec{b}_0 = (x_1, x_2, \dots, x_n)$ and $\vec{b}_1 = (y_1, y_2, \dots, y_n)$ be the characteristic vectors of two vehicles' pseudonym-changing processes observed by an adversary. Then, the cosine-based similarity between $\vec{b}_0$ and $\vec{b}_1$ can be given by

$$\cos(\vec{b}_0, \vec{b}_1) = \frac{\vec{b}_0 \odot \vec{b}_0}{|\vec{b}_0| \cdot |\vec{b}_1|} = \frac{\sum_{i=1}^{n} x_i \cdot y_i}{\sqrt{\sum_{i=1}^{n} x_i^2} \cdot \sqrt{\sum_{i=1}^{n} y_i^2}}$$

Obviously, when $\vec{b}_0$ and $\vec{b}_1$ are identical, $\cos(\vec{b}_0, \vec{b}_1) = 1$. Because of the monitoring inaccuracy, if $|1 - \cos(\vec{b}_0, \vec{b}_1)| \leq \epsilon$, for some small confusion value $\epsilon > 0$, two pseudonyms changing processes can be regarded as indistinguishable in the eye of the adversary. Therefore, in order to protect location privacy with high quality, a vehicle should choose a proper scenario where as many as possible indistinguishable pseudonyms changing processes are taking place simultaneously.

In this chapter, to enable vehicles to achieve high-level location privacy in VANETs, we propose an effective *pseudonyms changing at social spots* (PCS) strategy [11]. In the PCS strategy, the social spots are the places where many vehicles temporarily gather, e.g., a road intersection when the traffic light turns red, or a free parking lot near a shopping mall. If all vehicles change their pseudonyms before leaving the spot, the first broadcasted *safety message* includes indistinguishable information Location= social spot, Velocity=0, and unlinkable Pseudonym. Then, the social spot naturally becomes a *mix zone*, and the location privacy can be achieved. Specifically, in this work, our contributions are threefold.

First, we utilize the unique feature of social spots, i.e., where many vehicles temporarily stop at the social spot, to propose the PCS strategy. In addition, as an important technical preliminary of PCS strategy, we present a practical key-insulated pseudonym self-delegation (KPSD) model, which securely generates many on-demand short-life keys and can mitigate the hazards due to vehicle theft.

Second, we take the anonymity set size (ASS) as the privacy metric (the larger the anonymity set size, the higher the anonymity achieved [4, 12]) to measure the quality of privacy (QoP) achieved in PCS strategy. To the best of our knowledge, most previously reported schemes [4, 10] use the simulations to gauge the achieved location privacy in VANETs, and thus our anonymity set-analytic models will shed light on this research line.

Third, to guarantee the PCS strategy can be effectively adopted in practice, we use the simplified game-theoretic techniques to formally prove the feasibility of the PCS strategy. As a result, the PCS strategy can really guide vehicles to intelligently change their pseudonyms for better location privacy at the right moment and place.

The remainder of this chapter is organized as follows. In Section 4.2, we formalize the problem by describing the network model and the threat model, and identifying the requirements of location privacy in VANETs. Then, we present the PCS strategy in Section 4.3, followed by the performance evaluations in Section 4.4. Finally, we draw our summary in Section 4.5.

4.2 PROBLEM DEFINITION

In this section, we define the problem by formalizing the network model, threat model, and identifying the requirements of location privacy in VANETs.

4.2.1 Network Model

We consider a VANET in the urban area, which consists of a large number of vehicles and a collection of social spots[1] as follows:

- *Vehicles.* In the urban area, a large number of vehicles are running on the road everyday. Each vehicle is equipped with an onboard unit (OBU) device, which allows one vehicle to communicate with other vehicles for sharing local traffic information to improve the overall safety driving conditions.

- *Social Spots.* The *social spots* in the urban area refer to the places where many vehicles gather, for example, a road intersection when the traffic light is red or a free parking lot near the shopping mall, as shown in Fig. 4.2. Since the session of red traffic light is typically short, (i.e., 30 or 60 seconds), the road intersection is called a *small social spot*. As a shopping mall usually operates for a whole day, where a number of customers' vehicles will stop at the parking lot for a long period, the free parking lot near the mall is hence called a *large social spot*. Notice that social spots usually hold many vehicles and if all vehicles indistinguishably change their pseudonyms in the spots, the social spots automatically become *mix zones*.

---

[1] We confine our problem to pseudonym changing in the V2V communication mode, and do not include roadside units (RSUs) in the current network model, although RSUs are still deployed to support V2R communication in the urban area.

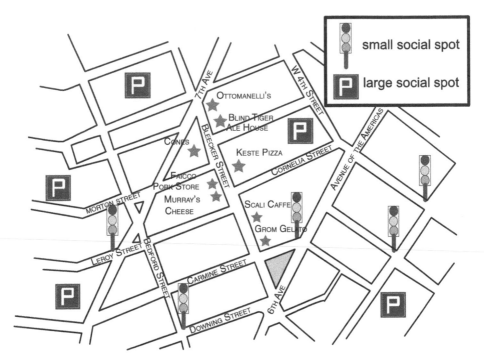

Figure 4.2. Social spots including the road intersection and free parking lots.

4.2.2 Threat Model

Unlike other wireless communication devices, the OBU devices equipped on the vehicles cannot be switched off once vehicles are running on the road [13]. Then, an eavesdropper, through the *safety messages* broadcasted by the OBU, can monitor the location information of a specific vehicle all the time. Specifically, in our threat model, we consider a global external adversary $\mathcal{A}$ equipped with radio devices to trace the vehicles' locations, where

- *Global* means the adversary $\mathcal{A}$ has the ability to monitor and collect all *safety messages* in the network with radio devices plus some special eavesdropping infrastructure [14], where each safety message includes Time, Location, Velocity, Content as well as Pseudonym. Since Pseudonym is unlinkable and Content could be set as irrelevant, the adversary $\mathcal{A}$ primarily tracks a vehicle in terms of Time, Location, Velocity, i.e., in a spatio-temporal way in our model.
- *External* denotes the adversary $\mathcal{A}$ can only passively eavesdrop the communications, but does not actively attempt to compromise the running vehicles.

Notice that an adversary $\mathcal{A}$ of course can track vehicles by using cameras in the urban area. However, the cost of *global* eavesdropping with cameras is much higher than that of radio-based eavesdropping [10]. Therefore, the topic of camera-based global eavesdropping is beyond the scope of this chapter.

4.2.3 Location Privacy Requirements

To resist the global external adversary's tracking and achieve the location privacy in VANETs, the following requirements must be satisfied:

- *R1.* Identity privacy is a prerequisite for the success of location privacy. Therefore, each vehicle should use a pseudonym in place of real identity to broadcast messages. Then, by concealing the real identity, the identity privacy can be achieved.
- *R2.* Each vehicle should also periodically change its pseudonyms to reduce the relation between the former and latter locations. In addition, pseudonym changing should be performed at an appropriate time and location to ensure that the location privacy is achieved.
- *R3.* Location privacy should be *conditional* in VANETs. If a broadcasted *safety message* is in dispute, the trusted authority (TA) can disclose the real identity; i.e., the TA has the ability to determine the location where a specific vehicle broadcasted a disputed *safety message*.

Recall that the social spots can serve as *mix zones* naturally. In what follows, we explore this feature and propose the PCS strategy for achieving location privacy in VANETs.

4.3 PROPOSED PCS STRATEGY FOR LOCATION PRIVACY

In this section, we present our PCS strategy for achieving location privacy in VANETs. Specifically, we develop two anonymity set-analytic models to investigate the location privacy level achieved in the PCS strategy, and use simplified game-theoretic techniques to discuss its feasibility. Before delving into the details of the PCS strategy, we first present a practical key-insulated pseudonym self-delegation (KPSD) model, which securely generates many on-demand short-life keys and serves as the basis of the proposed PCS strategy.

4.3.1 KPSD Model for PCS Strategy

To support the PCS strategy, a vehicle must hold a certain amount of pseudonyms. A simple and straightforward solution is proposed, [1], in which an OBU device equipped on a vehicle possesses a large number of anonymous short-time keys authorized by a trusted authority (TA). Obviously, this solution can achieve conditional location privacy when periodically changing the pseudonyms. However, it may take a large storage space to store these short-time keys in OBU device. GSIS [15] is a group-signature-based technique that can achieve conditional location privacy without pseudonym changing. However, the pure group signature verification is usually time-consuming, which may not be suitable for some time-stringent VANET applications. ECPP [15] is another anonymous authentication technique that combines group signature and ordinary signature. In ECPP, when a legal vehicle passes by an RSU, the RSU will authorize a group-signature-based short-life anonymous certificate to the vehicle. Then, the vehicle can use it to sign messages with ordinary signature techniques [16]. Once receiving a signed message, anyone can verify the authenticity of message by checking both the anonymous certificate and message signature. Note that, when the vehicle signs many messages, any verifier only needs to execute one group signature verification operation on certificate; thus ECPP is more efficient than GSIS. Similar to ECPP, Calandriello et al. [17], inspired by the idea of pseudonymous PKI for ubiquitous computing [18], also combine group signature and ordinary signature techniques to achieve anonymous authentication in VANETs. Because the short-life anonymous certificate is generated by the vehicle itself, their scheme is very flexible. However, once a vehicle is stolen, the vehicle thief can arbitrarily generate valid short-life anonymous certificates before being detected. Then, the potential hazards could be large. To mitigate such negative affects, we propose a practical key-insulated pseudonym self-delegation (KPSD) model.

As shown in Fig. 4.3, in KPSD model, TA does not directly preload an authorized anonymous key to the vehicle; instead, it provides the authorized anonymous key to the user—the owner of the vehicle. The user usually stores the authorized anonymous key in a secure environment, i.e., at home. When s/he prepares for travel (fuels the car with gasoline, etc.), s/he first generates required self-delegated short-life keys, and installs them in the OBU device. Later, when the vehicle is running in the urban area, these

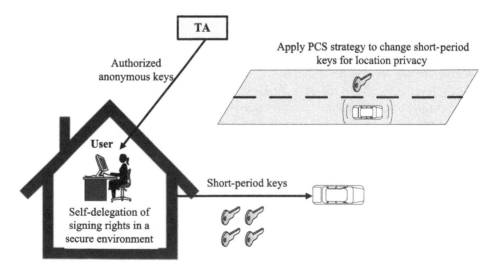

Figure 4.3. Practical KPSD model for location privacy in VANETs.

short-life keys can be used to sign messages. Because vehicle theft is still a serious concern (e.g., statistics show that there have been over 170,000 vehicles stolen each year in Canada [19]), these short-life keys could be mishandled by the thieves, once the vehicle is stolen. However, different from the previous work [1,14,15,17], the authorized anonymous key in KPSD model is not stored in the vehicle. Thus, the vehicle thieves cannot generate more short-life keys. As a result, the hazards due to vehicle theft can be mitigated in KPSD model. Note that if the authorized anonymous key is protected by a password-based tamperproof device, Calandriello et al.'s scheme [17] can fall into our key-insulated pseudonym self-delegation model, but the cost will increase accordingly.

In the following, we construct an efficient KPSD scheme with asymmetric bilinear groups [20], which serves as the basis of the PCS strategy.

4.3.1.1 Construction. Our proposed KPSD scheme is based on Boneh-Boyen short signature [21] and the conditional privacy preservation authentication technology [15, 22], which mainly consists of the following four parts: system initialization, key generation, pseudonym self-delegated generation, and conditional tracking.

System Initialization. Similar to the notations used in Ref. 20, let k be a security parameter, G, G' and G_T be three (multiplicative) cyclic groups of the same large prime order q generated by $\mathcal{AGen}(k)$, where $|q| = k$. Suppose G, G' and G_T are equipped with a pairing, i.e., a non-degenerated and efficiently computable bilinear map $e : G \times G' \rightarrow G_T$ such that $e(g_1^a, g_2^b) = e(g_1, g_2)^{ab} \in G_T$ for all $a, b \in \mathbb{Z}_q^*$ and any $g_1 \in G_1, g_2 \in G_2$. Let ψ be a one-way (easy to compute, but hard to invert) isohomomorphic mapping from G' to G. TA first chooses two random numbers $u, v \in \mathbb{Z}_q^*$ as the *master key*, and computes $U_1 = g_1{}^u$, $U_2 = g_2{}^u$, and $V_1 = g_1{}^v$. In addition, TA also chooses a public collision-resistant hash function: $H : \{0, 1\}^* \rightarrow \mathbb{Z}_q^*$. In the end, TA publishes the system parameters $params = (q, G, G', G_T, e, g_1, g_2, U_1, U_2, V_1, H)$.

Key Generation. When a user $\mathcal{U}_i$ with identity ID_i joins the system, TA first chooses a random number $s_i \in \mathbb{Z}_q^*$ such that $s_i + u \neq 0 \bmod q$, computes $A_i = g_1^{\frac{1}{s_i+u}}$. Then, TA stores (ID_i, A_i^u) in the tracking list and returns $ASK_i = (s_i, A_i = g_1^{\frac{1}{s_i+u}})$ as the authorized anonymous key to the user.

Pseudonym Self-Delegated Generation. After receiving the authorized anonymous key ASK_i, $\mathcal{U}_i$ places it in a secure environment (e.g., at home). When $\mathcal{U}_i$ starts to travel in the city, she first runs the following steps to generate the required anonymous short-life keys used for the travel, which is very analogous to the fueling of a vehicle before a travel:

1. $\mathcal{U}_i$ first chooses l random numbers $x_1, x_2, \ldots, x_l \in \mathbb{Z}_n^*$ as the short-life private keys and computes the corresponding public keys $Y_j = g^{x_j}$, for $j = 1, 2, \ldots, l$ for the travel.

2. For each short-life public key Y_j, $\mathcal{U}_i$ computes the anonymous self-delegated certificate $Cert_j$ as follows:
   - Randomly choose $\alpha, r_\alpha, r_x, r_\delta \in \mathbb{Z}_q^*$ and compute $T_U, T_V, \delta, \delta_1, \delta_2, \delta_3$, where

$$\begin{cases} T_U = U_1^\alpha, T_V = A_i \cdot V_1^\alpha, \delta = \alpha \cdot x_i \bmod q \\ \delta_1 = U_1^{r_\alpha}, \delta_2 = T_U^{r_x}/U_1^{r_\delta} \\ \delta_3 = e(T_V, g_2^{r_x})/e(V_1, U_2^{r_\alpha \cdot g_2^{r_\delta}}) \end{cases} \tag{4.1}$$

   - Compute $c = H(U_1||V_1||Y_j||T_U||T_V||\delta_1||\delta_2||\delta_3)$ and $s_\alpha, s_x, s_\delta \in \mathbb{Z}_q^*$, where

$$\begin{cases} s_\alpha = r_\alpha + c \cdot \alpha \bmod q, s_x = r_x + c \cdot x_i \bmod q \\ s_\delta = r_\delta + c \cdot \delta \bmod q \end{cases} \tag{4.2}$$

   - Set $Cert_j = \{Y_j||T_U||T_V||c||s_\alpha||s_x||s_\delta\}$ as the certificate.
3. After all anonymous self-delegated certificates $Cert_j$, $j = 1, 2, \ldots, l$, are generated, $\mathcal{U}_i$ installs them in the vehicle, i.e., implanting all $x_j||Y_j||Cert_j$, $j = 1, 2, \ldots, l$, into the OBU device.

Later, when driving the vehicle in the city, $\mathcal{U}_i$ can use one short-life key $x_j||Y_j||Cert_j$ to authenticate a message M by signing $\sigma = g_2^{\frac{1}{x_j + H(M)}}$, and broadcast

$$msg = (M||\sigma||Y_j||Cert_j) \tag{4.3}$$

On receiving $msg = (M||\sigma||Y_j||Cert_j)$, everyone can check the validity by the following process.

1. If the certificate $Y_j||Cert_j$ has not been checked, the verifier first computes

$$\begin{cases} \delta_1' = U_1^{s_\alpha}/T_U^c, \delta_2' = T_U^{s_x}/U_1^{s_\delta} \\ \delta_3' = \dfrac{e(T_V, g_2^{s_x} \cdot U_2^c)}{e(V_1, U_2^{s_\alpha} \cdot g_2^{s_\delta})e(g_1, g_2^c)} \end{cases} \tag{4.4}$$

and checks whether

$$c = H(U_1||V_1||Y_j||T_U||T_V||\delta_1'||\delta_2'||\delta_3') \tag{4.5}$$

If it does hold, the certificate $Y_j||Cert_j$ passes the verification. The corrections are as follows: (a) $\delta_1' = U_1^{s_\alpha}/T_U^c = U_1^{r_\alpha + c \cdot \alpha}/U_1^{c \cdot \alpha} = \delta_1$; (b) $\delta_2' = T_U^{s_x}/U_1^{s_\delta} = T_U^{r_x + cx_i}/U_1^{r_\delta + c\delta} = \delta_2$; (c) $\delta_3' = e(T_V, g_2^{s_x} \cdot U_2^c)/e(V_1, U_2^{s_\alpha} \cdot g_2^{s_\delta})e(g_1, g_2^c) = e(T_V, g_2^{r_x})/e(V_1, U_2^{r_\alpha} \cdot g_2^{r_\delta}) = \delta_3$.

2. Once the certificate $Y_j || Cert_j$ passes the verification, the verifier checks

$$e(Y_j \cdot g_1^{H(M)}, \sigma) \stackrel{?}{=} e(g_1, g_2) \tag{4.6}$$

If it holds, the message M is accepted; otherwise, M is rejected, since $e(Y_j \cdot g_1^{H(M)}, \sigma) = e(g_1^{x_j + H(M)}, g_2^{\frac{1}{x_j + H(M)}}) = e(g_1, g_2)$. Note that the value of $e(g_1, g_2)$ can be computed in advance.

Conditional Tracking. Once an accepted message M under the certificate

$$Cert_j = \{Y_j || T_U || T_V || c || s_\alpha || s_x || s_\delta\}$$

is disputed, TA uses the master key (u, v) to compute

$$T_V^u / T_U^v = A_i^u \cdot V_1^{u\alpha} / U_1^{v\alpha} = A_i^u \cdot g^{uv\alpha} / g^{uv\alpha} = A_i^u \tag{4.7}$$

and then can efficiently trace the real identity ID_i by looking up the entry (ID_i, A_i^u) in the tracking list.

4.3.1.2 Security.
Since both the short signature [21] and conditional privacy preservation authentication [15] are secure, the security of the proposed KPSD scheme can be guaranteed; i.e., it can effectively achieve anonymous authentication with conditional tracking to fulfill the requirements of location privacy. In addition, the proposed KPSD scheme can also mitigate the hazards due to vehicle theft, since the authorized anonymous key ASK_i is *key-insulated*; i.e., it is stored in a secure environment, so that vehicle thieves cannot obtain ASK_i from the stolen vehicle, and consequently cannot generate new self-delegated short-life keys arbitrarily.

4.3.1.3 Performance.
In VANETs, it is very difficult for a vehicle to verify many signed messages in a short time, e.g., within 300 ms. Let T_{pair}, T_{exp-1}, T_{exp-2} be the time costs for pairing operation, exponentiation in $\mathbb{G}$, and $\mathbb{G}'$, respectively. Then, to check n messages from the same source, where $n \geq 1$, the verification cost of the proposed KPSD anonymous authentication and the pure group signature-based (GSB) anonymous authentication are $(3 + n)T_{pair} + (4 + n)T_{exp-1} + 5T_{exp-2}$ and $3nT_{pair} + 4nT_{exp-1} + 5nT_{exp-2}$, respectively. Since T_{pair} is dominant over T_{exp-1} and T_{exp-2}, we set T_{pair} at 4.5 ms as in Ref. 15 and compare them in Fig. 4.4. It can be seen when n is large, the proposed anonymous authentication is much more efficient than the pure GSB anonymous authentication.

4.3.2 Anonymity Set Analysis for Achieved Location Privacy

With the above KPSD scheme, each vehicle can hold a number of pseudonyms on the road, and then it can apply the PCS strategy, as shown in Algorithm 3, to protect its

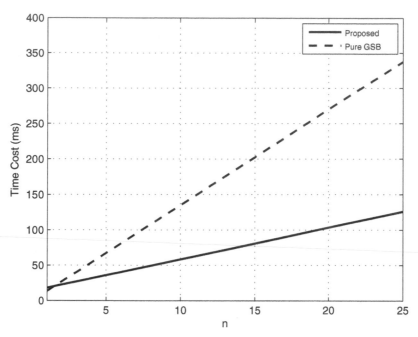

Figure 4.4. Time cost comparison.

Algorithm 3: Pseudonym Changing at Social Spots Strategy

---

begin

    if *Small social spot* **then**

        A vehicle V_i stops at road intersection when the traffic light turns red. When the traffic light turns to green, V_i changes its pseudonym.

    end

    if *Large social spot* **then**

        A vehicle V_i stops at a free parking lot near a shopping mall. When leaving the parking lot, V_i changes its pseudonym.

    end

end

---

location privacy. To gauge the benefits from the PCS strategy, we next develop two anonymity set-analytic models to investigate the location privacy achieved in small social spots and large social spots, respectively.

4.3.2.1 Anonymity Set Analysis at Small Social Spots. As shown in Fig. 4.5, when the traffic light turns red, the road intersection can be regarded as a *small social spot*, since a fleet of vehicles will stop at the intersection [10]. Assume that all vehicles will simultaneously change their pseudonyms when the traffic light turns green. Then, the road intersection becomes a *mix zone*. Let S_a be the number of vehicles stopped at

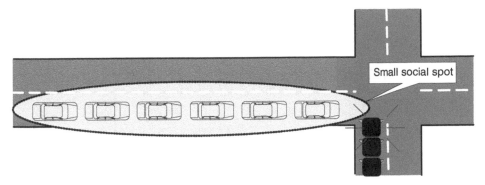

Figure 4.5. Pseudonym changing at an intersection.

the intersection, we will have the expected anonymity set size (ASS) = S_a. Clearly, the larger the anonymity set size ASS is, the greater the anonymity is offered in the small social spot. We can use a trivial anonymity set-analytic model on ASS to investigate the anonymity level provided by the small social spot.

Let $T_s = t$, where $t = 30, 60$ seconds, be the fixed stop time period of a specific road intersection. Let *vehicle arrival* (VA) at the road intersection be a Poisson process, and t_a be the interarrival time for VA, where t_a has an exponential distribution with the mean $\frac{1}{\lambda}$. Let X be the random variable of vehicles arriving at the road intersection during the period T_s. Then, based on Refs. 23 and 24, the probability $X = x$ during $T_s = t$ can be expressed as

$$\Pr[X = x | T_s = t] = \frac{(\lambda t)^x}{x!} e^{-\lambda t} \tag{4.8}$$

and the expected number of X can be computed as

$$E[X|T_s = t] = \sum_{x=1}^{\infty} x \Pr[X = x | T_s = t] = \lambda t \tag{4.9}$$

Since all vehicles leave the intersection after the traffic light turns to green,[2] the anonymity set size ASS is

$$ASS = S_a = E[X|T_s = t] = \lambda t \tag{4.10}$$

if all vehicles follow the PCS strategy.

---

[2] Note that when the number of waiting vehicles is larger than some threshold, only some of the waiting vehicles can leave the intersection after the traffic light turns to green, and some vehicles have to wait for the next green light. In this case, the number of waiting vehicles (N_v) can be regarded as the initial value for the next anonymity set size at intersection, i.e., $ASS = N_v + \lambda t$.

Figure 4.6. Pseudonym changing at a free parking lot.

4.3.2.2 Anonymity Set Analysis at Large Social Spots.

As shown in Fig. 4.6, a large social spot could be a free parking lot near a shopping mall [19]. Because a parking lot usually holds many vehicles, and each vehicle randomly leaves the parking lot at the user's own will, such a parking lot also naturally becomes a *mix zone* if all users change their pseudonyms in the parking lot and leave the parking lot after a random delay. Because a parking lot can obfuscate the relation between the arriving and leaving vehicles, the location privacy of user can be achieved.

Let S_a be the number of vehicles in the parking lot when a vehicle is ready to leave. Then, the anonymity set size denotes ASS $= S_a$. In the following, we propose an anonymity analytic model on ASS to investigate the anonymity level provided by the large social spot.

For a specific vehicle $\mathcal{V}$ that has entered a parking lot near a shopping mall for changing pseudonyms, we consider the time period from the mall's opening time, e.g., 8:00 AM, to the vehicle $\mathcal{V}$'s leaving time after pseudonyms changing T_S, as shown in Fig. 4.7, is exponentially distributed with the density function $f(t)$, the mean $\frac{1}{\mu}$, and the Laplace transform $f^*(s) = \left(\frac{\mu}{\mu+s} \right)$. On the other hand, other vehicles enter/leave a

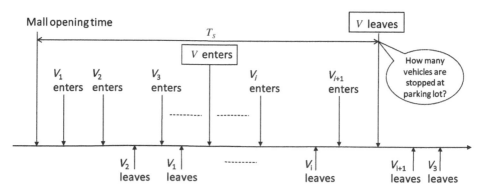

Figure 4.7. Timing diagram (there is no vehicle stopping in the parking lot initially).

parking lot at the drivers' own will; for example, a driver may determine when and how long he will stop at the mall. Let *vehicle arrival* (VA) at the parking lot be a Poisson process, and t_a be the interarrival time for VA. Then, t_a has an exponential distribution with the mean $\frac{1}{\lambda}$. In addition, the time period between the time when a vehicle arrives at the parking lot and the time when it leaves t_u is assumed to have the density function $f_u(\cdot)$, the mean $\frac{1}{\omega}$ and the Laplace transform $f_u^*(s)$. Let X be the random variable of vehicles arriving at the parking lot during the time period T_s. Then, the probability $X = x$ during the period $T_s = t$ follows $\Pr[X = x | T_s = t] = \frac{(\lambda t)^x}{x!} e^{-\lambda t}$, and for $t \geq 0$, we obtain

$$
\begin{aligned}
\Pr[X = x] &= \int_{t=0}^{\infty} \Pr[X = x | T_s = t] f(t) dt \\
&= \int_{t=0}^{\infty} \frac{(\lambda t)^x}{x!} e^{-\lambda t} f(t) dt \\
&= \left(\frac{\lambda^x}{x!}\right) \int_{t=0}^{\infty} t^x e^{-\lambda t} f(t) dt \\
&= \left(\frac{\lambda^x}{x!}\right) \left[(-1)^x \frac{d^x f^*(s)}{ds^x} \right]\Big|_{s=\lambda} \\
&= \frac{\mu \lambda^x}{(\mu + \lambda)^{x+1}}
\end{aligned}
\tag{4.11}
$$

and the expected number of X can be computed as

$$
E[X] = \sum_{x=1}^{\infty} x \Pr[X = x] = \frac{\lambda}{\mu}
\tag{4.12}
$$

Let χ be the time period between the time when a vehicle arrives at the parking lot and the time when the specific vehicle $\mathcal{V}$ leaves the parking lot after pseudonyms change. Since T_s is exponentially distributed, the density function $\sigma(\chi)$ for the distribution χ can be expressed as

$$
\sigma(\chi) = \mu \int_{t=\chi}^{\infty} f(t) dt = \mu[1 - F(t)]\Big|_{t=\chi} = \mu e^{-\mu \chi}
\tag{4.13}
$$

During the period T_s, many vehicles may leave the parking lot before $\mathcal{V}$ leaves, i.e., $t_u < \chi$, while others leave after $\mathcal{V}$, i.e., $t_u \geq \chi$. Assume that Y is the number of vehicles leaving the parking lot before $\mathcal{V}$; then the probability $\Pr[Y = y | X = x]$ can be computed as

$$
\Pr[Y = y | X = x] = \binom{x}{y} (\Pr[t_u < \chi])^y (\Pr[t_u \geq \chi])^{x-y}
\tag{4.14}
$$

Then, the probability $\Pr[t_u \geq \chi]$ can be calculated as

$$
\begin{aligned}
\Pr[t_u \geq \chi] &= \int_{t_u=0}^{\infty} \int_{\chi=0}^{t_u} \mu e^{\mu \chi} d\chi f_u(t_u) dt_u \\
&= \int_{t_u=0}^{\infty} (1 - e^{-\mu t_u}) f_u(t_u) dt_u \\
&= 1 - \int_{t_u=0}^{\infty} f_u(t_u) e^{-\mu t_u} dt_u = 1 - f_u^*(\mu)
\end{aligned}
\tag{4.15}
$$

and $\Pr[t_u < \chi]$ can be derived from $\Pr[t_u \geq \chi]$ as

$$
\Pr[t_u < \chi] = 1 - \Pr[t_u \geq \chi] = 1 - (1 - f_u^*(u)) = f_u^*(u)
\tag{4.16}
$$

After that, Eq. (4.14) can be rewritten as

$$
\Pr[Y = y | X = x] = \binom{x}{y} (f_u^*(u))^y (1 - f_u^*(u))^{x-y}
\tag{4.17}
$$

and the expected number of Y can be computed as

$$
\begin{aligned}
E[Y] &= \sum_{x=1}^{\infty} \sum_{y=1}^{x} \{ y \Pr[Y = y | X = x] \Pr[X = x] \} \\
&= \sum_{x=1}^{\infty} \left\{ \left\{ \sum_{y=1}^{x} y \binom{x}{y} (f_u^*(u))^y (1 - f_u^*(u))^{x-y} \right\} \right. \\
&\quad \left. \times \left[\frac{\mu \lambda^x}{(\mu + \lambda)^{x+1}} \right] \right\}
\end{aligned}
\tag{4.18}
$$

Therefore, the expected anonymity set size ASS for a specific vehicle $\mathcal{V}$'s pseudonym changing is

$$
\begin{aligned}
ASS = S_a &= E[X] - E[Y] \\
&= \frac{\lambda}{\mu} - \sum_{x=1}^{\infty} \left\{ \left\{ \sum_{y=1}^{x} y \binom{x}{y} (f_u^*(u))^y (1 - f_u^*(u))^{x-y} \right\} \right. \\
&\quad \left. \times \left[\frac{\mu \lambda^x}{(\mu + \lambda)^{x+1}} \right] \right\}
\end{aligned}
\tag{4.19}
$$

Since the exponential distribution has been widely used in modeling many realistic scenarios [23], we assume that t_u also follows the exponential distribution. Then, the Laplace transform $f_u^*(u)$ becomes

$$f_u^*(u) = \left(\frac{\omega}{\omega + \mu} \right) \tag{4.20}$$

As a result, S_{anony} can be rewritten as

$$
\begin{aligned}
ASS &= \frac{\lambda}{\mu} - \sum_{x=1}^{\infty} \left\{ \left\{ \sum_{y=1}^{x} y \binom{x}{y} \left(\frac{\omega}{\omega + \mu} \right)^y \left(1 - \frac{\omega}{\omega + \mu} \right)^{x-y} \right\} \right. \\
&\quad \left. \times \left[\frac{\mu \lambda^x}{(\mu + \lambda)^{x+1}} \right] \right\} \\
&= \frac{\lambda}{\mu} - \sum_{x=1}^{\infty} \left\{ x \cdot \frac{\omega}{\omega + \mu} \times \left[\frac{\mu \lambda^x}{(\mu + \lambda)^{x+1}} \right] \right\} \\
&= \frac{\lambda}{\mu} - \frac{\omega \mu}{(\omega + \mu)(\mu + \lambda)} \sum_{x=1}^{\infty} x \cdot \left(\frac{\lambda}{\mu + \lambda} \right)^x \\
&= \frac{\lambda}{\mu} - \frac{\omega \lambda}{\mu(\omega + \mu)} = \frac{\lambda}{\omega + \mu}
\end{aligned}
\tag{4.21}
$$

4.3.3 Feasibility Analysis of PCS Strategy

In the anonymity set analyses presented above, we assume that all vehicles change their pseudonyms. In this section, we use the simplified game-theoretic technique to show the feasibility of PCS strategy; i.e., we prove that each vehicle is really willing to change the pseudonym at social spots to achieve its location privacy in practice.

Let the anonymity set size ASS be $N = n + 1$, where $n \geq 0$, at social spots, which can be estimated by the above anonymity set analyses. Then, we investigate a rational scenario where all vehicles' location privacies are to be protected. At social spots, each vehicle V_j, $1 \leq j \leq N$ has two possible actions: change (C) the pseudonym with probability p_j and keep (K) the pseudonym with probability $1 - p_j$. If V_j keeps its pseudonym at the social spot, it will still be tracked with probability 1. Then, the loss of V_j's location privacy is unchanged, and the payoff in this action is a normalized location privacy loss of $-d_j$, where $d_j \in (0, 1)$ is the V_j's self-evaluation on the importance of location privacy. On the other hand, when V_j changes its pseudonym at the social spot, if there are other vehicles taking the same action as well, the anonymity set size will become S. After this social spot, V_j remains being tracked only with probability $\frac{1}{S}$. As such, the loss of location privacy in this case is reduced to $-\frac{d_j}{S}$. Let $c_j \in (0, 1)$ be V_j's normalized cost of changing a pseudonym, so the payoff in this action is $-\frac{d_j}{S} - c_j$. For all vehicles except V_j, let p_m be the minimum of all probabilities $\{p_i | 1 \leq i \leq N, i \neq j\}$.

Then, when V_j is ready to change its pseudonym at social spots, it can estimate the lower bound of the average anonymity set as

$$S = \sum_{i=0}^{n} \binom{n}{i} \cdot p_m^i \cdot (1 - p_m)^{n-i} \cdot (i + 1)$$

$$= np_m + 1$$

As a result, the payoff function of vehicle V_j can be summarized as

$$Payoff = \begin{cases} -\dfrac{d_j}{np_m+1} - c_j, & \text{if action C is taken} \\ \\ -d_j, & \text{else if action K is taken} \end{cases} \qquad (4.22)$$

Since vehicle V_j is rational and its goal is to protect its location privacy, the condition that V_j changes its pseudonym at the social spot is

$$-\frac{d_j}{np_m + 1} - c_j > -d_j \Rightarrow c_j < \frac{np_m d_j}{np_m + 1} \qquad (4.23)$$

With the adopted KPSD scheme, all vehicles generate and manage their pseudonyms by themselves. If they can generate enough pseudonyms before travel, then the cost of changing pseudonym can be very low. Nevertheless, when np_m is 0, in equation (4.23) does not hold, which indicates when there is no neighboring vehicle changing its pseudonym; V_j also does not change its pseudonym. However, when np_m is larger than 0, V_i is always able to reduce the cost c_j such that $c_j < \frac{np_m d_j}{np_m+1}$. Then, V_j can actively change the pseudonym at social spots. We define each vehicle V_j's location privacy gain (LPG) function as

$$LPG_j = -\frac{d_i}{np_m + 1} - (-d_i) = \frac{np_m}{np_m + 1} \cdot d_j$$

Then, LPG_j is an increasing function in terms of p_m. When $p_m = 1$, that is, when all vehicles change their pseudonyms at social spots, LPG_j can reach its maximal gain $\frac{n}{n+1} \cdot d_j = \frac{(N-1)}{N} \cdot d_j$. Since each vehicle is rational to maximize its location privacy gain, there would be a win–win situation when they all change their pseudonyms. As a result, the feasibility of PCS strategy in practice is demonstrated.

4.4   PERFORMANCE EVALUATION

In this section, we evaluate the location privacy level achieved in the PCS strategy. In particular, extensive simulations are conducted to demonstrate the impacts of different

TABLE 4.1. Simulation Settings in PCS

Parameter	Values
T_S: time period at small social spot	30, 60 seconds
$1/\lambda$: at small social spot	$[2, 4, 6, 8, 10, 12]$ seconds
$1/\mu$: mean of T_S at large social spot	$[1, 2, \ldots, 10]$ hours
$1/\lambda$: at large social spot	$[2, 4, 6]$ minutes
$1/\omega$: at large social spot	$[10, 20, \ldots, 90]$ minutes
d_i: a vehicle's self-evaluation on the importance of its location privacy	Normalized

parameters on the performance metrics in terms of the anonymity set size (ASS) and location privacy gain (LPG). Our simulations are based on a discrete-event simulator coded in C++, where the simulation parameters are listed in Table 4.1 under two scenarios: the small social spot and the large social spot. For each case, we repeat the simulation 100 times with different random seeds and calculate the average value with 95% confidence intervals. In addition, we compare the simulation results (denoted as Sim) with the numerical ones (denoted as Ana) to validate the developed analytical models.

We first validate the location privacy level achieved at small social spot, i.e., a road intersection when the traffic light turns red. Consider the stopping time period to be $T_S = 30, 60$ seconds for a low-traffic intersection and a high-traffic intersection, respectively. Figure 4.8 shows the ASS and LPG versus $1/\lambda$ varying from 2 seconds to 10 seconds with increase of 2. From the figure, it can be seen that ASS and LPG decrease with the increase of $1/\lambda$. The reason is that with a large $1/\lambda$, fewer vehicles drive at the road intersection when the traffic light is red, which leads to a small number of vehicles gathering at the intersection; as a result, this causes a smaller ASS as well as a lower LPG. In addition, a large T_S also has a positive impact on ASS and LPG.

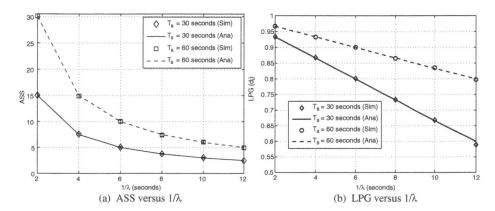

(a) ASS versus $1/\lambda$ (b) LPG versus $1/\lambda$

Figure 4.8. ASS and LPG versus $1/\lambda$ with different T_S at small social spot.

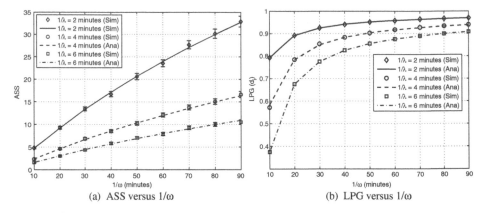

Figure 4.9. ASS and LPG versus $1/\omega$ with $1/\mu = 4$ hours at large social spot.

Therefore, to achieve a high location privacy level, a large intersection with high traffic is a good choice for vehicles, which tallies with our common sense.

To evaluate the location privacy level achieved at large social spot, we consider a free parking lot near a shopping mall. Parameterized with $1/\mu = 4$ hours, Fig. 4.9 shows the impacts of $1/\omega$ on the performance metrics in terms of ASS and LPG. From the figure, it can be seen that, as $1/\omega$ increases, both ASS and LPG increase. The reason is that the larger $1/\omega$, the more vehicles will park at the parking lot. In addition, the smaller $1/\lambda$ also achieves a larger ASS and a higher LPG. Therefore, when a vehicle changes its pseudonyms in a parking lot near a prosperous shopping mall (with small $1/\lambda$ and large $1/\omega$), high location privacy level can be guaranteed. From the figure, it can also be seen that the simulation and analysis results match very well, which justifies the accuracy of the analytic model.

Figure 4.10 shows the impact of the parameter $1/\mu$ on ASS and LPG. As we can see, except during the first 2 hours, with the increase of $1/\mu$, both ASS and LPG

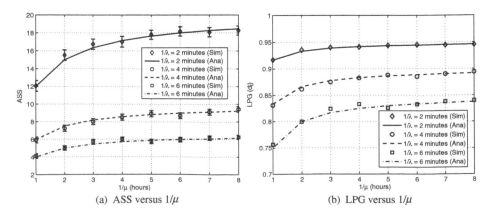

Figure 4.10. ASS and LPG versus $1/\mu$ with $1/\omega = 40$ minutes at large social spot.

smoothly increase. The results indicate that a vehicle can change its pseudonyms the most of daytime for better location privacy at a large social spot, in either the morning or afternoon. In the figure, the gaps between the simulation results and the analytical results are small, which can be further reduced if a larger number of simulation runs are conducted.

4.5 CONCLUDING REMARKS

In this chapter, we have proposed an effective pseudonym changing at social spots (PCS) strategy for location privacy in VANETs. In particular, we developed two anonymity set-analytic models in terms of ASS to formally analyze the achieved location privacy level, and we used game-theoretic techniques to prove its feasibility. In addition, we introduced a practical KPSD model to mitigate the hazards caused by vehicle theft. To the best of our knowledge, most previously reported works on *mix-zone*-based pseudonyms changing *only* use the simulations to evaluate the achieved location privacy. Therefore, our analytic models on location privacy at social spot *shed light on* this research line.

REFERENCES

1. M. Raya and J.-P. Hubaux, "Securing vehicular ad hoc networks," *Journal of Computer Security, Special Issue on Security of Ad Hoc and Sesnor Networks*, vol. 15, no. 1, pp. 39–68, 2007.

2. M. Raya, P. Papadimitratos, and J.-P. Hubaux, "Securing vehicular communications," *IEEE Communications Magazine*, vol. 44, no. 10, pp. 8–15, 2006.

3. C. Zhang, X. Lin, R. Lu, P.-H. Ho, and X. Shen, "An efficient message authentication scheme for vehicular communications," *IEEE Transactions on Vehicular Technology*, vol. 57, no. 6, pp. 3357–3368, 2008.

4. L. Buttyan, T. Holczer, and I. Vajda, "On the effectiveness of changing pseudonyms to provide location privacy in VANETs," *Proc. European Society for Applied Superconductivity (ESAS)*, 2007, ser. Lecture Notes in Computer Science, vol. 4572. Springer-Verlag, 2007, pp. 129–141.

5. A. Beresford and F. Stajano, "Mix zones: User privacy in location-aware services," *Proc. 2nd IEEE Annual Conference on Pervasive Computing and Communications Workshops*, IEEE, March 2004, pp. 127–131.

6. L. Huang, H. Yamane, K. Matsuura, and K. Sezaki, "Towards modeling wireless location privacy," *Proc. Privacy-Enhancing Technologies Conference (PET)*, ser. Lecture Notes In Computer Science, vol. 3856. Springer-Verlag, 2005, pp. 59–77.

7. L. Huang, H. Yamane, K. Matsuura, and K. Sezaki, "Silent cascade: Enhancing location privacy without communication qos degradation," *Proc. Statistical Process Control Conference (SPC)* 2006, ser. Lecture Notes in Computer Science, vol. 3934. Springer-Verlag, 2006, pp. 165–180.

8. M. Li, K. Sampigethaya, L. Huang, and R. Poovendran, "Swing & swap: User-centric approaches towards maximizing location privacy," *Proc. Workshop on Privacy in the Electronic Society (WPES)*, ACM, 2006, pp. 19–28.

9. K. Sampigethaya, L. Huang, M. Li, R. Poovendran, K. Matsuura, and K. Sezaki, "CARAVAN: Providing location privacy for VANET," *Proc. Embedded Security in Cars (ESCAR)*, IS-ITS, 2005.

10. J. Freudiger, M. Raya, and M. Feleghhazi, "Mix zones for location privacy in vehicular networks," *Proc. WiN-ITS 2007*, Vancouver, British Columbia: ACM, Aug. 2007.

11. R. Lu, X. Lin, T. H. Luan, X. Liang, and X. Shen, "Pseudonym changing at social spots: An effective strategy for location privacy in vanets," *IEEE Transactions on Vehicular Technology*, vol. 61, no. 1, pp. 86–96, Jan. 2012.

12. A. Pfitzmann and M. Köhntopp, "Anonymity, unobservability, and pseudonymity—a proposal for terminology," *Proc. Workshop on Design Issues in Anonymity and Unobservability*, ser. Lecture Notes in Computer Science, vol. 2009. Springer-Verlag, 2000, pp. 1–9.

13. P. Papadimitratos, A. Kung, J. P. Hubaux, and F. Kargl, "Privacy and identity management for vehicular communication systsms: A position paper," *Proc. Workshop on Standards for Privacy in User-Centric Identity Management*, 2006.

14. X. Lin, X. Sun, P.-H. Ho, and X. Shen, "GSIS: A secure and privacy-preserving protocol for vehicular communications," *IEEE Transactions on Vehicular Technology*, vol. 56, no. 6, pp. 3442–3456, 2007.

15. R. Lu, X. Lin, H. Zhu, P. Ho, and X. Shen, "ECPP: Efficient Conditional Privacy Preservation Protocol for Secure Vehicular Communications," *Proc. 27th IEEE International Conference on Computer Communications, Joint Conference of the IEEE Computer and Communications Societies, (INFOCOM'08), Phoenix April 13–18, 2008*, IEEE, 2008, pp. 1229–1237. (Available online at: http://dx.doi.org/10.1109/INFOCOM.2008.179.)

16. W. Mao, *Modern Cryptography: Theory and Practice*, Prentice-Hall Professional Technical Reference, 2003.

17. G. Calandriello, P. Papadimitratos, J.-P. Hubaux, and A. Lioy, "Efficient and robust pseudonymous authentication in VANET," *Proc. VANET' 07*, Montreal, Quebec: ACM, Sept. 2007, pp. 19–28.

18. K. Zeng, "Pseudonymous pki for ubiquitous computing," *Proc. EuroPKI'06*, Turin: Springer, June 2006, pp. 207–222.

19. R. Lu, X. Lin, H. Zhu, and X. Shen, "SPARK: A new vanet-based smart parking scheme for large parking lots," *Proc. 28th IEEE International Conference on Computer Communications, Joint Conference of the IEEE Computer and Communications Societies, 2009, INFOCOM'09 Rio de Janeiro, Brazil*, IEEE, April 19–25, 2009, pp. 1413–1421. (Available online at http://dx.doi.org/10.1109/INFCOM.2009.5062057.)

20. D. Boneh, B. Lynn, and H. Shacham, "Short signatures from the weil pairing," *Journal of Cryptology*, vol. 17, no. 4, pp. 297–319, 2004.

21. D. Boneh and X. Boyen, "Short signatures without random oracles and the sdh assumption in bilinear groups," *Journal of Cryptology*, vol. 21, no. 2, pp. 149–177, 2008.

22. R. Lu, X. Lin, and X. Shen, "SPRING: A social-based privacy-preserving packet forwarding protocol for vehicular delay tolerant networks," *Proc. INFOCOM'10*, San Diego, IEEE, March 2010, pp. 1229–1237.

23. L. Kleinrock, *Queueing Systems Vol. 1: Theory*. New York: Wiley, 1975.

24. S.-M. Cheng, W.-R. Lai, P. Lin, and K.-C. Chen, "Key management for umts mbms," *IEEE Transactions on Wireless Communications*, vol. 7, no. 9, pp. 3619–3628, 2008.

5

RSU-AIDED MESSAGE AUTHENTICATION

5.1 INTRODUCTION

As we continue to benefit from technological advancements, for example, VANETs whose prospects of ensuing safety on the roads, people are increasingly cynical about the security and privacy of their personal information. Security and privacy issues in vehicular communication networks have to be well addressed in order to develop such technologies. First, message integrity must be achieved so that messages sent by vehicles cannot be tampered with by adversaries. Second, message senders should be authenticated to prevent impersonation attacks. In addition, privacy concerns must also be addressed; otherwise, the identity, the position, and the whole movement track of a specific vehicle are exposed to the third party.

Numerous studies [1–4] have been done on security and privacy issues in VANETs. However, even though these existing solutions meet different security and privacy requirements, they did not take scalability into consideration and the communication overhead caused by security mechanisms used. First, there is a stringent time requirement for a vehicle to verify all message signatures sent by its neighboring vehicles, especially when the traffic density increases. What's more, the packet length is dramatically increased, due to message signatures and public key certificates attached with

Vehicular Ad Hoc Network Security and Privacy, First Edition. Xiaodong Lin and Rongxing Lu.
© 2015 The Institute of Electrical and Electronics Engineers, Inc. Published 2015 by John Wiley & Sons, Inc.

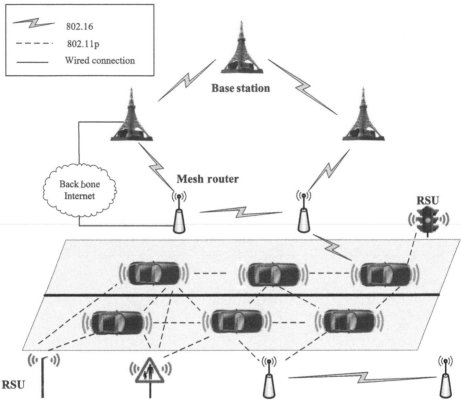

Figure 5.1. VANET infrastructure.

each message. Therefore, these cryptographic operations incur high computation and communication overhead when securing VANETs. The next four chapters address the aforementioned issues by taking a cooperative approach in which vehicles and RSUs work together to ensure security and privacy of vehicular communications.

An example of VANET infrastructure is illustrated in Fig. 5.1. It mainly comprises two kinds of nodes: vehicles and roadside units (RSUs). The vehicles are usually equipped with some wireless communication devices, called *onboard units* (OBUs), which can communicate with each other or with RSUs. The RSUs are stationed at critical points of road infrastructure (for example, at intersections) to provide wireless interfaces to vehicles within their radio coverage. More importantly, RSUs are usually rich in resources, including powerful computing capabilities and large local storage. These resource-rich RSUs are capable of handling computation-intensive tasks, and therefore, this chapter addresses aspects of RSU-assisted message authentication, in which resource-rich RSUs assist nearby vehicles to authenticate the messages they received.

Motivated by the aforementioned facts, in this chapter we will propose an *R*SU *ai*ded *m*essage *au*thentication scheme, termed RAISE [5]. In RAISE, each vehicle first anonymously authenticates itself to an RSU when approaching it within its transmission range. Then, a secure channel is established between the RSU and the vehicle. RSUs assign each vehicle a unique shared secret key and a pseudo-ID that may be shared with other vehicles. Vehicles will then send the message together with its corresponding *message authentication code* (MAC) generated by its secret key to their associated RSUs. RSUs are responsible for verifying the incoming messages from vehicles within its communication range, assembling them as a single packet, and sending it out after signing it by their private keys. As such, vehicles only need to authenticate messages coming from RSUs, and in such a case, only a few public key signature verifications are required. Further, since vehicles do not have to sign each message with asymmetric signature scheme, no public key certificate or message signatures are included in the message. With the RAISE protocol, not only are the communication and computation overhead reduced; the movement tracking attack is also eliminated.

The remainder of the chapter is organized as follows: Section 5.2 briefly introduces system model and preliminaries, including assumptions, the problem statement, and security objectives. Section 5.3 presents the proposed RAISE in detail. The performance evaluation and security analysis of RAISE are given in Section 5.4 and Section 5.5, respectively. Finally, we draw conclusions in Section 5.6.

5.2 SYSTEM MODEL AND PRELIMINARIES

In this section, we first introduce the system model for VANET, and then present several reasonable assumptions and the security requirements.

5.2.1 System Model

Vehicular ad hoc networks consist of two hierarchical layers. The upper layer is composed of application servers (ASs) and roadside units (RSUs), as shown in Fig. 5.2. AS can connect with RSUs through a secure channel, such as transport layer security (TLS) protocol with either wired or wireless connections. ASs provide application data for RSUs, and RSUs work as gateways to deliver data to the lower layer. The lower layer is composed of RSUs and vehicles. In our work, we aim to address the security issues in the lower layer.

5.2.2 Assumption

According to the abovementioned system model, this chapter is based on the following reasonable assumptions: (1) RSUs are trusted, and cannot be compromised—RSUs have higher computation capability than vehicles; (2) it is better to have RSUs cover all roads, but it is not necessarily the case—RSUs can be located at points where the density of vehicles is high, such as intersections (traditional public-key-based security protocols can be used in less dense roads since in such scenarios, scalability and communication overhead issues become less of a barrier to adopt public-key cryptosystems to secure VANETs); and (3) the radio communication range of RSUs can be twice as wide as the vehicles'.

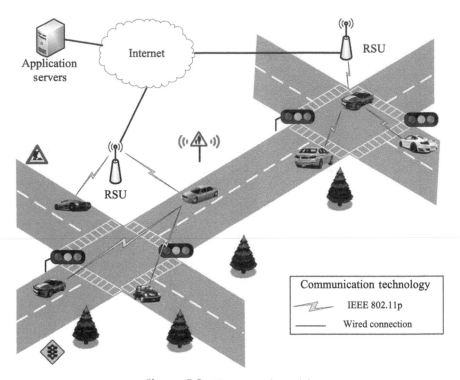

Figure 5.2. The network model.

5.2.3 Problem Statement

The current IEEE trial use standard [6] for VANETs' security provides us a detailed documentation, including the choice of cryptosystems. To authenticate a message's sender and guarantee the message's integrity, OBUs or RSUs should sign messages with their private keys before they are sent. Figure 5.3 shows the format of a signed message according to Ref. 6. We can observe that a 125-byte certificate and a 56-byte ECDSA signature have to be attached for each 69-byte traffic message. Obviously, the cryptographic overhead (the certificate and the signature) takes up a significant portion of the packet size.

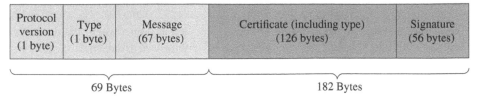

Figure 5.3. The format of the signed message.

Cryptographic operations also lead to high computation burden for receivers who wish to consume these messages. According to DSRC [7], a vehicle sends each message within a time interval of 100–300 ms. Generating a signature every 100 ms is not a problem for current pubic-key-based signature schemes. However, in cases where 50–200 cars are within the communication range, the receiver needs to verify around 500–2000 messages per second. Public key certificates have to be verified as well sometimes. Signing and verifying each message can certainly achieve secure communication; however, these cryptographic operations make the security protocol unscalable to the traffic density. Therefore, the verification algorithms have to be very fast, such that the incoming messages can be processed with limited message loss. Unfortunately, all current signature schemes for VANETs based on public key infrastructure (PKI) or group signature schemes cannot satisfy this stringent time requirement.

What's more, existing PKI-based security protocols violate the location privacy requirement. For ease of presentation, we simply use public keys as pseudonyms. The movement path of any vehicle can be easily traced by malicious global message observers, even if the public keys do not contain the real ID information and are updated frequently. This is because each public key has a lifetime of several minutes [2] and different vehicles update their public keys at different times. Therefore, the public key that changes at a particular time t is sure to be sent from the same source who uses a different public key before the moment t, because public keys used by other vehicles remain the same before and after time t. In this way, messages sent by the same vehicle can be connected and thus the whole movement of a vehicle can be traced. In other words, as discussed in Ref. 8, it is insufficient to simply use pseudonyms and even change pseudonyms in order to prevent vehicle tracking and provide unlinkability. In VANETs, because vehicles constantly broadcast traffic-related information including their locations, it is trivial to link an old pseudonym of a vehicle with its new pseudonym without any type of mix [4]. We need to have a way of letting vehicles cooperatively change their pseudonyms and go through a short silent period, which is an interval of time during which vehicles stop broadcasting messages and resume broadcasting simultaneously afterward.

5.2.4 Security Objectives

To address the issues, mentioned above, in this section we propose the following security objectives:

Message Integrity and Source Authentication. All messages should be delivered unaltered. Also, the origin of the messages should be verified to ensure that the received data originated from the claimed source and were not from a fraudulent source, to defend against impersonation attack.

Low Communication Overhead and Fast Verification. The security protocol should be efficient with small communication overhead and acceptable processing latency. A large number of message signatures should be verified in a short interval.

Identity Privacy Preservation. The identities of vehicles should be hidden from normal message receivers during the authentication process to protect the senders' private information, such as position, license plate number, and movement route.

Identity Traceability. The identities should be revealed under exceptional circumstances such as liability investigation. For example, capable of being law authorities may want to discover the identity of the message sender to help find witnesses or determine the cause of an accident.

Location Privacy Preservation. The adversaries should not be able to link multiple messages sent by the same vehicle in distinct locations and thus trace the movement of vehicles.

Prevention of Internal Attack. Normal vehicles holding their own keying materials cannot trace the movement of other vehicles (but cf. Ref. 4).

5.3 PROPOSED RSU-AIDED MESSAGE AUTHENTICATION SCHEME

5.3.1 Overview

In this section, we first overview the proposed *RSU-ai*ded me*s*sage ath*e*ntication scheme, termed RAISE.

RAISE is motivated by the following two factors: (1) compared with previous message authentication schemes [2, 3], which consider only vehicle-to-vehicle (V2V) communications, RAISE makes use of the characteristics of VANETs, and employs RSUs to assist vehicles to authenticate messages; and (2) unlike public-key-based message authentication schemes, which use asymmetric computation to sign messages, RAISE employs a keyed hash message authentication code (HMAC)-based symmetric encryption scheme to authenticate messages.

With RAISE, when a RSU is detected nearby, vehicles process association with the RSU, and then the RSU assigns a distinct symmetric key to each vehicle. A vehicle within the radio range of the RSU sends messages with the symmetric MAC code instead of PKI-based message signature. Vehicles receiving the messages sent by other vehicles cannot verify their authenticity immediately. However, they can verify them after receiving a notice from the RSU about these messages' authenticity. RSUs know the authenticity of messages because only they (RSUs) know the MAC encryption keys shared with vehicles. Note that, in cases where there is no RSU nearby, vehicles use the traditional PKI-based scheme to sign and verify messages. In this chapter we focus on the scenario where RSUs exist. The details of RAISE will be presented below. For ease of presentation, the notations used throughout this chapter are listed in Table 5.1.

5.3.2 Mutual Authentication and Key Agreement between RSUs and Vehicles

Once an oncoming vehicle V_i detects the existence of an RSU R_i (e.g., through hello messages of R_i), V_i initiates mutual authentication and establishes a shared secret key

TABLE 5.1. Notations Used in RSU-Aided Message Authentication

Notation	Descriptions
R_i	ith RSU
V_i	ith vehicle
M_i	Message sent by V_i
K_i	Key shared between V_i and R_i
ID_i	Pseudoidentity of V_i assigned by R
U	An entity, which could be an RSU R or a vehicle V_i
PK_U	Public key of U
SK_U	Private key of U
C_U	U's certificate
$\{M\}_{SK_U}$	U's digital signature on M
$H(.)$	A one-way hash function such that SHA-1
$HMAC(.)$	A keyed-hash message authentication code
$\|\|$:	Message concatenation operation, which appends several messages together in a special format

with R_i. This can be achieved by adopting Diffie–Hellman key agreement protocol [9] secured with public-key-based signature scheme to help defend against man-in-the-middle (MITM) attacks. The mutual authentication and key agreement processes are shown as follows:

$$V_i \longrightarrow R: \quad g^a, \{g^a\}_{SK_{V_i}}, C_{V_i}$$
$$R \longrightarrow V_i: \quad ID_i \| g^b, \{ID_i \| g^a \| g^b\}_{SK_R}, C_R$$
$$V_i \longrightarrow R: \quad \{g^b\}_{SK_{V_i}}$$

where g^a and g^b are elements of the Diffie–Hellman key agreement protocol,[1] and the shared key between R_i and V_i is $K_i \leftarrow g^{ab}$. When receiving the first message from V_i, R_i can verify V_i's public key certificate C_{V_i}. On successful verification, R_i can obtain V_i's public key PK_{V_i} from certificate C_{V_i}, and then uses PK_{V_i} to verify the signature $\{g^a\}_{SK_{V_i}}$ on g^a. In a similar manner, V_i authenticates R_i. If the above three flows pass, the mutual authentication succeeds. At the same time, in the second flow, R_i assigns a pseudoidentity ID_i to the vehicle V_i. The pseudo-ID_i uniquely links with K_i. (To protect the location privacy, cannot vehicles have unique pseudo-IDs. This case will be discussed in Section 5.3.5. For ease of representation, we explain the protocol under the assumption that vehicles are allocated with unique pseudo IDs in this subsection). With ID_i, R_i can know which vehicle sends the message, and can further verify the authenticity of the message with their shared symmetric key. Therefore, R_i maintains an ID-key table in its local database, as shown in Fig. 5.4(a). Vehicles update their anonymous certificates once they get out of the radio range of an RSU. For instance,

---

[1] Let p be a large prime, g be a generator of $\mathbb{Z}_p^*$, and $a, b \in \mathbb{Z}_p^*$. Here, to facilitate presentation, we let g^a (or g^b, g^{ab}) denote g^a (or g^b, g^{ab}) mod p.

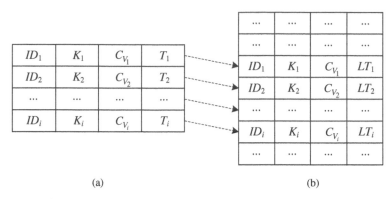

Figure 5.4. (a) The ID-key table; (b) the trace evidence table.

vehicles choose a new public/private key pair [2] to sign messages. In Fig. 5.4(a), T_i denotes the time when R receives the latest message from V_i. T_i is used to determine the freshness of a record. If the interval between the current time of R and T_i exceeds a predefined threshold, the record corresponding to T_i will be removed from the ID-key table and stored into the trace evidence table as shown in Fig. 5.4(b), which will be used for the purpose of traceability. The LT_i in Fig. 5.4(b) is used to control how long trace evidence is kept. In reality, it is decided by the authority, and is much larger than the T_i in Fig. 5.4(a). The details of the trace process will be discussed in the following section.

Further, indexes will be created on both tables for speeding up searches and queries so that RSUs can quickly locate data corresponding to a pseudo-ID.

5.3.3 Hash Aggregation

Once vehicle V_i obtains the symmetric key K_i from the RSU R, V_i can use K_i to compute the message authentication code $MAC_{K_i}(ID_i||M_i||TS_i)$ on $ID_i||M_i||TS_i$, where ID_i is V_i's pseudoidentity assigned by R, M_i is the message to be sent, and TS_i is a timestamp that records the current time when sending the message M_i. TS_i is used to thwart the replay attack. Then, V_i one-hop broadcasts $ID_i||M_i||TS_i||MAC(ID_i||M_i||TS_i)$. Because K_i is only known by R in addition to V_i itself, only R can verify M_i. Thus, to enable other vehicles to verify the authenticity of M_i, and at the same time to reduce communication overhead, the RSU R is responsible for aggregating multiple authenticated messages in a single packet and sending it out. The detailed process is shown as follows:

1. R checks whether the time interval between the current time and the time when R sent the last message authenticity notification packet is less than a predefined threshold Δt. If so, go to step 2. Otherwise, go to step 4.
2. When R receives a message, $\langle ID_i||M_i||TS_i||MAC_{K_i}(ID_i||M_i||TS_i)\rangle$ sent by the vehicle V_i, R first checks whether ID_i is in R's ID-key table. If yes, go to step 3. Otherwise, go to step 4.

3. R uses ID_i's K_i to verify $MAC_{K_i}(ID_i||M_i||TS_i)$. If it is valid, R computes $H(ID_i||M_i||TS_i)$. In this case, go to step 1. Otherwise, drop the packet.

4. R aggregates all hashes generated at step 3, i.e., $HAggt = H(ID_1||M_1||TS_1)$ $||H(ID_2||M_2||TS_2)||$ $\cdots$ $||H(ID_n||M_n||TS_n)$, and signs it with its private key SK_R. Then, R one-hop broadcasts $\langle HAggt||\{HAggt\}_{SK_R}\rangle$ to vehicles within its communication range.

The predefined threshold Δt in the above algorithm can affect message authentication delay, which will be further discussed in Section 5.4.2. In addition, the above algorithm supports the identity traceability property. Since there is a one-to-one mapping between the key K_i and the certificate C_{V_i} in the trace evidence table, the RSU can distinguish the unique sender of a message. Thus, in cases where a malicious vehicle sends a bogus message (e.g., the context of the message is found to be fake after a while), the RSU can trace back to the message sender by finding its certificate. The RSU could also report the certificate to a trusted authority (TA) for further investigation.

5.3.4 Verification

When a vehicle receives messages sent by other vehicles, it only buffers the received messages in its local database without verifying them immediately. The buffered record has the following format: M_i, ID_i, TS_i, $H(ID_i||M_i||TS_i)$ [note that $H(ID_i||M_i||TS_i)$ is computed by the receiver]. Once vehicles obtain the signed packet $\langle HAggt||\{HAggt\}_{SK_R}\rangle$ from the RSU, they are able to verify the buffered messages one by one. First, vehicles use the RSU's public key PK_R to verify the signature $\{HAggt\}_{SK_R}$. If it is valid, vehicles will check the validity of the previously received messages buffered in the record in the local database. This is done by determining whether there is a match between the buffered record with the de-aggregated message. For example, V_i checks whether $H(ID_i||M_i||TS_i)$ coming in $HAggt$ has been buffered in any record before. If so, M_i is consumed. Otherwise, V_i waits to see if M_i will be in the next $HAggt$ packet. If $H(ID_i||M_i||TS_i)$ does not appear in two[2] successive aggregated $HAggt$ packets, M_i is regarded as invalid. The reason why $H(ID_i||M_i||TS_i)$ is double-checked is that the RSU may have not aggregated the message M_i yet when V_i receives the first $HAggt$ packet from the RSU. In addition, a vehicle has to be capable of verifying all incoming messages sent by neighboring vehicles, which means that all messages received by the vehicle can be received by its corresponding RSU as well. However, if the communications between the RSU and a vehicle [or RSU-to-vehicle communications (RVC)] has the same distance limit as that of IVC, a vehicle will lose the messages sent by the vehicles that have not been in the eligible distance with the RSU. Figure 5.5 illustrates this scenario. Let the distance limit of RVC be r. The RSU can communicate with vehicles V_1 and V_2. Since V_3 has not associated with the RSU, V_2 cannot verify messages

---

[2] Suppose that a vehicle V_i receives a message M_j sent by V_j, and then immediately receives an aggregate $HAggt$ sent by an RSU R. Since the R could not receive M_j at all before the R sends the $HAggt$, $H(M_j)$ will appear at the following $HAggt$.

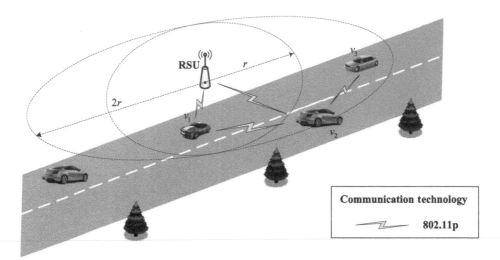

Figure 5.5. The radio range of the RSU.

from V_3 even though the two vehicles are supposed to be communicable. To overcome this problem, we require the distance limit for RVC to be 2 times longer than that for IVC. The distance between vehicles and vehicles and between vehicles and RSUs can be derived from GPS coordinates, because the GPS coordinates can be contained in the messages of vehicles.

5.3.5 Privacy Enhancement

With RAISE, if a vehicle does not change its pseudo-ID all the time during the association period, an adversary can trace the vehicle movement trajectory according to the vehicle's unchanged ID. Therefore, the vehicle's trace privacy is violated during the small time duration.

To preserve the trace privacy, we employ the concept of *k-anonymity* (*k* entities are not distinguishable) [10] in the proposed RAISE scheme to mix *k* vehicles. With RAISE, RSUs assign a common pseudo ID to *k* vehicles, where the *k* vehicles (as a group) will take the same pseudo-ID when communicating with the RSU. Thus, the ID-key table resembles Fig. 5.6.

When an adversary intends to trace a specific vehicle through the pseudo-ID, s/he will easily get lost after the group of vehicles passes through an intersection (where an RSU is allocated). In other words, the route of a specific vehicle cannot be identified. The biggest value of *k* would be the total number of vehicles within the coverage range of an RSU, in which all vehicles' messages are mixed and cannot be distinguished. Notice that such a scenario is equivalent to the case where vehicles have no identity at all.

In the *k-anonymity* RAISE, RSUs can still identify a vehicle by finding the symmetric key shared with the vehicle, and each pseudo-ID corresponds to *k* unique symmetric keys. Suppose that a vehicle V_i sends $\langle ID||M_i||TS_i||MAC_{K_i}(ID||M_i||TS_i)\rangle$ to RSU R. R

	K_{11}	C_{11}	T_{11}
ID_1	•••••••	•••••••	•••••••
	K_{1k}	C_{1k}	T_{1k}
	K_{2l}	C_{2l}	T_{2l}
ID_2	•••••••	•••••••	•••••••
	K_{2k}	C_{2k}	T_{2k}
...	...	...	...
	K_{il}	C_{il}	T_{il}
ID_i	••••••••	••••••••	••••••••
	K_{ik}	C_{ik}	T_{ik}

Figure 5.6. The ID-key table in the *k-anonymity* RAISE.

first finds out k possible keys corresponding to the pseudoidentity ID. Then, R sequently checks whether $MAC_{K_i}(ID||M_i||TS_i)$ is equal to $MAC_K(ID||M_i||TS_i)'$ to be generated by one of the k symmetric keys. If there is a match, the message is considered to be valid. Since a vehicle holds a distinct key shared with the RSU, the key that makes the above comparison can be used to find the message sender's anonymous certificate that was used during the first mutual authentication process. This can be done by looking up the RSU's local ID-key table. Being able to find out the anonymous certificate used during the mutual authentication process is to support the future ID traceability property.

However, if there is still no match with the two MAC values after R has tried all possible k keys, the message is considered as invalid and will be dropped. After this process, R can continue the message aggregation process as presented in Section 5.3.3.

With the adoption of *k-anonymity*, the verification process remains the same as before. Vehicles compare whether there is a match between the deaggregated $H(ID_i||M_i||TS_i)$ from $HAggt$ and the buffered $H(ID_i||M_i||TS_i)$ value in any record. Here, the cost of comparison computation can be neglected compared with message verification of the PKI-based scheme in Ref. 2.

5.4 PERFORMANCE EVALUATION

In this section, we use the ns-2 simulator [11] to evaluate the performance of RAISE in terms of the message loss ratio, the message end-to-end delay, and the communication overhead, respectively, compared with the group signature scheme in Ref. 3 and the standard PKI-based signature scheme in Ref. 6. We simulated a crowded traffic scenario in which an RSU is located at an intersection and 30–200 vehicles are under the coverage range of the RSU. The intervehicular distance varied from 7.5 to 15 m to simulate different traffic densities. The communication range of each vehicle is 300 m, and the transmission range of the RSU is twice that of the vehicles'. Messages are sent every 300 ms. IEEE 802.11a is used to simulate the MAC layer transmission protocol as was done in Ref. 2. The channel bandwidth is 6 Mb/s. The group signature verification delay is taken as 11 ms,[3] the ECDSA signature verification delay as 3.87 ms,[4] and MAC verification delay as 0.5 ms. All possible cryptographic time intervals are represented as equal time delays in the simulation.

5.4.1 Message Loss Ratio

Average message loss ratio (LR) is defined in Eq. (5.1), where N represents the total number of vehicles in the simulation. For the group signature and PKI signature schemes, M_{mac}^i represents the total number of messages received by the vehicle i in the MAC layer, and M_{app}^i represents the total number of messages consumed by the vehicle i in the application layer. For RAISE, M_{mac}^i represents the total number of messages received directly from other vehicles in the MAC layer; M_{app}^i represents the total number of $H(ID_i||M_i)$s that are sent by the RSU, and are consumed by the application layer. Here, for group signature and the PKI signature scheme, we consider only the message loss incurred by delays due to the security protocol rather than the wireless transmission channel. Since RAISE needs two-hop communication, we considered the loss caused by wireless communications between the RSU and vehicles:

$$ LR = \frac{1}{N} \sum_{i=1}^{N} \left(M_{app}^i / M_{mac}^i \right) \tag{5.1} $$

Figure 5.7 shows the relationship between the message loss ratio and the traffic load (the number of vehicles associated with an RSU). RSU periodically broadcasts an aggregation of $H(ID_i||M_i||TS_i)$s every 10 ms. Clearly, we can observe that the message loss ratio of the three schemes increases as the traffic load increases. The group signature scheme has the highest loss ratio, and the PKI-based scheme ranks in the middle. Our RAISE protocol has the lowest loss ratio. Also, from the simulation, we observed that most of the message losses comes from the two-hop wireless transmission.

5.4.2 Message Delay

Average message delay (MD) is defined in Eq. (5.2), where N represents the total number of vehicles in the simulation, M is the number of messages sent by vehicle i, and K is the number of adjacent vehicles within i's communication range. $T_{recv}^{i,k,m}$ represents the moment that the vehicle k in the application layer receives the mth message from the

---

[3] For efficiency's consideration, the curve we used to estimate the short group signature scheme is the MNT curve [12] with embedding degree $k = 6$ and 163-bit prime order p. As in Ref. 13, the verification process of the group signature includes 1 nonpreprocessable pairing plus 4 nonpreprocessable multiexponentiations in G_1, plus 1 preprocessable multiexponentiation in G_2, and 1 nonpreprocessable multiexponentiation in G_T. The timings to do these operations are estimated based on the numbers provided by Scott [14] with a 3-GHz Pentium IV system.

[4] The 224-bit ECDSA cryptographic delays are quoted from the MIRACL cryptographic library [15] with the 3-GHz Pentium IV system.

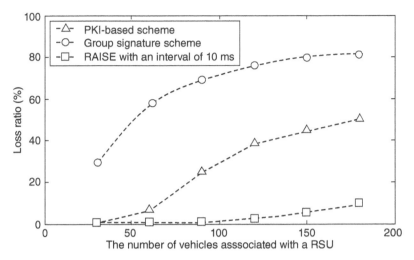

Figure 5.7. Average loss ratio vs. traffic load

vehicle i. $T_{send}^{i,k,m}$ represents the moment that the vehicle i in the application layer sends the mth message to the vehicle k.

$$MD = \frac{1}{N} \sum_{i=1}^{N} \frac{1}{MK} \sum_{m=1}^{M} \sum_{k=1}^{K} \left(T_{recv}^{i,k,m} - T_{send}^{i,k,m} \right) \tag{5.2}$$

Figure 5.8 shows the relationship between the message delay and the traffic load. Again, the group signature scheme has the highest message delay. The reason is due to the high delay used to verify a message signature. The PKI-based scheme and RAISE

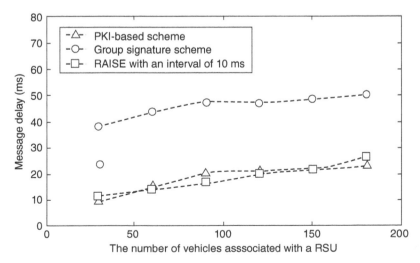

Figure 5.8. Average message delay vs. traffic load.

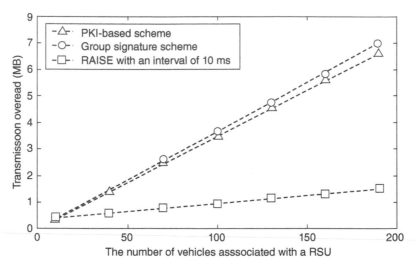

Figure 5.9. Communication overhead vs. traffic load.

have nearly the same message delays. Since the comparison computation is very fast, the delay of RAISE is determined primarily by the packet release interval of RSUs; e.g., in Fig. 5.6, the packet release interval is 10 ms. To reduce the message delay, we can decrease this time interval; however, further reducing the message delay is at the cost of increasing the communication overhead and bringing more conflict to the media access control (MAC) layer wireless communications, which will be further discussed in Section 5.4.3.

5.4.3 Communication Overhead

First, we list the communication overhead used by the ECDSA in Ref. 6, the group signature in Ref. 3, and *HMAC* in RAISE, respectively. With ECDSA, for each massage, the additional overhead caused by cryptographic operations is 181 bytes, which includes a certificate and an ECDSA signature, as shown in Fig. 5.3. With the group signature scheme, the additional communication overhead is 184 bytes.[5]

With RAISE, the additional communication overhead is 128 bits + 128 bits + $(56+2)/n$ bytes, where the first 128 represents the length of a *HMAC* that is sent by a vehicle, the second 128 represents the length of a $H(ID_i||M_i)$ packet that is sent by an RSU, 56 is the length of an ECDSA signature [6] signed by the RSU, and 2 is the length of a message header as shown in Fig. 5.3. Here, 56+2 is shared by n messages, because in RAISE n messages are batched and signed once. Note that n is determined by the density of vehicles and the packet release interval for the RSU to broadcast a batched packet.

Figure 5.9 shows the relationship between the overall communication overhead in 1 minute and the traffic load within an RSU. Clearly, we can observe that RAISE with

---

[5] As discussed in footnote 2, since p is a 163-bit prime and the elements of G_1 are 164 bits long,the length of a group signature is therefore 184 bytes. The computations can be referred from Ref. 13.

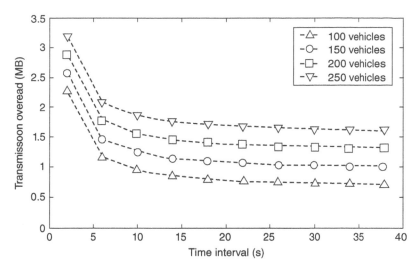

Figure 5.10. Communication overhead vs. time interval.

the time interval of 10 ms has much lower communication overhead than the PKI-based signature scheme and the group signature scheme. Further, as observed from Fig. 5.9, we can compute that the communication overhead caused by RAISE is 24.94% of that of the PKI-based signature scheme and 23.64% of the group signature scheme. To further illustrate the effect of the time interval on RAISE, Fig. 5.10 shows the relationship between the time interval and the overall communication overhead, caused by 100, 150, 200, and 250 vehicles, respectively in 1 minute. Clearly, as the time interval increases, particularly from 2 to 10 ms, the communication overhead decreases sharply. However, when the time interval is 10 ms or larger, the time interval has very little effect on the communication overhead. From Fig. 5.8, we also observe that the communication overhead increases approximately 0.3 MB every time the number of vehicles increases by 50.

5.5 SECURITY ANALYSIS

In this section, we analyze the security of the proposed scheme in terms of message integrity and source authentication, prevention of internal attack, replay attack resistance, and conditional privacy preservation.

Message Integrity and Source Authentication. With RAISE, a vehicle generates a MAC for each message originating from it. The MAC can only be generated by the vehicle that has the key assigned by the RSU. If an adversary tampers with a message, the RSU cannot find a corresponding validation key that can compute a matching MAC for the message, and therefore the garbled message will be ignored. In addition, for each vehicle, there is a unique key stored in the ID-key table at the RSU side. If an RSU can find out a key to verify a MAC, the RSU can know the identity of the message sender, and therefore the source is authenticated. Because of the nature of message integrity and source authentication, typical attacks such as bogus attack and impersonation attack [2] can be prevented.

Prevention of Internal Attack. RAISE is robust against not only the external attacks but also the internal attacks. Even if a vehicle is compromised and its symmetric secret session key shared with an RSU is exposed to an adversary, the adversary cannot trace other vehicles' movement because it cannot distinguish the vehicles that use the same pseudo ID with the compromised vehicle. Therefore, RAISE can resist key-compromise impersonation attack.

Location Privacy Preservation. As discussed in Section 5.3.5, the location privacy is achieved under the concept of *k-anonymity* in our scheme. Multiple vehicles using the same pseudoidentity are mixed and unable to be distinguished. To maximize the anonymity, all vehicles can use the same identity. Thus, an adversary cannot map a position to a particular vehicle; that is, an adversary cannot trace a particular vehicle's movement route.

Replay Attack Resistance. With a replay attack, an adversary replays intercepted messages in order to impersonate a legitimate vehicle. Obviously, this impersonation cannot work with RAISE because a timestamp TS_i is attached with the corresponding M_i and all vehicles keep time synchronization. Suppose an adversary intercepts a message $\langle ID_i||M_i||TS_i||MAC_{K_i}(ID_i||M_i||TS_i)\rangle$, and launches a replay attack at the time TS_j. Because the time period $|TS_j - TS_i| > \Delta T$, where ΔT is a mutually agreed transmission delay, the receiver will reject the message. Therefore, RAISE is robust to resist the replay attack.

Conditional Privacy Preservation. RAISE makes vehicles use pseudoidentities to protect their real identities. As such, the identity privacy of vehicles is protected. Nevertheless, RSUs are able to know the anonymous certificate corresponding to a pseudoidentity, and a trusted authority is capable of tracing the real identity of a vehicle from its anonymous certificate. For example, a vehicle V_i sends a bogus message, which contains the pseudoidentity ID_i that an RSU allocates. Once the RSU finds out that the content of the message is bogus, the RSU can know the anonymous certificate of the V_i from the trace evidence table in which the ID_i uniquely maps the anonymous certificate C_{V_i} as shown in Fig. 5.4(b). Further, the RSU gives the certificate C_{V_i} to a trust authority, which has the ability to trace the real identity of the V_i from C_{V_i}. Therefore, in RAISE, vehicles cannot tell their real identities each other, while RSUs can distinguish whether two messages are sent by the same vehicle. By the cooperation of the trust authority and the RSUs, the real identity of the message sender can be traced.

5.6 CONCLUDING REMARKS

In this chapter, an RSU-aided message authentication scheme, called *RAISE*, is proposed. In RAISE, RSUs are responsible for verifying the authenticity of messages sent from vehicles and notifying the results back to all vehicles within its communication range.

The RAISE protocol is advantageous because it needs less computation and communication overhead; it also protects the vehicle's location privacy. Extensive simulations were conducted, which showed that RAISE indeed had the lowest message loss ratio and communication overhead than both the PKI-based and the group-signature-based schemes.

REFERENCES

1. J.-P. Hubaux, S. Capkun, and J. Luo, "The security and privacy of smart vehicles," *IEEE Security & Privacy Magazine*, vol. 2, no. LCA-ARTICLE-2004-007, pp. 49–55, 2004.

2. M. Raya and J.-P. Hubaux, "Securing vehicular ad hoc networks," *Journal of Computer Security*, vol. 15, no. 1, pp. 39–68, 2007.

3. X. Lin, X. Sun, P.-H. Ho, and X. Shen, "GSIS: A secure and privacy-preserving protocol for vehicular communications," *IEEE Transactions on Vehicular Technology*, vol. 56, no. 6, pp. 3442–3456, 2007.

4. J. Freudiger, M. Raya, M. Félegyházi, P. Papadimitratos, et al., "Mix-zones for location privacy in vehicular networks," *Proceedings 1st International Workshop on Wireless Networking for Intelligent Transportation Systems (WIN-ITS)*, ACM, 2007.

5. C. Zhang, X. Lin, R. Lu, and P. Ho, "RAISE: An efficient RSU-aided message authentication scheme in vehicular communication networks," *Proc. IEEE International Conference on Communications, ICC 2008,* Beijing: IEEE, May 19–23, 2008, pp. 1451–1457. (Available online at http://dx.doi.org/10.1109/ICC.2008.281)

6. Intelligent Transportation System (ITS) Committee et al., "IEEE trial-use standard for wireless access in vehicular environments-security services for applications and management messages," *IEEE Vehicular Technology Society Standard*, vol. 1609, p. 2006, 2006.

7. "Dedicated short range communications (DSRC)," http://grouper.ieee.org/groups/scc32/dsrc/index.html.

8. K. Sampigethaya, L. Huang, M. Li, R. Poovendran, K. Matsuura, and K. Sezaki, *Caravan: Providing Location Privacy for VANET*, DTIC Document, Technical Report, 2005.

9. W. Diffie and M. E. Hellman, "New directions in cryptography," *IEEE Transactions on Information Theory*, vol. 22, no. 6, pp. 644–654, 1976.

10. L. Sweeney, "*k*-anonymity: A model for protecting privacy," *International Journal of Uncertainty, Fuzziness and Knowledge-Based Systems*, vol. 10, no. 5, pp. 557–570, 2002.

11. "University of south california, the network simulator ns-2," http://nsnam.isi.edu/nsnam/index.php/User_ Information.

12. M. Scott and P. S. Barreto, "Generating more MNT elliptic curves," *Designs, Codes and Cryptography*, vol. 38, no. 2, pp. 209–217, 2006.

13. D. Boneh, X. Boyen, and H. Shacham, "Short group signatures," *Proc. Advances in Cryptology–CRYPTO 2004*. Springer, 2004, pp. 41–55.

14. M. Scott, "Implementing cryptographic pairings," *Lecture Notes in Computer Science*, vol. 4575, p. 177, 2007.

15. "Shamus software. MIRACL library," http://www. shamus.ie/index.php?page=Elliptic-Curve-point-multiplication.

6

TESLA-BASED BROADCAST
AUTHENTICATION

6.1 INTRODUCTION

In the previous chapter we discussed an RSU-aided message authentication scheme
named *RAISE*, where RSUs are responsible for verifying the authenticity of the messages
originated from vehicles, and for notifying the vehicles of their results. Since *message
authentication codes* (MACs) are used for authenticating inter-vehicle communication
with the aid of RSUs, the message authentication process is suitable for vehicular
communication. However, because it requires direct involvement of RSUs in the process
of message authentication, it becomes ineffective when RSUs are not widely available,
e.g., in the early stage of VANETs deployment.

In this chapter, we explore ways to use fast symmetric cryptography to protect
vehicular communications, but without direct involvement of RSUs. In particular, we
adopt TESLA (*timed efficient stream loss-tolerant authentication*) authentication protocol [1], which is commonly used in securing broadcast and multicast communication.
As such, the proposed scheme needs to only perform symmetric MAC operation at the
receiver, which is sufficient to authenticate the source of the message and ensure data
integrity, instead of performing any computation-intensive asymmetric verification. In
addition, since only a short MAC tag is attached to each message, the extra message

Vehicular Ad Hoc Network Security and Privacy, First Edition. Xiaodong Lin and Rongxing Lu.
© 2015 The Institute of Electrical and Electronics Engineers, Inc. Published 2015 by John Wiley & Sons, Inc.

length and the bandwidth overhead due to the security mechanism can be significantly reduced. Moreover, the proposed scheme is much more effective than any of the other reported PKI-based schemes in terms of the resultant packet loss ratio, which is found to be almost independent of the traffic density. Results of extensive simulation studies demonstrate that the proposed scheme reduces packet loss ratio significantly more than the existing PKI-based security schemes, especially when the traffic becomes denser while maintaining acceptable packet latency. The proposed scheme is feasible because of the unique features of VANETs, such as a fixed message release interval, and temporally stable geographic groups, which will be discussed later.

In this chapter we present the design of a TESLA-based broadcast authentication scheme for vehicular communication, termed TSVC [2]. We begin by giving a brief introduction to the techniques used here, which serve as the basis for the proposed scheme, and then present the scheme. Finally, the chapter analyzes security through rigorous analysis and conduct performance evaluations through extensive simulation. The chapter concludes with Section 6.5.

6.2 TIMED EFFICIENT AND SECURE VEHICULAR COMMUNICATION SCHEME

6.2.1 Preliminaries

6.2.1.1 One-Way Hash Chain. The one-way hash chain was first proposed in 1981 [3] for secure password authentication, which quickly became an important cryptographic primitive in many other applications, such as micropayment systems [4], secure data forwarding in wireless ad hoc networks [5], and stream data authentication [6]. A one-way hash chain is a repeated application of a hash function $H(x)$ with a randomly selected seed S, which has the following properties:

- $H(x)$ can take a message of arbitrary-length input and produce a message digest of a fixed-length output.
- Given x, it is easy to compute $y = H(x)$. However, it is hard to compute $x = H^{-1}(y)$, when given y.
- Given x, it is computationally infeasible to find $x' \neq x$ such that $H(x') = H(x)$.
- It is computationally infeasible to find any two pair x and x' such that $x' \neq x$ and $H(x') = H(x)$.

The operation result of the hash function for $n - 1$ times is denoted as $h_1, h_2, \ldots, h_n$, respectively, where $h_1 = H(h_2)$, $h_{i-1} = H(h_i)$, $h_n = S$, $1 < i \leq n$. h_1 is called the *tip* or the *commitment* of the chain. Then, the holder of the hash chain can release the chain elements in reverse order to the chain being generated. In this way, any hash chain element can be kept secret until it's released, and on receiving a chain element, its authenticity can be easily validated by the receiver with a simple hash operation. For example, we can verify that h_j is part of the chain if we know that h_i is the ith element of the chain ($i < j$); then we check that $h_i = H^{j-i}(h_j)$.

A one-way hash chain can always be used to reduce the authentication load of a series of messages. However, the main problem of the hash chain mechanism is in the ability to handle message loss. Furthermore, the traditional one-way hash chain has a fixed length, but the number of messages varies with applications. In addition, the messages to be authenticated should be known in advance, which incurs a big constraint for most real-time applications.

6.2.1.2 *TESLA Authentication Protocol.*
TESLA is an efficient and message-loss-tolerant protocol for broadcast authentication with low communication and computation overhead [1]. It is widely used in areas of sensor networks [7]. It uses a one-way hash chain where the chain elements are the secret keys to compute MAC. With TESLA, a sender sends data packets at a predefined schedule, which has been known in advance to the receivers as well as the commitment to a hash chain as a key commitment. Each hash chain element of a MAC key corresponds to a certain time interval. For each packet, the sender attaches a MAC tag to it. This MAC tag is derived using the next corresponding MAC key in the hash chain, based on the negotiated key disclosure delay schedule between the sender and the receiver. Obviously, on receiving the packet, the receiver cannot verify the authenticity of the packet. After a key disclosure delay, the sender discloses the MAC key, and then the receiver is able to authenticate the message after verifying that the released MAC key is indeed the corresponding element of the chain. One requirement for the TESLA scheme is loose synchronization among the nodes. The disadvantage is the delayed message authentication, which is susceptible to denial-of-service (DoS) attacks because the messages received must be buffered at the receiver side before they are authenticated. This can lead to a serious security problem if malicious attackers send a large amount of messages. It can easily gobble up receivers' memory, and as a result, the receivers have to drop incoming messages that arrive afterward. Many DoS-attack-resilient enhancements of TESLA-based broadcast authentication protocols have been proposed [8–11]. For simplicity, we will not consider DoS attack prevention in the proposed scheme.

6.2.1.3 *Bloom Filter.*
A Bloom filter is a hash-based space-efficient probabilistic data structure used for querying a large set of items to determine whether a given item is included as a member of the set. It is developed by inserting a given set of items $E = \{e_1, e_1, \ldots, e_n\}$ into a bit string of length m, $B = (b_1, b_2, \ldots, b_m)$, which are initially all set to be 0. K independent hash functions $(H_1, H_2, \ldots, H_k)$ are applied to each item in the set to produce k hash values (or index values) $(V_1, V_2, \ldots, V_k)$, and all corresponding bits in the bit string are set at 1, as illustrated in Fig. 6.1. When we query an item in the Bloom filter, false-negative matches are not possible; in other words, an element has no chance of being incorrectly recognized as a member of the set. However, false positives—when an element is indicated to be a member of the set but, in reality, not a part of it—can occur with a predetermined acceptable false-positive rate. Thus, a Bloom filter is used more effectively in environments where it tests whether an element is actually not present instead of testing whether an element is presented because no false-negative is guaranteed. It also uses less space when representing a set than do other data structures such as binary search trees, arrays, or hash tables.

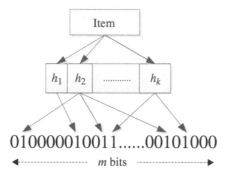

Figure 6.1. Example of an *m*-bit standard Bloom filter. The filter begins as a bit string of all zeros. Each item in the set is hashed *k* times, with each hash yielding an index value of the bit string; these corresponding bits are set to 1.

The main properties of a Bloom filter are summarized as follows [12]: (1) the space for storing the Bloom filter is very small as well as the size of a bit string B; (2) the time to query whether an element is in the Bloom filter is constant and is not affected by the number of items in the set; (3) false negatives are impossible; and (4) false positives are possible, but the rate can be controlled. Nevertheless, the lower the false positive rate is, the more storage space is required. As a space-efficient data structure for representing a set of elements, the Bloom filter has been widely used in web cache sharing [13, 14], package routing [15], compact representation of a differential file [16], and so on.

6.2.2 System Formulation

Let each vehicle act as a leader and form a dynamic group with the current neighboring vehicles that are within its transmission range. In Fig. 6.2, vehicles O_1, N_1, N_2, and N_3 form a vehicle group with vehicle O_1 acting as the leader. Obviously, a vehicle

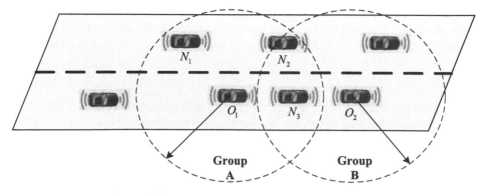

Figure 6.2. Dynamic virtual vehicle group formation.

may belong to many dynamic groups; e.g., vehicle N_3 belongs to group B with vehicle O_2 acting as the leader as well. We assume that the maximum delay of a message traveling within a typical transmission range over a wireless channel can be estimated. In Ref. 17, the estimated communication latency is identified to be about 10 ms. Also, all the vehicles are loosely synchronized, which can easily be achieved by some time synchronization protocols [1, 18, 19]. Currently, there exist two methods for the sender and the receivers to be time-synchronized: direct time synchronization and indirect time synchronization [20]. Considering the high mobility of vehicles in VANETs and loose time synchronization requirement, we prefer that all the vehicles synchronize securely via an external time reference, i.e., indirect time synchronization. For example, each vehicle is equipped with a highly accurate atomic clock, and then the clock can be synchronized to a central time server during its annual or biannual vehicle check, such as license renewal or emission test. We divide the message authentication into two categories based on the message type: routine message and emergency message, where the former one obviously dominates the total traffic amount while the latter one is much less frequently. In this text, we concentrate on solving the former one.

The general idea of the proposed scheme for the routine traffic related messages is described as follows. As a sender, a hash chain is generated in advance before using the chain elements as encryption keys to generate MAC codes. A signature is produced for the first message with the conventional public key signature technique. For the following messages, on the other hand, the MAC tag of each message is computed with the corresponding encryption key in the hash chain, which is disclosed after a short delay. Messages can be authenticated when the encryption keys are released. According to the expected transmission delay of each message along with the serial number of the key used in a hash chain, the receiver can check whether the next hash key used to generate the MAC tag of the received message has been released. If the next hash key is released, the message should be discarded to prevent message forgery attack.

Emergency messages that are sent with a much lower frequency are processed at higher priority. Normal digital signature and verification schemes are adopted, where the best security assurance and a constant delay can be achieved.

6.2.3 Proposed TSVC Scheme

6.2.3.1 Vehicle Group Formation. One of the unique features of VANETs is that the vehicles driving on the highway maintain a temporally stable relative distance with the neighboring vehicles. Since the communication range is typically 250–1000 m [21], this neighborhood relationship may last from several seconds to several minutes or even longer according to the driving speed of individual vehicles, and the road and weather conditions. By taking advantage of this property, we can group the vehicles according to their physical locations. For a specific vehicle O_1, all the other vehicles within its one-hop communication range are defined to be in the same group as O_1. The group relationship is dynamic and is updated when any other vehicle comes into the communication range or any group member leaves the group. The majority of the group members remain stable for a comparatively long time.

6.2.3.2 *TSVC Scheme.* Let all the vehicles be installed with a list of anonymous public–private key pairs $< PK_i, SK_i >$ in the vehicle registration phase or during annual checkup, where the corresponding anonymous certificates are $Cert_i$ with pseudoidentities $PVID_i$ as its certificate identities [22]. For the purpose of traceability, vehicle registration authority keeps records of those anonymous certificates and their corresponding real identities. Each pair of keys has a short lifetime, e.g., a few minutes. Each vehicle has to generate a hash chain $h_1, h_2, \ldots, h_n$ initiated from a random seed S, where $h_n = S$, and $h_i = H^{j-i}(h_j)$ with $i < j$. Each element in the hash chain is in charge of generating a number of MAC codes for a number of messages as the cryptographic keys and will be released after a short delay δ, which is called *key disclosure delay*. Without loss of generality, we assume that the number of messages each encryption key works on is 1; thus, each hash element will generate one MAC code for one message. Also, we set the time interval in TESLA authentication protocol as the packet release interval, which means that each data packet and its corresponding key release packet are generated during one time interval.

The length of the hash chain can be predetermined according to the lifetime of each anonymous certificate and the message-sending interval. Once the anonymous public key pairs are updated, a new chain is initiated and comes into play. Note that all the hash chains can be initialized in advance before going into function to reduce system operation delay. Let the routine safety messages sent by a vehicle be denoted as $M_1, M_2, \ldots, M_k$, and M_i is encapsulated in packet P_i, $1 \leq i \leq k$. Further, let packets be launched with a fixed interval of 300 ms. The packet authentication process is shown in Fig. 6.3.

There are two categories of packets. The first category is called a *data packet*, denoted as P_i, which is specialized in sending data information, while the second category is the *key release packet* (KRP), denoted as kr_P_i, which is dedicated for releasing the encryption keys h_i. Such a design is to reduce the packet end-to-end delay, since the interval between two traffic safety packets are usually longer than the maximum tolerable human reaction latency. KRP is disclosed a fixed time δ after the previous data packet is released.

The proposed security scheme is illustrated in Fig. 6.4. For an arbitrary sender O, it generates the MAC tags of the messages using h_j as the encryption keys, where $1 \leq h_j \leq n$. Therefore, the data packet to be sent has the following format:

$$P_j = \langle PVID, M_j, MAC_{h_j}(M_j || T_j), T_j, index \rangle, j \geq 1 \tag{6.1}$$

* h_i is the hash element encapsulated in the key release packet $K_r\_P_i$, and also is the key used to calculate MAC of the data packet P_i.

Figure 6.3. Relationship between a hash chain and the corresponding packets.

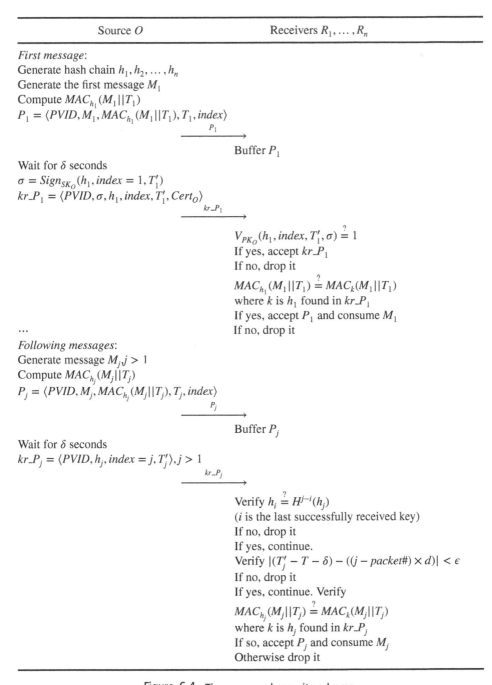

Source O	Receivers $R_1, \ldots, R_n$
First message:	
Generate hash chain $h_1, h_2, \ldots, h_n$	
Generate the first message M_1	
Compute $MAC_{h_1}(M_1 \| T_1)$	
$P_1 = \langle PVID, M_1, MAC_{h_1}(M_1 \| T_1), T_1, index \rangle$	
$\xrightarrow{P_1}$	
	Buffer P_1
Wait for δ seconds	
$\sigma = Sign_{SK_O}(h_1, index = 1, T_1')$	
$kr\_P_1 = \langle PVID, \sigma, h_1, index, T_1', Cert_O \rangle$	
$\xrightarrow{kr\_P_1}$	
	$V_{PK_O}(h_1, index, T_1', \sigma) \overset{?}{=} 1$
	If yes, accept kr_P_1
	If no, drop it
	$MAC_{h_1}(M_1 \| T_1) \overset{?}{=} MAC_k(M_1 \| T_1)$
	where k is h_1 found in kr_P_1
	If yes, accept P_1 and consume M_1
...	If no, drop it
Following messages:	
Generate message $M_j, j > 1$	
Compute $MAC_{h_j}(M_j \| T_j)$	
$P_j = \langle PVID, M_j, MAC_{h_j}(M_j \| T_j), T_j, index \rangle$	
$\xrightarrow{P_j}$	
	Buffer P_j
Wait for δ seconds	
$kr\_P_j = \langle PVID, h_j, index = j, T_j' \rangle, j > 1$	
$\xrightarrow{kr\_P_j}$	
	Verify $h_i \overset{?}{=} H^{j-i}(h_j)$
	(i is the last successfully received key)
	If no, drop it
	If yes, continue.
	Verify $|(T_j' - T - \delta) - ((j - packet\#) \times d)| < \epsilon$
	If no, drop it
	If yes, continue. Verify
	$MAC_{h_j}(M_j \| T_j) \overset{?}{=} MAC_k(M_j \| T_j)$
	where k is h_j found in kr_P_j
	If so, accept P_j and consume M_j
	Otherwise drop it

Figure 6.4. The proposed security scheme.

Here, M_j is the safety message; $PVID$ is the pseudo ID of vehicle O, which is kept in accordance with the ID that is being used in the current public key certificate $Cert_O$; and T_j is the time when the sender sends the data packet, which is used to defeat any replay attack.

Then, the sender O prepares the first key release packet (KRP) by signing the *commitment* of the hash chain h_1 according to the traditional public-key-based signature techniques, and the first key release packet has the format

$$kr\_P_1 = \langle PVID, Sig_{SK_O}(h_1, index, T_1'), h_1, index, \atop T_1', Cert_O \rangle, \tag{6.2}$$

where h_1 is the key, which is used to generate the MAC tag for the first message M_1, $Cert_O$ is the currently used anonymous public key certificate, SK_O is the corresponding private key of $Cert_O$, T_1' is the time when the sender sends the first key release packet, and *index* represents the index of the current hash value in the hash chain when O is releasing in the packet, i.e., 1 for the first key release packet. It is worth pointing out that the KRP is released δ seconds later than the previous data packet. The following key release packets have the following format:

$$kr\_P_j = \langle PVID, h_j, index = j, T_j' \rangle, \ j > 1, \tag{6.3}$$

where h_j is used to generate the MAC tag for message M_j. On receiving the first data packet, the receivers simply put the received packet in the buffer and wait until the first key release packet arrives.[1] After receiving the first key release packet that is signed by the source of the message, the receivers perform the following verification after validating the sender's anonymous certificate $Cert_O$:

$$\begin{cases} V_{PK_O}(h_1, index, T_1', Sig_{SK_O}(h_1, index, T_1')) \overset{?}{=} 1, \\ \text{where } index = 1; \\ MAC_{h_1}(M_1||T_1) \overset{?}{=} MAC_k(M_1||T_1), \end{cases} \tag{6.4}$$

where k is the h_1 contained in the first key release packet.

Therefore, it is crucial for vehicle O's neighboring vehicles to receive the first key release packet in order to authenticate the data packets from O. Basically, there are two ways to accomplish this, by either using any mobile reliable broadcast protocol [23] or treating the missed vehicles as newly joining group members, which will be discussed in Section 6.2.5.3.

---

[1] Whenever receiving any packet, the receivers first check whether the timestamp found in packet is reasonable, and if so, continue. Otherwise, the receivers drop the packet since the receivers could be subject to replay attack.

TABLE 6.1. Cache Table at the Receiver Side

packet#	Source	c	T	Lifetime
...	...	...	...	...

The receivers then store information such as the *PVID* and T_1 in order to synchronize the latter packets that are sent by the same source. If the verification fails, the packet is dropped. Otherwise, every receiver keeps an entry (*packet#, source, c*,T,*Lifetime*) in its local cache table (Table 6.1) corresponding to sender O, where it stores the packet index, i.e., 1, to field *packet#*, *PVID* to the field source, the authenticated hash chain element h_1 to field c, and the time T_1 when the sender sends the data packet to field T. *Lifetime* serves as a timer controlling how long the entry is active. If the timer hits 0, the entry expires, and will be removed from the receiver's cache table. Whenever a new packet arrives from a source, the receivers update the timer of the corresponding entry in the table.

When receiving data packet $P_j, j > 1$, the receivers simply put the received packet in the buffer without trying to verify it. As soon as the next key release packet kr_P_j arrives, the receivers will start to verify the previous data packet. At first, the receivers will check the legitimacy of the received hash chain member, which is done by checking if the following equation holds:

$$H^{j-packet\#}(h_j) = c \qquad (6.5)$$

Here, h_j is included in the key release packet kr_P_j, and c and *packet#* are from the entry corresponding to *PVID*, which is found in its local cache table. If Eq. (6.5) does not hold, the packet kr_P_j is dropped; otherwise, it checks whether h_j received should be released during the current transmission time interval. This can be checked using the equation

$$|(T_j' - T - \delta) - ((j - packet\#) \times d)| < \epsilon \qquad (6.6)$$

where T_j' is the time when the sender sends out the key release packet, d is the packet release interval, δ is *key disclosure delay*, T is from the local cache table entry corresponding to *PVID*, and ϵ is the clock error (offset). If Eq. (6.6) doesn't hold, then the packet is considered to be unsafe and will be dropped since an adversary attempts to forge a message using a key already released. Otherwise, the receivers start to validate the data packet P_j by checking whether $MAC_k(M_j||T_j) = MAC_{h_j}(M_j||T_j)$, where M_j, T_j and $MAC_{h_j}(M_j||T_j)$ are the previously buffered values of the data packet, and k is the hash element h_j in kr_P_j. If the verification succeeds, P_j is accepted and consumed by the application layer, and then, in the entry corresponding to *PVID*, the receivers update the first, third, and fourth fields with *index*, h_j, and T_j along with a new timer for the last field; otherwise, P_j is dropped.

In summary, the proposed scheme can achieve the same guarantee on the message integrity, anonymity, and authenticity as the traditional PKI based schemes, which will be detailed in Section 6.3. In spite of the anonymity among the public, the scheme can well maintain a conditional traceability property for the authorities such as the police, because all the accepted messages can be uniquely tied to an anonymous public key certificate of its sender. Thus, by checking this unique public key certificate, the authority can trace the unique real-world identity of the message sender as that in the traditional PKI-based schemes.

6.2.3.3 *Security Requirement and Key Disclosure Delay δ.* The security requirement to prevent the message forgery attack for the TSVC scheme is that the key release waiting time should be longer than the time for a message to travel from the source to all the recipients. If any receiver r can receive the released key before the original data packet arrives at another receiver, e.g., $\bar{r}$, receiver r who holds the key can forge a message by generating a valid MAC tag to this message and sending the tagged message to $\bar{r}$. Note that this forged message can pass $\bar{r}$'s verification. This situation can be avoided by properly choosing the key disclosure delay δ. In the vehicular communications with IEEE 802.11p, since the longest transmission range is about 1000 m [21], δ should be slightly greater than the time duration for a message to travel for 1000 m in the wireless channel. The communication latency is identified as ~10 ms [17]. In our scheme, therefore, δ is set to be 100 ms, which is about 10 times the communication latency needed to achieve absolute safety that also can meet the requirement for the maximum allowable latency. This parameter setting will be verified through simulation as presented in Section 6.4.

Before a normal message authentication process (as discussed above) is performed, validity of the messages needs to be checked to see if the security requirement can be met. This means the receivers have to know which interval that packet belongs to and whether the corresponding key has already been released. If not, the packet is dropped without trying to authenticate it. Note that, due to the stringent time requirement of the real-time applications in VANETs, late or outdated messages should be dropped. Therefore, if a message arrives after the maximum allowable latency such as the maximum human's reaction time, the message should be dropped without putting it into the buffer.

6.2.4 Enhanced TSVC with Nonrepudiation

Besides DoS attacks [8–11], the original TESLA is also susceptible to repudiation. At the TESLA's core is the need to divide the time into uniform intervals of duration and to assign one element from a one-way hash chain as a MAC key to each time interval of duration in the reverse order of chain generation. The sender defines a disclosure time δ for the keys, usually of the order of a few time intervals. Then the sender constructs each packet as $M_j||MAC_k(M_j)$, where M_j is a message to be sent, $MAC_k(M_j)$ is a MAC of M_j using key k, and the $||$ stands for message concatenation. The receiver buffers the received packet, while the MAC key is still secret. After disclosure time δ, the sender discloses the MAC key k in successive packets and the receiver checks whether the disclosed key should be released at this time interval and is correct (using previously released keys, and its security is guaranteed by the irreversible property of one-way hash function). Then, the receiver checks the correctness of the MAC of the buffered packet to ensure that the packet has not been modified or altered.

As can easily be seen, a packet can be forged after the MAC key is disclosed. Anyone including the sender who knows the key is able to forge a packet M'_j and calculate a correct MAC code, $MAC_k(M'_j)$, using the known key k. Hence, the proposed TSVC scheme does not provide nonrepudiation because only symmetric key cryptosystems are used to protect communications over VANETs. As such, it allows a sender to deny the fact that s/he sent a message in the past; therefore, it would be very difficult to prosecute offenders. Nevertheless, it is worth pointing out that the real identity of the message sender can be still revealed, but we cannot prove that the message indeed originates from the sender, making investigating and prosecuting offenders a challenge. This is because the message can be forged since the hash key (or hash chain element) is released or broadcast across the network. Nevertheless, not many vehicle applications, particularly nonsafety applications like in-vehicle infotainment (e.g., music and video streaming services) and advertising, currently need nonrepudiation since it is not critical for these applications to run properly. For instance, advertising is commonly seen on roadsides, and the method of marketing them has enhanced through vehicle-to-RSU communications. Local businesses or retailers now promote their products or services by broadcasting offers using RSUs. However, false advertising (or deceptive advertising) will often appear, for example, claiming a special deal offer or product in their description to entice the customers (drivers and passengers) to their store. But customers, on arriving at the store, might recognize the scam (e.g., quality of the product does not match the description), based on their past experiences. Even those who fall for the scam would have proof (transaction history like a sales slip or receipt) to file a complaint against the fraudulent business or service. Hence, nonrepudiation is not needed here.

However, because fraud is becoming more prominent on the roads and costly to resolve, there is a need to enable nonrepudiation for vehicular communication. In this section, we further extend our proposed TSVC scheme into a scheme supporting non-repudiation and give two solutions for the problem, which will be elaborated on next.

6.2.4.1 *In-Data-Packet Bloom Filter–Based Chained Packages Signature.* Many mechanisms and solutions have started to incorporate nonrepudiation to TESLA-like schemes. One such example is the Efficient Multichained Stream Signature (EMSS) protocol [24], where each augmented packet (AP) contains hash values of some predecessor packets (approximately 100–1000), as shown in Fig. 6.5. To provide nonrepudiation service to the sender, a signature packet containing the signature of a few hash values must be sent at a constant rate, which could lead to a significant increase in communication overhead. This is due to the fact that the size of communication overhead is proportional to the number of the predecessors of the augmented packet. For example, we assume that digital signatures are 2048 bits long. If the number of the predecessors is 99 and the SHA-1 hash function is adopted, a total of 195.5 kB overhead will be introduced for every 100 packets. In EMSS, communication overhead is caused mainly by two parts: the hash values of all the predecessors and the signature packets.

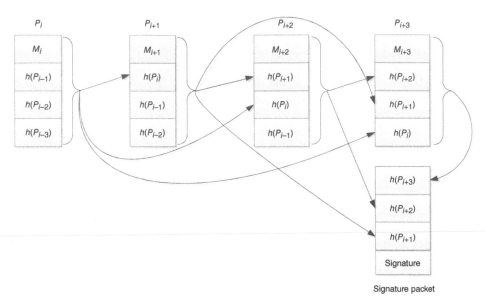

Figure 6.5. An EMSS protocol case where each augmented packet contains the digests of its three predecessors.

Obviously, the bigger the number of predecessors is, the larger communication overhead will be. However, in such a case, we need lesser signature packets.

To solve the communication overhead issue, we introduce an in-data-packet Bloom filter based the chained packages signature protocol. In the proposed protocol, each augmented packet only contains a Bloom filter, which represents all the preceding packets as well as itself. In order to provide nonrepudiation to the sender, a signature packet containing the signature of the Bloom filter is sent from time to time. Figure 6.6 illustrates an example of such a case, where the signature packet is sent every three packets. The Bloom filter is excellent because it doesn't store the actually packets that could have incurred significant communication overhead (e.g., additional spaces). In other words, the size of the communication overhead can be reduced by using a Bloom filter; thus, performance improves and still retaining the security properties from the TESLA-like schemes.

Next, we analyze the communication overhead of the proposed protocol by comparing it to EMSS as shown in Fig. 6.7. We assume that the RSA signature scheme is adopted here. The larger the RSA key size is, the more secure the RSA signature scheme will be. In fact, the recommended key size should be at least 2048 bits to ensure a high level of security. As a result, the digital signature size is 256 bytes. In addition, we assume that the SHA-1 hash function is adopted here and the size of the Bloom filter is 16 bits. Henceforth, we investigate the communication overhead of every n packets for both EMSS and the proposed protocol with the notion that each augmented packet contains the digests of its $(n-1)$ predecessors in EMSS. It was observed that the communication overhead of the proposed protocol is proportional to the number of packets being sent.

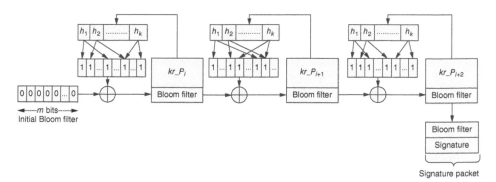

Figure 6.6. A proposed protocol case where the signature packet is sent every three packets (assume that the size of the Bloom filter is *m* bits).

Furthermore, the communication overhead of EMSS significantly increases as the number of packets—whose hash values are contained in each augmented packet—increases, and eventually, the communication overhead of EMSS becomes much larger than that of the proposed protocol. Obviously, with the proposed protocol, the size of communication overhead can be significantly reduced without compromising the security.

6.2.4.2 Nonrepudiation Using Trusted Devices. Another way to effectively provide nonrepudiation in TSVC is to use tamperproof devices (TPDs). Each vehicle is equipped with a TPD to store cryptographic key, data, and code, which is secure

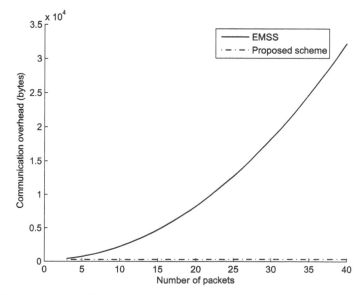

Figure 6.7. Comparison of communication overhead between the proposed scheme and EMSS.

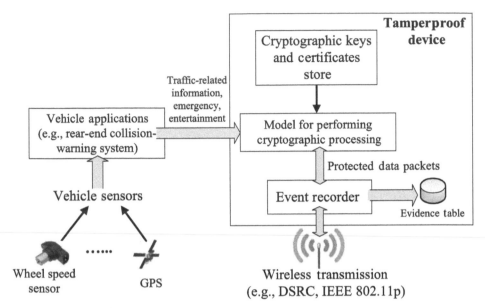

Figure 6.8. Architecture of an OBU system using a TPD.

against any compromised attempt such that an attacker cannot extract any data stored in the device. To reduce the risk of its compromise by attacks, the devices should have its own battery, which can be recharged from the vehicles. Access to this device should be restricted to authorized people. Several commercial products have these features, e.g. [25, 26]. Further, to protect the drivers' privacy rights, authorized people must also obtain a search warrant in order to access this device.

As shown in Fig. 6.8, the TPD would have two main functionalities: (1) to perform cryptographic operations, for example, securing outgoing packets and verifying the MAC tags of incoming packets; and (2) to record any data launched from and received by the vehicle. It is similar to a blackbox, which can often be found in an aircraft for the purpose of facilitating the investigation of aviation accidents.

When receiving a data packet P_j, the OBU will send it to the TPD. The TPD simply caches it. As soon as the next key release packet kr_P_j arrives at the TPD, it will start to verify the previously cached data packet P_j. We assume the verification succeeds following the procedures illustrated in Fig. 6.4, and the data packet P_j is accepted. Afterward, the hash value of the data packet is calculated and then stored into the evidence table along with a timestamp when the data packet is received, as shown in Table 6.2, which will be used for the purpose of nonrepudiation. Also, a parameter is used to control how long evidence is kept in the evidence table. By embedding the parameter (or expiration date) into the table, all the corresponding records of the expired data packets in the table can thus be removed, thereby reducing the storing and searching cost. In reality, it is decided by the authority. Expired data will be automatically removed from the table. Similar regulations already exist for surveillance videos. For example, all

TABLE 6.2. Evidence Table in a TPD

The Hash for Data Packet	Timestamp
0x387a87d3948772dd9746d2917043fbf2	1419197712
0x5ec962b4eafcac61f803ddb08add65bc	1281190212
...	...

financial institutions, including banks and automated teller machines (ATMs), will need to store their surveillance videos for at least 180 days. The details of the nonrepudiation protection will be discussed in the following text.

In some cases of repudiation the sender denies having sent a data packet in the past and claims to have sent another different data packet that in reality is forged by him/her later. The dispute can be easily resolved by searching the hash values of these data packets against the evidence tables of involved vehicles. If a match is found, we can simply figure out the truth. If we get a hit for the data packet that the sender has sent, it proves the sender falsely denies the truth.

Next, we analyze the storage cost of the proposed system using trusted devices. Assuming that the MD5 hash function is adopted here and the timestamp is 32 bits of milliseconds, we can estimate that the size of an evidence table entry for each data packet is 160 bits. According to DSRC [21], a vehicle sends each message with a time interval from 100 to 300 ms. In the case where 10 cars are within the communication range of a vehicle, the vehicle receives up to 100 messages per second, which would necessitate at least 2000 bytes of storage space every second. The longer the evidence is kept, the larger storage space is needed. Assume that we follow current strict regulations for financial sectors, and the evidence must be kept for at least 180 days. The total storage space needed is approximately 29 GB, which can be easily achieved by today's hard disk technology at a very low cost (according to statisticbrain.com [27], the average cost per gigabyte have fallen dramatically, reaching \$0.03 per gigabyte in 2014). Also, given the fact that the average car is parked most of the time (approximately 95% of the time [28]), the actual amount of storage space needed is going to be far less than the above estimates.

6.2.5 Discussion

6.2.5.1 *The Capability to Deal with Message Loss.* Wireless communication channels are lossy in nature. Inherited from TESLA, which is packet-loss-tolerant, our scheme is also packet-loss-tolerant. If a data packet is lost, no further action will be taken. On the other hand, if the KRP kr_P_i is lost, the legitimacy of the previous message can still be verified on receiving kr_P_j with $j > i$. The broken hash chain can be connected by applying the hash function $H(x)$ $j - i$ times and checking if $H^{j-i}(h_j) = h_i$. If so, the newly arrived hash value h_j is acceptable. However, if multiple continuous packets are lost such that the time to wait for the new key release packet is longer than the maximum tolerable message delay, M_j is neglected. In that case, the subsequent messages can still be authenticated when new data packets arrive, as we discuss in Section 6.4.

6.2.5.2 Bandwidth Efficiency. We analyze the reduction of bandwidth consumption due to the decrease of the average packet size compared with the regular public key based protocols.

For a signed message, additional load caused by security is the length of the certificate of the public key[2] and the digital signature of the message. Among the existing digital signature schemes such as RSA, DSA, ECDSA, and BLS, the most appropriate candidate for the VANET application in terms of the packet overhead and verification time is ECDSA.[3] The minimum additional space caused by ECDSA is 181 bytes for each message, including the digital signature and public key certificate. Thus, the total length of a traditional signed packet is around 281 bytes, including the message payload, which is around 100 bytes [17].

To evaluate the average cost of delivering a message in our scheme, we assume that the first KRP is signed with the ECDSA scheme and the secure hash algorithm used is SHA-1; the lifetime of an anonymous certificate is 10 minutes; routine traffic messages are sent every 300 ms. Thus, the total number of routine traffic messages N_{total} is 2000. The length of data packet is

$$
\left\{
\begin{aligned}
L_{P_i} &= L_{M_i} + L_{PVID} + L_{MAC} + L_T + L_{index} \\
&= 100 + 4 + 20 + 4 + 4 \\
&= 132 \text{ bytes}
\end{aligned}
\right. \tag{6.7}
$$

where *timestamp* and *PVID* are taken as 4 bytes each, respectively. The length of the first KRP is

$$
\left\{
\begin{aligned}
L_{kr\_P_1} &= L_{PVID} + L_{sig} + L_{hash} + L_{index} \\
&\quad + L_T + L_{Cert} \\
&= 4 + 56 + 20 + 4 + 4 + 125 \\
&= 157 \text{ bytes}
\end{aligned}
\right. \tag{6.8}
$$

and the length of the subsequent KRP is

$$
\left\{
\begin{aligned}
L_{kr\_P_i} &= L_{PVID} + L_{hash} + L_{index} \\
&= 4 + 20 + 4 \\
&= 28 \text{ bytes}, \ i > 1
\end{aligned}
\right. \tag{6.9}
$$

---

[2] We assume that a signing certificate for an OBU is used in our scheme, and the size of an OBU signing certificate is about 125 bytes [29].

[3] We assume that ECDSA-224 is used.

where *index* is taken as 4 bytes. Therefore, the average packet length due to the crypto-graphic algorithm in our scheme is:

$$
\begin{cases}
L_{avgP} = (L_{kr\_P_1} + L_{P_i} \times N_P + L_{kr\_P_i} \\
\qquad \times (N_{kr\_P} - 1))/N_{total} \\
\qquad = (157 + 132 \times 2000 + 28 \times 1999)/2000 \\
\qquad \approx 160 \text{ bytes,}
\end{cases}
\tag{6.10}
$$

which is much shorter than that of the traditional PKI-based digital signature schemes.

6.2.5.3 Tolerating Group Membership Fluctuation.

We investigate how to mitigate the impact due to dynamic vehicle group membership fluctuation while maintaining acceptable communication consumption and authentication delay.

The member of a group may fluctuate when a vehicle joins or leaves the group. Clearly, the case where the vehicle leaves the transmission range can be easily handled by removing the group leader's entry in its local cache table after a time threshold. The reason that the leaving vehicle keeps the information record of the group leader briefly is to avoid temporary group membership changes. On the other hand, when a vehicle (denoted as A) newly joins the group of vehicle (denoted as O), A needs to catch up with the authentication key information contained in the first key release packet kr_P_1 in order to authenticate any possible message received from O. Intuitively, this issue could be easily solved if A could obtain the first authenticated tip of hash chain kr_P_1 from O, by which A can verify this signed tip of the encryption key h_1 and subsequently authenticate any received message from O. Therefore, it is straightforward and effective in dealing with the membership fluctuation when the fluctuation rate is low; however, it may be subject to heavy signaling and processing overhead when the membership fluctuation is serious. In the following, we introduce an alternative approach where the first authenticated tip of the hash chain kr_P_1 with key release packets is periodically broadcast by each vehicle group, in order to allow a newly joining vehicle to authenticate its received messages at the expense of additional bandwidth assumption in the periodical broadcasting as well as longer authentication delay. It is clear that determining the length of the broadcasting period becomes an issue of design, where taking a larger (or smaller) broadcast interval leads to less (or more) bandwidth consumption yet longer (or shorter) authentication delay. Note that the traffic routine/safety messages are designed to provide early warning to the other drivers, and the late arrival of routine/safety messages may significantly diminish their effectiveness. Thus, it is challenging to initiate a graceful tradeoff between the authentication latency and the bandwidth consumption in the effort of periodically broadcasting the tip of the hash chain.

We first consider a single-lane highway scenario as shown in Fig. 6.9, where vehicle A is entering the transmission range of O. We are interested in how many vehicles are affected by the test slot in the proposed security mechanism. Assume that each vehicle is at the center of an imaginary cell defined by its transmission range R, and vehicle locations on the highway are randomly distributed according to a uniform distribution with density η vehicles per kilometer. This assumption has been widely adopted in traffic

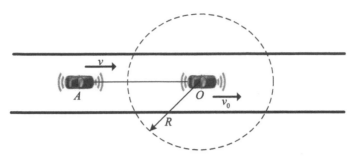

Figure 6.9. Single-lane highway scenario.

flow modeling [30–32]. The probability density function of the distance between vehicle A and reference vehicle O is given by

$$f(l) = \frac{1}{T(v - v_o)_{max}}, \quad 0 \le l \le T(v - v_0)_{max} \tag{6.11}$$

where l denotes the distance between A and O, and v_0 and v are the reference velocity and entering velocity, respectively. This assumption is reasonable because (1) in any time snapshot all vehicles may have equal probabilities of being placed on the lane segment (2) regularly, there are few hotspots on the highway that have higher density than other areas on the road. In the city, we can frequently see that some areas are crowded with cars, such as taxi loading/unloading areas, but vehicles seldom gather on the highway under normal situations. Moreover, v is assumed to follow a truncated Gaussian distribution with parameter $(\bar{v}, \sigma)$. On the highway, drivers must observe the speed restrictions; however, there are still a few overspeeding vehicles and low-speed vehicles. Khoury and Hobeika [33] used the Federal Highway Administration Highway Statistics 2002, and applied the Monte Carlo simulation model as well as a closed-form analytic estimation model to demonstrate that vehicle speed on highways fits into a truncated Gaussian distribution. Thus, the probability that A enters the O's virtual cell in test time T is denoted as $P(l - R < (v - v_0)T|v)$, and can be expressed as

$$\begin{cases} P_T = Prob\{\text{one vehicle enters the} \\ \qquad\qquad \text{transmission range within T}\} \\ \quad = \displaystyle\int\int P(l < (v - v_0)T + R|v)f(v)\,dl\,dv \\ \quad = \dfrac{1}{\sigma\sqrt{2\pi}T(v - v_0)_{max}} \displaystyle\int_{v_L}^{v_H} ((v - v_0)T \\ \qquad + R)\cdot exp(-\dfrac{v - \bar{v}^2}{2\sigma^2})\,dx, \text{ where } v > v_0 \end{cases} \tag{6.12}$$

or $P_T = 0$, $v \le v_0$. On a single lane, all vehicles have identical probabilities of entering the reference cell P_T, which can be regarded as a "success" trial; and the probability of not entering $1 - P_T$ can be regarded as a "failure" trial. If the number of vehicles on the lane, which is approximated by $\eta T(v - v_0)_{max}$, is supposed to be n independent trials, we can use the binomial distribution to model the distribution of the number of vehicles entering the reference cell. Then, the average number of entering vehicles is given by

$$E[k] = nP_T \tag{6.13}$$

where n is the number of vehicles on the lane, which can be approximated by $\eta T(v - v_0)_{max}$.

Note that with the assumption of uniform distribution for the vehicles along each lane, the single-lane scenario can be easily extended to a multi-lane scenario by multiplying the number of lanes to attain $E[k]$. Because of the radio reflection among vehicles, the virtual cell may be taken as a rectangle, which validates our assumption.

Figure 6.10 shows the average bandwidth consumption of each message corresponding to different broadcast intervals for disseminating the authenticated tip of hash chain. It is observed that the larger the broadcast interval is, the smaller the average bandwidth is consumed by each message. In addition, the bandwidth consumption decreases less significantly after the broadcast interval reaches around 10. More interestingly, the saving of bandwidth becomes steady after the broadcast interval is greater than 20. Thus, with the simulation configurations, it is suggested that the broadcast interval be set at approximately 6 seconds, which is the knee in the curve obtained in the analysis, such

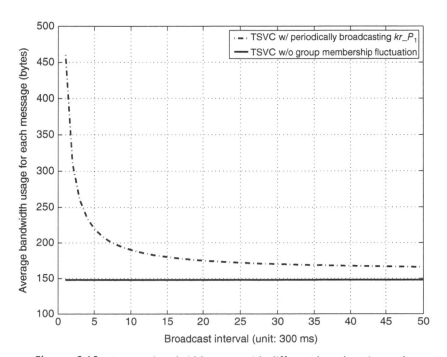

Figure 6.10. Average bandwidth usage with different broadcast intervals.

that the vehicles can fully enjoy the most rapid decrease of bandwidth consumption while increasing broadcast interval.

Also, from Fig. 6.10, we observe that conservation of bandwidth usage is very limited when $T = 20$ is used as the broadcast interval instead of 10. Based on the fact that a vehicle is able to sense the velocity of an approaching vehicle, our suggested policy for achieving adaptive authenticated tip broadcasting is described as follows. When a vehicle observes that there is a large velocity deviation among neighboring vehicles, it takes a small broadcast interval, such as $T = 10$, which can help to achieve an acceptable authentication delay at the expense of larger bandwidth consumption. Otherwise, it takes a normal broadcast interval such as $T = 20$ in order to obtain the optimal gain between the authentication delay and bandwidth consumption.

Next, we investigate the impact of adopting the proposed periodic broadcasting mechanism on newly joining vehicles. Let the average velocity $\bar{v}$ on a highway be 100 km/h. Figure 6.11 illustrates the average number of affected vehicles (denoted as $E[k]$) versus vehicle velocity standard deviation (denoted as σ) with respect to different broadcast intervals. It is observed that under small σ, the number of affected vehicle is moderate and does not necessarily increase significantly with the increase of σ. However, the number of affected vehicle increases significantly with the increase of σ when σ is large. This indicates that the length of broadcast interval may impose a significant impact on the proposed mechanism in terms of average number of affected vehicles, especially when σ is large.

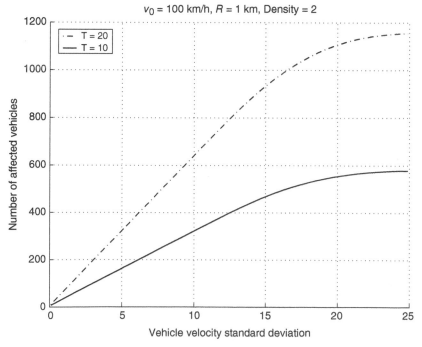

Figure 6.11. Affected vehicles due to vehicle velocity standard deviation.

6.3 SECURITY ANALYSIS

The security of the proposed TSVC scheme is analyzed as follows.

- *Data Source Privacy*. The privacy of the data source is well protected because each vehicle is preloaded with a list of anonymous public–private key pairs as well as their corresponding public key certificates at the initialization stage. When a vehicle broadcasts the data packets, it just needs to pick up one pair of keys, where the private key is used to sign the first key release packet. Therefore, the real identity will not be disclosed during the whole TSVC scheme since only the pseudo-ID of the data source has been used. Furthermore, since each anonymous public key certificate has a short lifetime, it is difficult to track an individual driver by way of an anonymous certificate.
- *Traceability*. The authorities can always reveal the real identities of the message senders by looking up the database for matching between a real identity and the pseudo-ID in order to guard the truth when there is any dispute.
- *Data Source Authentication*. With the proposed TSVC scheme, the data source can be efficiently authenticated to fit into the vehicular communication scenarios, which is described as follows. The first key release packet is signed by a private key corresponding to one anonymous public key certificate, where ECDSA is used. Since ECDSA is a secure and efficient digital signature scheme, anyone can explicitly authenticate the first key release packet. Afterward, the key enclosed in the first key release packet can then be used to authenticate the first data packet. At the same time, since the secure one-way function is employed in the scheme, the subsequently arriving data packets can also be fastly authenticated. If an adversary can forge the first authenticated key release packet, it will contradict with the hardness of the elliptic curve discrete logarithm problem. On the other hand, if an adversary can forge the latter authenticated packets, it will contradict with the one-way assumption of secure hash function. Therefore, the data source authentication can be achieved in our TSVC scheme.
- *Resilience to Replay Attack*. Because a timestamp is embedded into each packet to verify its validity, the replay attack is also prevented.

6.4 PERFORMANCE EVALUATION

Simulation is conducted to verify the efficiency and applicability of the proposed scheme using ns-2 [35]. We are interested in the system performance concerning the average *packet delay* (PD) and average *packet loss ratio* (PLR) under the proposed security scheme, which is further compared with a number of traditional public-key-based security schemes. For the PLR, we consider only the packet loss caused by security mechanisms instead of the lossy wireless channels.

Roadside communication on both scenarios of highway and city traffic supporting three lanes in each direction is simulated. In the highway scenario, each vehicle is first

Span 500 m
N 23400 m

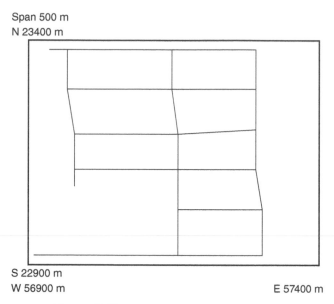

S 22900 m
W 56900 m   E 57400 m

Figure 6.12. A city map with span of 500 m.

located with an even intervehicle distance and then starts traveling with a uniformly random speed within a range of $v \pm 10$ km/h, where v is the average velocity of each vehicle in the simulation. In the city scenario, to fully estimate the real-world city road environment and vehicular traffic, we use the mobility model generation tool developed by Saha and Johnson [34], which is specialized to generate realistic traffic scenario files for vehicles in ns-2. This tool utilizes the publicly available *topologically integrated geographic encoding and referencing* (TIGER) database from the US Census Bureau, which contains detailed street maps for each city in the USA. The map adopted in the simulation is shown in Fig. 6.12, which corresponds to part of the Afton Oaks area in Houston. Vehicles are first scattered randomly on one intersection of the roads and repeatedly move toward another randomly selected intersection along the path constrained by the map. Vehicles are driving with a random fluctuation range of 5 mi/h according to the road speed limit of 35–75 mi/h. All simulation parameters are listed in Table 6.3.

We first run a simulation to test the message transmission time through the wireless channel based on the highway situation with IEEE 802.11p. Because most of the transmission delay is incurred by wireless channel contention, which means that the longest transmission time occurs when the density of the traffic is the highest, we simulate the crowded traffic scenario in which the communication range is set as 300 m, and the inter-vehicular distance is set as 5 m. From the simulation result, the longest transmission delay is 6.467 ms. Therefore, key disclosure delay δ for the latter experiments is conservatively set as 100 ms, which is much larger than the actual delay and thus ensures the absolute security.

TABLE 6.3. Simulation Configuration

Highway simulation range	2500 m * 50 m
City simulation range	500 m * 500 m
Communication range	300 m
Simulation time	100 s
Channel bandwidth	6 MB/s
Wireless protocol	802.11
Pause time	0 s
Digital signature signing delay	1.52 ms
Message verification delay	4.14 ms
MAC generation/verification delay	1 ms
Length of TSVC data packet	120 bytes
Length of signed message	200 bytes
Buffer size for TSVC	80 packets[a]
Buffer size for PKI	2 packets

[a]The buffer size should be large enough to store the number of messages that will be received during the key disclosure delay δ.

We then run two sets of simulations. The first set of simulations investigates the impact of the vehicle's moving speed in highway scenario, whereas the second set of simulations investigates the impact of vehicle's density in both highway and city (surface street) scenarios.

The metric of PD is composed of all the periods from the moment that the data packet is formed at the sender's side from the application layer to the moment that the receiving vehicle has the opportunity to react to the received data. Therefore, the latency for a successful transmission of a message is given by

$$t_{sign}(M) + t_{trans} + t_{queue} + t_{verify}(Cert) + t_{verify}(M) \qquad (6.14)$$

for the traditional public key based protocols, and

$$t_{trans} + t_{queue} + t_{verify}(MAC) + t_{1-hash} \qquad (6.15)$$

for the TSVC scheme. The delay induced by any cryptographic operation in the proposed scheme is automatically considered as ns-2 simulation delay according to measurement of those algorithms based on cryptographic library MIRACL [36].

6.4.1 Impact of Vehicle Moving Speed

In the first set of simulations, v (i.e., the average speed of the vehicles) varies between 10 and 40 m/s (36 and 144 km/h). The initial intervehicle distance is 30 m. The simulation results on the PD and PLR are shown in Fig. 6.13. In both of the schemes, the variation of speed does not affect much on PD and PLR. It can be seen that the proposed TSVC scheme yields larger PD, which is negligibly higher than the key disclosure

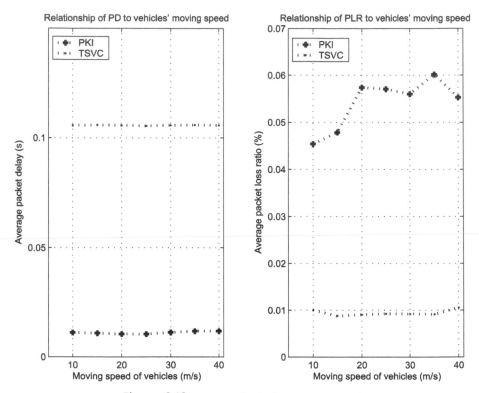

Figure 6.13. Impact of vehicles' moving speed.

delay δ. The delay for TSVC is slightly higher than 100 ms. According to [17], the maximum allowable message latency is around 100 ms to meet the driver's reaction. Thus, both of the two schemes can meet this requirement. For PLR, TSVC yields much lower packet loss ratio compared with that of PKI-based schemes under this normal traffic density.

6.4.2   Impact of Vehicle Density

In the second set of simulations, the impact of node density for both highway and city traffic is studied. The city traffic has different traffic model with highway scenario and is usually denser than that on the highway. From Fig. 6.14, it can be seen that TSVC has higher but acceptable packet delay than PKI. Moreover, the packet delay for both of the two schemes does not vary a lot with the increase of the traffic density. From Fig. 6.15, the traditional public-key-based protocol suffers a much higher packet loss ratio, reaching 47% when the vehicle density is greater than 40, which makes it infeasible in practical use; however, our TSVC scheme maintains stable packet loss ratio that is not affected by the increase of the vehicle density.

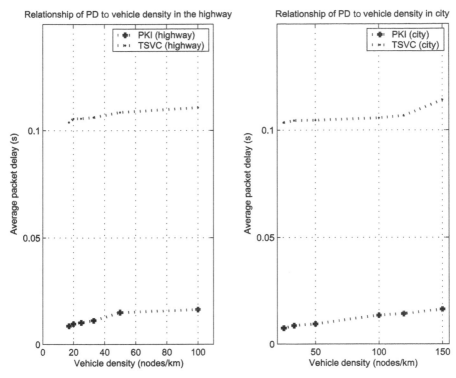

Figure 6.14. Relationship between PD and vehicle density.

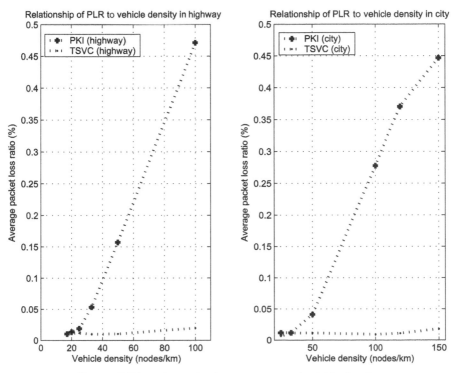

Figure 6.15. Relationship between PLR and vehicle density.

6.5 CONCLUDING REMARKS

In this chapter, we have proposed a novel TSVC security scheme for achieving efficient and secure vehicular communication, which not only meets the various security requirements and the drivers' conditional privacy requirement but also achieves high efficiency in terms of packet overhead and computation latency. We have demonstrated its practicality to the real-world applications through rigorous analysis and extensive simulation.

REFERENCES

1. A. Perrig, R. Canetti, J. D. Tygar, and D. Song, "The TESLA broadcast authentication protocol," *CryptoBytes*, vol. 5 no. 2, pp. 2–13, 2002.
2. X. Lin, X. Sun, X. Wang, C. Zhang, P. Ho, and X. Shen, "TSVC: Timed efficient and secure vehicular communications with privacy preserving," *IEEE Transactions on Wireless Communications*, vol. 7, no. 12-1, pp. 4987–4998, 2008. (Available online at http://dx.doi.org/10.1109/T-WC.2008.070773.)
3. L. Lamport, "Password authentication with insecure communication," *Communications of the ACM*, vol. 24, no. 11, pp. 770–772, 1981.
4. R. L. Rivest and A. Shamir, "Payword and micromint: Two simple micropayment schemes," *Proc. Security Protocols Conference*. Springer, 1997, pp. 69–87.
5. Q. Huan, I. C. Avramopoulos, H. Kobayashi, and B. Liu, "Secure data forwarding in wireless ad hoc networks," *Proc. IEEE International Conference on Communications, 2005. (ICC'05)*, IEEE, 2005, vol. 5, pp. 3525–3531.
6. P. Golle and N. Modadugu, "Authenticating streamed data in the presence of random packet loss," *Proc. Network and Distributed System Security (NDSS) Symposium*, Internet Society, 2001, vol. 1, pp. 13–22.
7. A. Perrig, R. Szewczyk, J. Tygar, V. Wen, and D. E. Culler, "Spins: Security protocols for sensor networks," *Wireless Networks*, vol. 8, no. 5, pp. 521–534, 2002.
8. A. Studer, F. Bai, B. Bellur, and A. Perrig, "Flexible, extensible, and efficient VANET authentication," *Journal of Communications and Networks*, vol. 11, no. 6, pp. 574–588, 2009.
9. A. Perrig, R. Szewczyk, J. Tygar, V. Wen, and D. E. Culler, "Spins: Security protocols for sensor networks," *Wireless Networks*, vol. 8, no. 5, pp. 521–534, 2002.
10. P. Ning, A. Liu, and W. Du, "Mitigating dos attacks against broadcast authentication in wireless sensor networks," *ACM Transactions on Sensor Networks*, vol. 4, no. 1, p. 1, 2008.
11. Q. Li and W. Trappe, "Staggered TESLA: A multicast authentication scheme resistant to DoS attacks," *Proc. Global Telecommunications Conference, 2005 (GLOBECOM'05)*, IEEE, 2005, vol. 3, pp. 1670–1675.
12. C. Antognini and A. Trivadis, "Bloom filters," http://antognini.ch/papers/BloomFilters 20080620. (pdf), 2008.
13. L. Fan, P. Cao, J. Almeida, and A. Z. Broder, "Summary cache: A scalable wide-area web cache sharing protocol," *IEEE/ACM Transactions on Networking*, vol. 8, no. 3, pp. 281–293, 2000.

14. B. D. Davison, "A web caching primer," *Internet Computing, IEEE*, vol. 5, no. 4, pp. 38–45, 2001.

15. A. Broder and M. Mitzenmacher, "Network applications of bloom filters: A survey," *Internet Mathematics*, vol. 1, no. 4, pp. 485–509, 2004.

16. J. K. Mullin, "A second look at bloom filters," *Communications of the ACM*, vol. 26, no. 8, pp. 570–571, 1983.

17. CVSC Consortium et al., *Vehicle Safety Communications Project: Task 3 Final Report: Identify Intelligent Vehicle Safety Applications Enabled by DSRC*," National Highway Traffic Safety Administration, US Department of Transportation, Washington DC, 2005.

18. M. K. Reiter, K. P. Birman, and R. Van Renesse, "A security architecture for fault-tolerant systems," *ACM Transactions on Computer Systems*, vol. 12, no. 4, pp. 340–371, 1994.

19. M. K. Reiter, K. P. Birman, and R. Van Renesse, "A security architecture for fault-tolerant systems," *ACM Transactions on Computer Systems*, vol. 12, no. 4, pp. 340–371, 1994.

20. V. Roca, A. Francillon, and S. Faurite, "The use of TESLA in the ALC and norm protocols," Internet Engineering Task Force (IETF) work in progress, 2007.

21. J. B. Kenney, "Dedicated short-range communications (DSRC) standards in the United States," *Proceedings of the IEEE*, vol. 99, no. 7, pp. 1162–1182, 2011.

22. M. Raya, P. Papadimitratos, and J.-P. Hubaux, "Securing vehicular communications," *IEEE Wireless Communications Magazine, Special Issue on Inter-Vehicular Communications*, vol. 13, no. LCA-ARTICLE-2006-015, pp. 8–15, 2006.

23. T. L. Willke and N. F. Maxemchuk, "Coordinated interaction using reliable broadcast in mobile wireless networks," *Proc. NETWORKING 2005. Networking Technologies, Services, and Protocols; Performance of Computer and Communication Networks; Mobile and Wireless Communications Systems*. Springer, 2005, pp. 1168–1179.

24. A. Perrig, R. Canetti, J. D. Tygar, and D. Song, "Efficient authentication and signing of multicast streams over lossy channels," *Proc. IEEE Symposium on Security and Privacy, 2000, S&P 2000*. IEEE, 2000, pp. 56–73.

25. "Tamper resistant security," https://www.thales-esecurity.com/solutions/by-technology-focus/tamper-resistant-security.

26. "Trusted computing group," http://www.trustedcomputinggroup.org/.

27. "Average cost of hard drive storage," http://www.statisticbrain.com/average-cost-of-hard-drive-storage/.

28. Cars are parked 95 percent of the time." Let's check!" http://www.reinventingparking.org/2013/02/cars-are-parked-95-of-time-lets-check.html.

29. D. Jiang and L. Delgrossi, "IEEE 802.11p: Towards an international standard for wireless access in vehicular environments," *Proc. Vehicular Technology Conference, 2008 (VTC'08). Spring 2008 IEEE*. IEEE, 2008, pp. 2036–2040.

30. M. Nekovee, "Modeling the spread of worm epidemics in vehicular ad hoc networks," *Proc. Vehicular Technology Conference, 2006 (VTC'06)*, IEEE, 2006, vol. 2, pp. 841–845.

31. F. Dion, H. Rakha, and Y.-S. Kang, "Comparison of delay estimates at under-saturated and over-saturated pre-timed signalized intersections," *Transportation Research Part B: Methodological*, vol. 38, no. 2, pp. 99–122, 2004.

32. J. Zhao, Y. Zhang, and G. Cao, "Data pouring and buffering on the road: A new data dissemination paradigm for vehicular ad hoc networks," *IEEE Transactions on Vehicular Technology*, vol. 56, no. 6, pp. 3266–3277, 2007.

33. J. E. Khoury and A. Hobeika, "Incorporating uncertainty into the estimation of the passing sight distance requirements," *Computer-Aided Civil and Infrastructure Engineering*, vol. 22, no. 5, pp. 347–357, 2007.

34. A. K. Saha and D. B. Johnson, "Modeling mobility for vehicular ad-hoc networks," *Proc. 1st ACM International Workshop on Vehicular Ad Hoc Networks*. ACM, 2004, pp. 91–92.

35. J. Lin, S. Sedigh, and A. Miller, "A general framework for quantitative modeling of dependability in cyber-physical systems: A proposal for doctoral research," *Proc. 33rd Annual IEEE International Computer Software and Applications Conference, 2009 (COMPSAC'09)*. IEEE, 2009, vol. 1, pp. 668–671.

36. M. Scott, "MIRACL–multiprecision integer and rational arithmetic C/C++ library," Shamus Software Ltd, Dublin, Ireland, URL¡ http://www.shamus.ie, 2003.

7

DISTRIBUTED COOPERATIVE MESSAGE AUTHENTICATION

7.1 INTRODUCTION

In previous chapters we have explored ways to allow vehicles and RSUs to work together to ensure the integrity and guarantee the authenticity of messages received by each individual vehicle. Chapter 5 presented an RSU-aided message authentication scheme, where RSUs are responsible for verifying the authenticity of the messages sent from vehicles, and for notifying the vehicles of the results. Since MACs are used for authenticating intervehicle communication with the aid of RSUs, the message authentication process is suitable for vehicular communication. This, however, requires direct involvement of RSUs in the message authentication processing phase; when RSUs are not widely available, in the early stage of the deployment phase of VANETs, for example, it becomes ineffective. Chapter 6 utilized fast symmetric cryptography, allowing vehicles to work cooperatively with each other to authenticate received messages. It is based on TESLA (timed efficient stream loss-tolerant authentication). In the proposed TESLA-Based scheme, a number of hash chains are generated in advance for a given vehicle. The vehicle selects one chain at random, and broadcasts the commitment of the chain to its neighbors, which is simply protected by a traditional PKI-based digital signature. Then, the vehicle uses the elements of the chain to generate message

Vehicular Ad Hoc Network Security and Privacy, First Edition. Xiaodong Lin and Rongxing Lu.
© 2015 The Institute of Electrical and Electronics Engineers, Inc. Published 2015 by John Wiley & Sons, Inc.

authentication codes (MACs) for messages originating from it. Its neighbors are able to authenticate the messages on the basis of these MACs; however, the high dynamics of topological structure for vehicular network could jeopardize the effectiveness of the proposed scheme.

In this chapter we will present an efficient cooperative message authentication scheme that does not directly involve a trusted authority (TA) [1]. This scheme is carried out by a set of neighboring vehicle users; with minimal intervehicle coordination, the scheme minimizes redundant authentication efforts of different vehicles working on the same message. It also encourages cooperation and resists free-riding attacks. First, we propose a cooperative authentication scheme that doesn't involve intervehicle interaction, using extensive simulations to derive the optimal strategy for vehicle users under different parameter settings. Second, in order to resist the free-riding attacks that do not use fake authentication efforts (hereafter referred to as *passive free-riding attack*), an evidence–token mechanism is added. This mechanism enables the TA to flexibly control the cooperational capability of vehicles, according to their cooperation history. An authentication proof is further required to be output by cooperative vehicles to resist the free-riding attacks where fake authentication efforts are involved (hereafter referred to as *active free-riding attack*). Without having free access to others' cooperation efforts, one's selfish behavior is effectively discouraged. Third, we evaluate the performance of the proposed scheme in a simulated VANET environment. From this point forward, we use the terms *"vehicle," "vehicle user," "driver"* and *"user"* interchangeably.

The remainder of this chapter is organized as follows: Section 7.2 gives the problem formulation, including network model, and the security model. A basic version of the cooperative authentication scheme is presented in Section 7.3, and its extended version with security concerns is introduced in Section 7.4. Security analysis and performance evaluation of the proposed schemes are provided in Section 7.5 and Section 7.6, respectively; and finally, the chapter concludes with Section 7.7.

7.2 PROBLEM FORMULATION

7.2.1 Network Model

We consider a VANET consisting of a large number of vehicles $\mathcal{V} = \{v_1, v_2, \ldots, v_\mu\}$. The OBUs equipped on the vehicles enable them to communicate with neighboring vehicles in range tr_v. A central TA provides registration to vehicle users during which vehicles' pseudonyms and corresponding secrets are updated and stored in the vehicles' OBUs. A limited number of RSUs are deployed in the VANET. The TA can talk to vehicle users via RSUs through wireless communication when the vehicles are close to the RSUs. The RSUs have both wireless and wired connections. The wireless connections with communication range $tr_r (> tr_v)$ can be used for contacting nearby OBUs. The wired connections allow RSUs to communicate with each other in a secure and reliable way.

The multiple-pseudonym technique is adopted to attain location privacy [2]. Specifically, vehicles are assigned a set of asymmetric key pairs, and the public keys serving as pseudonyms are alternatively used. Vehicles frequently change their pseudonyms used for authentication over time, and their location privacy preservation is attained through the unlinkability of old and new pseudonyms. If a vehicle uses up its pseudonyms, the TA will assign the vehicle new pseudonyms. Moreover, the pseudonyms can be linked to a specific vehicle by the TA so that the TA is able to trace and regulate the vehicle's behavior.

7.2.2 Security Model

In our security model, we assume that the TA is fully trusted by all vehicles and that it is infeasible for any attacker to compromise. We do not consider attacks by compromised vehicles or outside adversaries, and focus only on user selfish behavior in cooperative authentication. Since cooperative authentication is conducted in an unattended and autonomous environment, vehicles may behave selfishly to take advantages of others' authentication contributions and rarely make their own contributions. Such selfish behavior, referred to as *free-riding attack*, poses a serious threat to cooperative message authentication. On one hand, cooperative behavior can largely reduce authentication overhead for every vehicle; on the other hand, the desired benefits seem to come for free and possibly trigger free-riding attacks. We consider the security threats of the following three types:

1. *Linkability Attack.* Authentication linkability is necessary for the TA to identify misbehaving users. In a linkability attack, a malicious user falsely claims that it has verified multiple message–signature pairs, and it also disables the TA to trace its unique identifier so as to avoid punishment.
2. *Free-Riding Attack without Authentication Efforts* (*or Passive Free-Riding Attack*). Such an attack is launched by a malicious user who aims to enjoy the authentication efforts of other users at no cost, for example, by passively listening to the information sent from nearby users. It reduces the attacker's authentication overhead and breaks the fairness among users.
3. *Free-Riding Attack with Fake Authentication Efforts* (*or Active Free-Riding Attack*). Such an attack is launched by an active malicious user who participates in the cooperative authentication protocol by generating fake authentication efforts. Considering the asynchronism in a cooperative authentication process, the attacker checks the authentication efforts of other users and combines them to forge an authentication effort for itself. By doing so, it does not actually authenticate any original message but provides valid verification efforts, since these signatures have been checked by others. This attack is more intelligent than the second one. It can hardly be detected by nearby users or the TA.

In order to resist such attacks and stimulate cooperation among autonomous vehicles, it is important to ensure fairness during cooperation; specifically, the greater efforts that a vehicle makes, the more advantages the vehicle can obtain. In other words, any selfish user cannot take advantage of the others without contributing anything itself.

7.3   BASIC COOPERATIVE AUTHENTICATION SCHEME

We consider x vehicles that gather in a small area and are able to directly communicate with each other. There are y messages available to these vehicles, and each message contains a unique index and is attached with a signature. The x vehicles need to authenticate the y messages by verifying their attached signatures. Let C_v denote the cost of authenticating one signature, and C_s be the cost of generating one signature. In the following, we analyze the noncooperative authentication case and the cooperative authentication case, respectively.

> *Noncooperation Case.* Vehicles do not cooperate on message authentications. Each
> of them has to authenticate the y signatures alone. Per vehicle authentication cost
> is $C_1^{nc} = y \times C_v$, and the total cost of the x vehicles is $x \times y \times C_v$.
> *Cooperation Case.* The x vehicles cooperatively authenticate the y signatures. The
> cooperative strategy of vehicle v_i can be described as follows:
>
>   1. Based on (x, y), vehicle v_i authenticates $v_{x,y}$ randomly chosen signatures, where
> $0 \leq v_{x,y} \leq y$. Denote these signatures by $(s_{i,1}, \ldots, s_{i,v_{x,y}})$ and the corresponding
>   messages by $(m_{i,1}, \ldots, m_{i,v_{x,y}})$.
>   2. User v_i generates an integrated signature $s_{i,c}$ on the message $m_{i,c} =$
> $(m_{i,1}, pid_{i,1})|| \cdots ||(m_{i,v_{x,y}}, pid_{i,v_{x,y}})$, and then sends $(m_{i,c}, s_{i,c})$ together with the
>   indices of the original messages to neighboring vehicles.
>   3. User v_i authenticates the others' integrated signatures.
>   4. User v_i authenticates the remaining signatures that have not been covered by
>   the integrated signatures.

At steps 1 and 2, vehicle v_i does $v_{x,y}$ authentications and one signature generation. The authentication overhead is not reduced in these two phases. However, at step 3, for the remaining $y - v_{x,y}$ signatures, vehicle v_i does not need to do $y - v_{x,y}$ authentications. Instead, it authenticates the integrated signatures, each covering multiple original signatures. Here, we consider that all vehicles choose the same value $v_{x,y}$ in step 1 and a vehicle authenticates all integrated signatures. The authentication overhead per vehicle is $C_1^c = (x - 1 + v_{x,y}) \times C_v + C_s$; the total cost of all vehicles is $x \times ((x - 1 + v_{x,y}) \times C_v + C_s)$.

Figure 7.1 shows the cooperation gain in message authentication, where $x = 10$ users have $y = 100$ common message–signature pairs. The number of messages that have been verified by a vehicle is shown in terms of the number of authentications that have been performed by the vehicle. The circle and plus lines represent the performance of cooperative/noncooperative authentications. The shaded area shows the gain that can be achieved by cooperative authentication. We take an example as follows: if a vehicle authenticates 39 signatures in a noncooperative way, it obtains 39 authenticated messages; if a vehicle authenticates $30 + 9$ signatures by cooperative authentication introduced above, it will receive 87 authenticated messages. It can be seen that vehicles can receive larger

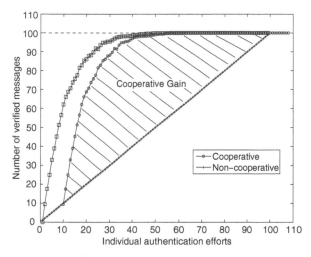

Figure 7.1. Cooperative gain.

benefits by authenticating 9 integrated signatures. The square line represents the number of original signatures that have been covered by integrated signatures in terms of $v_{x,y}$.

When each vehicle wishes to authenticate all the y messages, we run a 100000-round simulation to obtain the optimal $\rho = v_{x,y}$ for each vehicle to maintain a minimal authentication overhead. We choose $x = 2, 4, 6, 8, 10, 15, 20$ and $y = 100$. The authentication overhead per vehicle is $f(\rho) = (x - 1 + \rho + 100 - c_\rho) \times C_v + C_s$, where c_ρ is the number of original signatures that covered all the integrated signatures. Notably, $(x - 1) \times C_v$ overhead is for authenticating integrated signatures. Figure 7.2 shows the simulation results, which are to be adopted in Section 7.6 for performance evaluation.

7.4 SECURE COOPERATIVE AUTHENTICATION SCHEME

In this section, we improve the basic scheme to deal with selfish behavior. It is observed that if a vehicle does not generate integrated signatures, it can always consume less for message authentication than those who do. Since VANETs are highly dynamic environments and the privacy of vehicles needs to be guaranteed by pseudonyms, the cooperation among vehicles can be regarded as a nonrepeated game where defection is always the optimal strategy for individual vehicles. In order to overcome the incentive to defect, we introduce an evidence–token mechanism and an identity-based signcryption scheme. We then propose a secure cooperative authentication scheme that provides an efficient and secure cooperation platform for vehicles. In the last part, we additionally require vehicles output cooperation proofs so that they can verify the originality of authentication efforts made by each other. The generation of such proofs is to prevent free-riding attacks with fake authentication efforts (or active free-riding attack) at a reasonable cooperation cost.

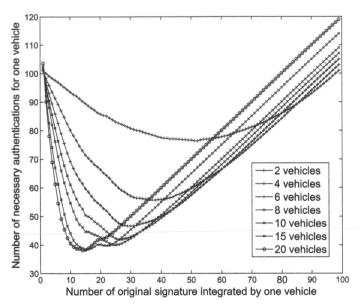

Figure 7.2. Optimal number of original signatures.

7.4.1   Evidence and Token for Fairness

The basic principle of the evidence–token mechanism is to balance the effort that vehicles make over time with the advantages that vehicles take from others. The mechanism requires time to be slotted. The TA will be responsible for maintaining the balance according to the time slots. It receives the evidences from vehicles via RSUs when vehicles pass by the RSUs, and sends the tokens back to vehicles, based on the evaluation of their authentication efforts in the past time slots. The evidences will not be repeatedly used to count their effort. The TA generates and distributes tokens to vehicles in order to enable them to verify other vehicles' integrated signatures. The tokens must be of timeliness; otherwise vehicles may disconnect from RSUs after obtaining enough tokens. Specifically, we describe the evidence–token mechanism as shown in Fig. 7.3.

7.4.1.1   Evidence Collection by Vehicles. In step 1 of the basic scheme, a vehicle authenticates some of the original signatures received and generates an integrated signature at a time slot. It then creates an evidence for its authentication effort, which includes the time slot, the number of cooperative vehicles x, the number of original signatures y, and the number of original signatures $v_{x,y}$ included in the integrated signature. It transmits the integrated signature and the evidence to others. Note that the evidence cannot be forged and will be publicly verified by the receiver vehicles. Since evidence generation and transmission consume energy, the number of evidences generated per vehicle should be limited. Next, we devise a distributed approach based on geographic information in order for vehicles to be locally aware of their responsibilities of evidence generation. The approach randomly and fairly distributes the workload

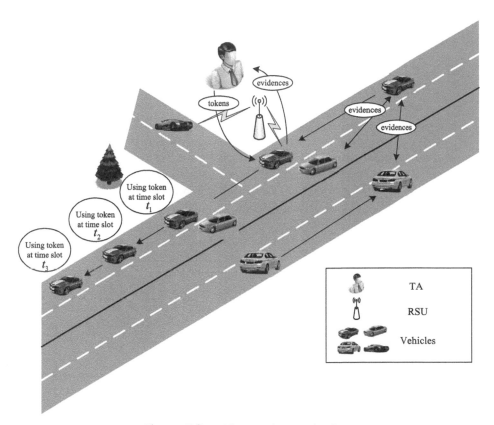

Figure 7.3. Evidence–token mechanism.

of evidence generation and minimizes the number of evidences. It also enables good vehicles to monitor the potential malicious behavior.

We consider that vehicle users $\{v_1, \ldots, v_x\}$ are all aware of the geographic information $(L_1, \ldots, L_x)$, where L_i is a (latitude, longitude)-tuple representing the location of user v_i. User v_i builds a polar coordinate system with itself as the origin and the east direction as axis, as shown in Fig. 7.4. Another user v_j has its unique polar coordinates (r_j, a_j) in this coordinate system, where r_j is the distance between v_i and v_j and a_j is the angle. All the other vehicles can be sorted in an increasing order $od_i = \{v_{i,1}, \ldots, v_{i,x-1}\}$

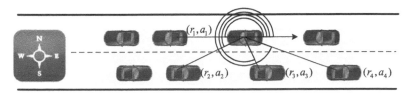

Figure 7.4. Polar coordinates of vehicles.

based on their polar coordinates. od_i can be obtained by all x users. We set a time upper bound for evidence generation. The evidence generation for user v_i is started by $v_{i,1}$.

- If user $v_{i,1}$ generates an evidence in the given time bound, user $v_{i,2}$ will check the validity of the evidence based on user v_i's effort. If the evidence is incorrect, user $v_{i,2}$ will continue to wait.
- If user $v_{i,2}$ does not receive a valid evidence from user $v_{i,1}$ in the given time bound, user $v_{i,2}$ records this irresponsible behavior together with the current pseudonym of user $v_{i,1}$. It then takes over the evidence generation responsibility of v_i in the following time period. User $v_{i,3}$ will be invoked in turn if $v_{i,2}$ fails to do so. Since every user knows its order in od_i and the time upper bound is fixed, user v_j will be responsible for checking v_i's evidence if v_{j-1} outputs the evidence. If the check fails, user v_j then generates the evidence.

Since the geographic information of vehicles is totally random and unpredictable, vehicle users will fairly share the evidence generation load. The number of evidences is minimum; i.e., it is equal to the number of vehicles. If any vehicle does not generate an evidence as required, another vehicle will record its malicious behavior and report it to the TA. Such behavior will also be considered selfish. Note that, an exceptional case is that all the $x - 1$ vehicles are irresponsible, which exists with a very small probability.

7.4.1.2 Token Generation by TA.

The TA balances the workload of vehicles and the advantages the vehicles taken from each other. Based on the evidences, it checks the number of integrated signatures $s_{i,c}$ that are generated by user v_i in previous time periods. Then, it assigns user v_i with multiple tokens according to the provided evidences. Each token is valid for only a specific time slot. If user v_i provides enough evidences to confirm its proper behavior, the TA will assign a large number of tokens to user v_i so that v_i can benefit from other vehicles in a long time period. On the other hand, if v_i does not provide the expected number of evidences, the TA will assign less tokens to v_i so that v_i does not have enough tokens before contacting the next encountered RSU.

Now, we adopt an identity-based signcryption (IBSC) technique [3,4] into the secure cooperative authentication. An IBSC scheme can be used to control the capability of verification. For example, after verifying a group of original signatures, a user could encrypt an integrated signature such that others know which signatures it has verified after the corresponding decryption. Specifically, the IBSC scheme consists of the following five algorithms: SETUP, KEY GENERATION, TOKEN GENERATION, SIGNECRYPTION, and DECRYPTION-AND-VERIFICATION.

SETUP—The TA chooses $\mathbb{G}$ and $\mathbb{G}_T$ to be two finite cyclic groups of the same large order q. Suppose $\mathbb{G}$ and $\mathbb{G}_T$ are equipped with a pairing, i.e., a nondegenerated and efficiently computable bilinear map $e : \mathbb{G} \times \mathbb{G} \rightarrow \mathbb{G}_T$ such that $\forall g, h \in \mathbb{G}, \forall a, b \in \mathbb{Z}_q$, $e(g^a, h^b) = e(g, h)^{ab}$ [3]. The TA chooses a generator g of group $\mathbb{G}$. In addition, it also chooses random exponents $\beta \in \mathbb{Z}_q$, and two cryptographic hash functions $H : \{0, 1\}^* \rightarrow \mathbb{G}$ and $H_1 : \mathbb{G}_2 \rightarrow \{0, 1\}^n$. The TA sets $g_{pub} = g^\beta$. The system public parameters are $(\mathbb{G}, \mathbb{G}_T, e, q, g, g_{pub}, H, H_1, n)$.

KEY GENERATION—The TA assigns user v_i with pseudo-identity pid_i with a secret key $psk_i = Q_i^\beta = H(pid_i)^\beta$.

TOKEN GENERATION—If user v_j has provided enough evidence in the past time slot $t-1$, the TA assigns v_j with a token $tk_t = H(t)^\beta$ for time slot t.

SIGNENCRYPTION—After user v_i verifies a group of original signatures, it computes the following signing and encryption on the message m which denotes the group of corresponding indices. User v_i chooses a random number $r_s, r_e \in \mathbb{Z}_q$, generates an integrated signature $s_{i,c} = (s_1, s_2) = (g^{r_s}, psk_i \cdot H(m)^{r_s})$ and outputs a ciphertext $C = \{(m||s_{i,c}) \oplus H_1(e(g_{pub}^{r_e}, H(t))), g^{r_e}\}$.

DECRYPTION-AND-VERIFICATION—If user v_j has already obtained the token tk_t, it performs the decryption to obtain the integrated signature $s_{i,c}$ by $m||s_{i,c} = C \oplus H_1(e(g^{r_e}, tk_t))$, and then verifies the group of indices m by checking if $e(s_2, g) = e(H(pid_i), g_{pub}) \cdot e(H(m), s_1)$.

We design the evidence–token scheme based on the IBSC scheme such that any user without a valid token is unable to obtain the integrated signature. The IBSC scheme can effectively control the verification capability, but it still cannot resist free-riding attacks. For example, if a malicious user directly generates an integrated signature by using others' cooperation efforts, but it does not check the original signatures at all, other users are unable to detect this malicious behavior. In the following section, we require each user to additionally output an authentication proof to show their individual authentication efforts.

7.4.2 Authentication Proof

In Section 7.4.1, we introduced an approach to enable the offline TA to coordinate cooperation among users via RSUs. The TA balances the contributions from and rewards toward individual users so that cooperation is largely stimulated and users are treated fairly. However, the approach cannot resist free-riding attacks. Users are unable to distinguish fake authentication effort from a real one, and the TA still rewards the attackers with valid tokens. In this section, we consider the free-riding attacks with fake authentication efforts (or active free-riding attack). The attackers make use of other users' authentication efforts and refuse to contribute in the cooperation.

Specifically, consider a selfish user u_i who receives the cooperative authentication efforts $e_{j_1}, e_{j_2}, \ldots, e_{j_k}$ from multiple users $u_{j_1}, u_{j_2}, \ldots, u_{j_k}$, where e_{j_x} corresponds to a group of indices S_{j_x} that from u_{j_x}. By using IBSC scheme, if e_{j_x} contains any incorrect information, user u_{j_x} can be easily tracked. On the basis of this observation, user u_i assumes that the cooperation efforts from other users are valid, and thus selects a subset group of indexes $S_i \subseteq \bigcup_{x=1}^k S_{j_x}$, and generates a signature on the index set of S_i as its cooperative authentication effort e_i. In cases where all the signatures in S_i are good, such selfish behavior cannot be detected by other users. As such, the attack succeeds since user u_i does not check any original signature in S_i but obtains the maximum profits. We regard this as a free-riding attack with fake authentication efforts (or an active free-riding attack).

It is obvious that such selfish behavior of u_i is unfair to other participating users. A direct solution is to require users to output the cooperative authentication efforts at the same time. However, this time synchronization is extremely difficult in a distributed wireless communication scenario. In the following paragraphs, we will propose a novel authentication scheme that can effectively resist the selfish behavior mentioned above. For each message, a signature is attached. We adopt the Schnorr signature [5].

SETUP—Similar to the SETUP algorithm of IBSC, the TA $(G, G_T, e, q, g, g_{pub}, H)$. The TA additionally chooses a generator h of group G and calculates $h_{pub} = h^s$. It chooses $x \in \mathbb{Z}_q$, and generates $y = g^x$. (x, y) will be the private–public key pair for a user. The user also obtains the certificate $Cert_y$ on y.

We adopt the Schnorr signature [5]. Consider messages $m_1, m_2, \ldots, m_k$ attached with signatures $s_1, s_2, \ldots, s_k$, where $s_i = (\sigma_i, e_i, Q_i)$, $\sigma_i = r_i - xe_i$, $R_i = g^{r_i}$, $Q_i = g_{pub}^{r_i}$, and $e_i = H(m_i || R_i || Q_i)$.

Users cooperatively authenticate these k signatures. In each verification, a user will (1) calculate $R'_i = g^{\sigma_i} y^{e_i}$, and (2) determine whether $e_i \overset{?}{=} H(m_i || R'_i || Q_i)$. It is obvious that step 1 involves two exponential operations while step 2 takes one equality check.

Consider that a user u_i decides to make cooperative authentication efforts on messages m_x for $x \in \mathcal{I}$. u_i currently uses a pseudonym pid_i, and it has the secret key $psk'_i = H(pid_i)^{1/s}$. In order to persuade others that it does check the signature, u_i outputs a proof $F_i = (F_{i,1}, F_{i,2}) = (h^\alpha, (\prod_{x \in \mathcal{I}} R'_x)^\alpha \cdot psk'_i)$, where $\alpha \in \mathbb{Z}_p$ is chosen randomly. The proof will be embedded in the message (previously containing the indices of signatures only) of the integrated signature. Note that the authentication proof F_i does not include the index of signatures, and the verifier must use integrated signature to check the group of corresponding indices.

With the proof F_i, every other user is able to check whether u_i has checked the signatures by the following equation:

$$e(F_{i,2}, h_{pub}) = e\left(\left(\prod_{x \in \mathcal{I}} R'_x\right)^\alpha \cdot psk'_i, h_{pub}\right)$$

$$\overset{?}{=} e\left(\prod_{x \in \mathcal{I}} Q_x, F_{i,1}\right) e(H(pid_i), h)$$

Note that F_i is generated by using psk'_i and cannot be reused by other users. In order to provide a proof F_i, two exponential operations for each signature must be performed by the user itself. Then, user v_i has to consume the individual efforts to prove its cooperation efforts. Note that, since F_i does not disclose any index information, a user without a valid token is unable to get the correct index information. Thus, the verification capability is effectively controlled by the TA and the free-riding attack with fake authentication efforts (or active free-riding attack) can be effectively resisted.

7.4.3 Flows of Proposed Scheme

Consider some geographically close users with a common set of message–signature pairs. We summarize the secure cooperative authentication scheme as follows. As shown in Fig. 7.5, each user randomly picks and verifies $v_{x,y}$ original signatures, and generates

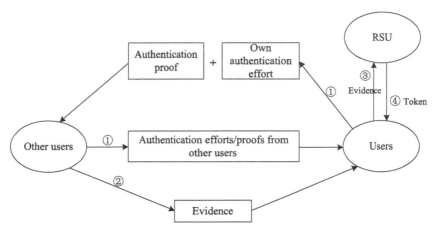

Figure 7.5. Flowchart of the secure cooperative authentication scheme.

an integrated signature as its own authentication effort. The value of $v_{x,y}$ can be calculated according to Section 7.3. In addition, the user also generates an authentication proof, which proves that it indeed verified the original signatures. After that, it shares its authentication proof with the public. Whenever a user is able to communicate with an RSU, it sends the authentication proof as evidence of others to the RSU. The RSU then checks the validity of the evidence and rewards the user with new token that can be used to verify the cooperative authentication efforts in the subsequent time slots.

7.5 SECURITY ANALYSIS

In this section, we analyze the security properties of our proposed scheme following the predefined security model. We will show how the scheme can effectively resist linkability and free-riding attacks.

7.5.1 Linkability Attack

In this attack, the attacker generates integrated signatures and disables the TA to trace the signatures to its identity. Because generating an integrated signature requires the attacker to input a pseudonym secret key psk_i, the generated signature is linked to the corresponding pseudonym. The TA records the mapping from pseudonyms to identities and is therefore able to recover the identity of the attacker. Hence, linkability attack is successfully prevented.

7.5.2 Free-Riding Attack without Authentication Efforts

In this attack, the attacker does not verify any original signature but obtains the authentication efforts from other cooperative users. In the basic cooperative authentication scheme (Section 7.3), we do not adopt any security mechanism to overcome this attack.

An evidence–token mechanism was then devised in Section 7.4.1 to deal with it. After sharing its authentication effort with nearby users, a user obtains an unforgeable evidence from a random neighbor. It then trades the evidence with the TA for new tokens. Only with the new tokens, it may enjoy the authentication efforts from nearby users in the following time slots. If the user does not cooperate at all, it will obtain no token and be unable to benefit from other users' authentication efforts. Hence, free-riding attack without authentication efforts (or passive free-riding attack) is resisted. We will demonstrate the effectiveness of the evidence–token mechanism through simulations in the next section.

7.5.3 Free-Riding Attack with Fake Authentication Efforts

In this attack, the attacker pretends to contribute to cooperative authentication by incorporating nearby users' authentication efforts into its own integrated signature. For example, two users generate two integrated signatures corresponding to index sets $\{1,2,3\}$ and $\{4,5,6\}$. The attacker may generate an integrated signature with index set $\{2,3,5\}$. We presented a defense mechanism in Section 7.4.2 by requiring users to output an authentication proof. The authentication proof is an evidence of the verification on original signatures. Recall that the original signature consists of three elements (σ_i, R_i, Q_i). The verification includes two steps: one is to calculate $R'_i = g^{\sigma_i} y^{e_i}$; and the other one is to check the equality $e_i \overset{?}{=} H(m_i||R'_i||Q_i)$. The main computational overhead of the verification comes from the two exponential operations. The authentication proof of user u_i is $F_i = (F_{i,1}, F_{i,2}) = (h^\alpha, (\prod_{x \in \mathcal{I}} R'_x)^\alpha \cdot psk'_i)$. If u_i outputs F_i, it must execute all the exponential operations for $(m_x, s_x)_{x \in \mathcal{I}}$. In addition, since the generation of F_i involves the pseudonym secret key psk'_i, the authentication proofs of different users must be processed independently. Therefore, the user cannot save its computational costs by generating fake authentication efforts. Free-riding attack with fake authentication efforts (or active free-riding attack) is effectively resisted.

7.6 PERFORMANCE EVALUATION

In order to present insight into the performance of the proposed secure cooperative authentication scheme, we have conducted a set of custom simulations using a Java simulator. In the following, we detail our simulation settings and present the simulation results.

7.6.1 Simulation Settings

We consider a relatively small and typical VANET, where $\mu = (20, 40, \dots, 200)$ vehicle users equipped with OBUs are uniformly deployed in a 10000 m $\times$ 10000 m area. The wireless transmission range of each OBU is 300 m. A set of 10 social spots indexed from 1 to 10, denoted as S_u, are randomly deployed into the area. At each of the four randomly selected social spots $4, 6, 8, 10$, a storage-rich RSU device with transmission radius of 1000 m is deployed, which helps users contact with the TA. Each vehicle user has a fixed social spot set $S_i \subset S_u$, where $6 \leq |S_i| \leq 10$. It randomly chooses a social

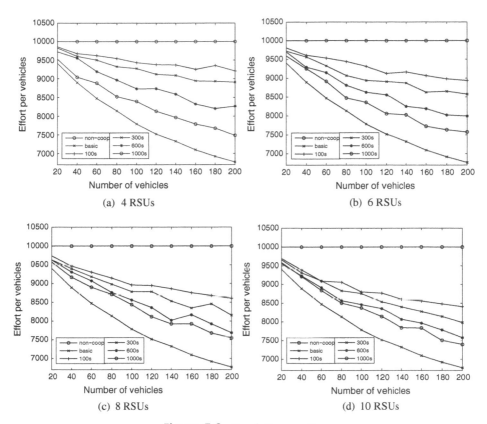

Figure 7.6. Simulation results.

spot from this set, and arrives there along the shortest path at the average velocity 10 m/s. After arriving at the social spot, it stays at most 5 minutes and then moves to another randomly chosen spot from its social spot set.

The simulation lasts 10000 seconds. For every 100 seconds, each user needs to authenticate 100 common messages using the noncooperative scheme, where users individually do the authentication, or our proposed cooperative scheme, where they cooperatively authenticate the signatures. These messages and the corresponding signatures can be obtained via V2V/V2I communications or 3G/cellular networks. The simulation parameters include the number of users (20, ... , 200), the number of RSUs (4, 6, 8, 10), and token lifetime (100, 300, 600, 1000) seconds. Using 100 simulation runs for each case, we obtain the average results of accumulated effort of $f(\rho)$ (defined in Section 7.3) over 10, 000 seconds. We plot the results in Fig. 7.6.

7.6.2 Simulation Results

Figure 7.6 shows the simulation results for three settings. The black line indicates the performance of the noncooperative authentication scheme. It can be seen that the average total efforts of the users over $10,000$ seconds is $10,000$. This is because each user has to do 100 message authentications every 100 seconds and $100 \times (10,000/100) = 10,000$ message authentications in total. The blue line shows the performance of the cooperative authentication scheme without selfish behavior. The users can obtain maximum cooperative gain since all of them behave according to the optimal approaches. The authentication effort made by users significantly decreases as the number of users increases.

The red lines impliy the performance of the cooperative authentication scheme with selfish concerns. In order to prevent selfish users from launching free-riding attacks, the TA adopts the proposed evidence–token mechanism to control the cooperation capability of users. It can be seen that by reducing the value of nt_i and the cooperation period decreases from 1000 s to 100 s in the 200-user setting, the authentication efforts per user increase by 1721, i.e., from 7485 to 9206. From Fig. 7.2, we observe that a user has to make effort 38 for the 100 message–signature pairs and 20-user cooperation setting. In this case, the maximal gain obtained by a selfish user v_i for a single valid period of 1000 seconds is $38 \times (1000/100) = 380 < 1383$. Therefore, the TA can set an nt_i to an appropriate value and adjust the token lifetime among 1000 s, 600 s, 300 s, and 100 s for user v_i. By doing so, the gain obtained by v_i can be reduced to 0 or a negative value, and its authentication effort is no less than that of other cooperative users. Thus, the proposed scheme overcomes the users' incentive to defect and effectively resists free-riding attack.

By comparing parts (a)–(d) in Fig. 7.6, it can be seen that when the number of RSUs is small, the difference in required efforts decreases. For example, in the case of 200 users and 100-second token lifetime, the required authentication effort in the 4-RSU setting is much larger than that in the 10-RSU setting. The main reason is that users have less probability to contact with RSUs in the former case. This indicates that users with 100-second-lifetime tokens may have less cooperations on authentication since they cannot update their tokens in time. Therefore, the determination of token lifetime should depend on not only the selfish behavior of users but also the number of users and the number of RSUs. The scheme must ensure that the reduction of token lifetime as punishment leads to the reduction of gain in cooperative authentication.

7.7 CONCLUDING REMARKS

In this chapter, we have presented a novel cooperative message authentication scheme for VANETs. By the proposed scheme, vehicle users can cooperatively authenticate a bunch of message–signature pairs without direct involvement of a trusted authority (TA). In addition, the free-riding attacks without authentication efforts (or passive free-riding attack) launched by selfish vehicle users can also be effectively resisted through an evidence–token approach; the free-riding attacks with fake authentication efforts (or active free-riding attack) can be prevented by enforcing vehicle users to output their authentication proofs. The TA strategically adjusts the valid period (lifetime) of tokens for each vehicle user based on the collected evidence, thereby controlling vehicle users' cooperation capabilities periodically. The simulation results confirm that the proposed scheme can significantly reduce the computational overhead on vehicle users for authenticating signatures and enable the TA to flexibly balance the advantages that a vehicle user takes from others and the efforts it offers to others during cooperative authentication.

REFERENCES

1. X. Lin and X. Li, "Achieving efficient cooperative message authentication in vehicular ad hoc networks," *IEEE Transactions on Vehicular Technology*, vol. 62, no. 7, pp. 3339–3348, 2013. (Available online at http://dx.doi.org/10.1109/TVT.2013.2257188.)

2. J. Freudiger, M. H. Manshaei, J.-P. Hubaux, and D. C. Parkes, "On non-cooperative location privacy: A game-theoretic analysis," *Proc. 16th ACM Conference on Computer and Communications Security*. ACM, 2009, pp. 324–337.

3. D. Boneh and M. K. Franklin, "Identity-based encryption from the weil pairing," *Proc. Advances in Cryptology—CRYPTO 2001, 21st Annual International Cryptology Conference*, Santa Barbara, CA, Aug. 19–23, 2001, ser. Lecture Notes in Computer Science, vol. 2139. Springer, 2001, pp. 213–229.

4. P. S. L. M. Barreto, B. Libert, N. McCullagh, and J.-J. Quisquater, "Efficient and provably-secure identity-based signatures and signcryption from bilinear maps," *Proc. ASIACRYPT*, 2005, pp. 515–532.

5. C. Schnorr, "Efficient identification and signatures for smart cards," *Proc. Advances in Cryptology—CRYPTO '89, 9th Annual International Cryptology Conference*, Santa Barbara, CA, Aug. 20–24, 1989, pp. 239–252. (Available online at http://dx.doi.org/10.1007/0-387-34805-0_22.)

8

CONTEXT-AWARE COOPERATIVE AUTHENTICATION

8.1 INTRODUCTION

Road emergencies are very common across the globe; this is due to a number of reasons, such as bad road condition, inappropriate vehicle design, improper roadway design, poor driving skill and/or impairment, and unhealthy driving habits (i.e. ignore traffic signs, speeding, etc.). Thus, it is very common to witness many more road accidents and injuries after major storms, as a driver's visibility decreases in these environments. What makes the situation much worse is the added danger caused by multi-vehicle collisions; these incidents quickly become worse when other approaching motorists are unable to stop in time, since they are unable to anticipate the dangerous situation in front of them. A perfect example of exactly what happens when all the wrong conditions are gathered is shown in Ref. 1. In Pennsylvania, a 50-car pileup occurred as a result of a winter storm and freezing rain. The road became slippery and visibility was very poor. Many drivers spun out of control because of the weather, and were unable to avoid a collision when approaching the car accident scene.

Severe accidents can result in financial loss, physical disability, and even death. However, if drivers are warned about approaching danger ahead of time via an alarm or a warning message, this would give the drivers enough time to react appropriately to the

Vehicular Ad Hoc Network Security and Privacy, First Edition. Xiaodong Lin and Rongxing Lu.

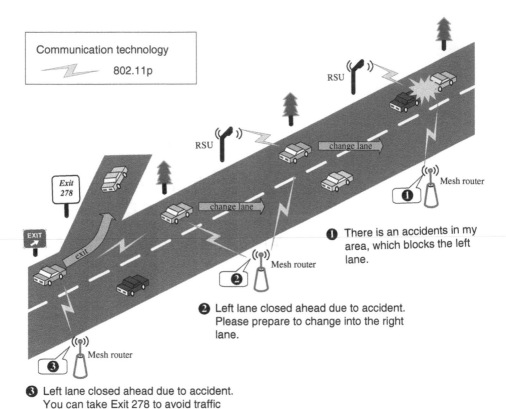

Figure 8.1. Example of a road emergency response operation using a VANET.

situation. Traffic collisions would be reduced as a result. There are many approaches out there that can prevent car accidents, and vehicular ad hoc network (VANET) technology has been envisioned as an excellent solution for improving road safety, through the use of a variety of vehicle applications enabled by communication between vehicles.

An example of such a scheme is shown in Fig. 8.1. An accident has occurred and blocks the left lane; a roadside unit (RSU) detects this, then relays the information to the other cars. Drivers that are close to the accident will be notified that the left lane is closed. Those that are further ahead will be instructed to exit the road early if possible, to reduce the growing volume of stopped vehicles in the area. As a result, emergency crews will also be able to reach the accident site faster and prevent further pileups from happening, since drivers are able to divert away from the accident site even before being able to see it.

While it is encouraging to see that VANET technologies improve road safety via vehicle-to-vehicle (V2V) and vehicle-to-infrastructure (V2I) data transmission, it is unfortunate that such a useful system can be easily abused if implemented without the

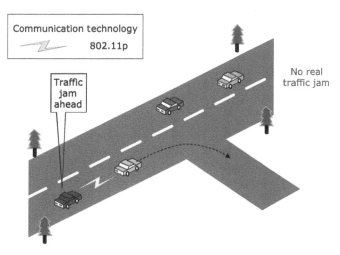

Figure 8.2. Bogus traffic information.

appropriate security measures. For example, emergency messages can be modified by a malicious driver—someone who wants fewer cars in the way, for example. It would be quite easy for such a driver to report false information, like claiming that there is a traffic jam ahead when, in reality, there is no traffic jam at all, and people unnecessarily leave the road as a result. This is demonstrated in Fig. 8.2.

As a result of these bogus messages, drivers may be less inclined to believe in emergency messages, and there has already been documented evidence of the occurrence of this type of behavior. Providing a true warning is critical for the general public's safety, and recently increasing moose–vehicle collisions in Newfoundland highlight the importance of trustworthiness of emergency messages [2]. The "false driver comfort" phenomenon is exactly what happened in Newfoundland, Canada, when a moose detection system was deployed on their roads. A light mounted on the moose detection system would blink to notify the driver that there is a moose wandering on the road; however, the computerized detection system failed to truthfully warn the driver, as it had a high false reporting rate (FPR). As a result, drivers gain a false sense of safety and approach the area at high speed thinking that there was no moose wandering around. Since the implementation of the moose detection system, there has actually been an increase in moose–vehicle collisions. To enable proper driver response, emergency messages must be trustworthy and protected. In this chapter, we will focus in particular on the trustworthiness of emergency messages in VANETs.

The remainder of the chapter is organized as follows. In Section 8.2, we discuss message trustworthiness issues in VANETs. In Section 8.3, we present the system model, attack model, and the design goals. Section 8.4 gives a review on some preliminary background. In Section 8.5, the proposed AEMAT scheme is presented in detail. Security analysis and performance analysis are given in Section 8.6 and Section 8.7, respectively. Finally, the chapter concludes with Section 8.8.

8.2   MESSAGE TRUSTWORTHINESS IN VANETS

Many trusted security mechanisms and protocols have been developed to protect messages over VANETs, and to ensure the integrity and origin of messages (also referred to as *message authentication* or *data origin authentication*). As for message authentication, if a message hasn't been modified during its transmission between the two parties (e.g., sender and receiver) and the receivers can be assured that the message indeed originated from the sender that the message claims to be from, then it is assumed that the message is authentic. Sadly, this way of thinking is flawed. Let's take the bogus traffic information scenario in Fig. 8.2 as our example. This problem stems from the fact that there is no way to guarantee that the individual (e.g., sender) is telling the truth; if it occurs in a VANET scenario, the consequences could be very costly, or even fatal.

While bogus emergency messages from external attackers can be filtered out easily with existing security mechanisms, protecting against internal attacks is more challenging. Nowadays, it is not unusual to witness some people drive aggressively; as a result, it is no surprise that legitimate users could become malicious, broadcasting fake emergency messages for their own advantage (for example, creating better driving conditions by telling other drivers to avoid a traffic jam that, in reality, doesn't exist). The properties of traceability and conditional privacy become important; with these factors built into the messages, the real identity of the abuser can be revealed when the emergency is proved to be fake. It will certainly curb these offenses to a certain extent, but the reality is, the problem will not disappear entirely. Law enforcement has put a lot of effort toward stopping aggressive driving through various campaigns, such as "stop aggressive driving," yet we still witness many aggressive drivers on the road, and it is partially because penalties for aggressive driving are not severe enough for certain offenders (a $500 fine, for example, does not impact an aggressive driver who also happens to be very rich). The same thing will certainly happen to fake emergency message offenders. More significantly, *a posteriori* countermeasures such as these are not acceptable for offenses against vehicular safety applications, especially when the nature of the emergency is life-threatening; it will be too late for these punishments to have a significant effect, since the damage has already been caused [3]. Also, in such a highly dynamic network environment, with a large number of potential vehicle nodes, conventional security mechanisms, such as public key certificate and digital signature, are not sufficient. Adversaries can still launch the attack by compromising one or several nodes, and then disseminating false emergency messages with the credentials of the other users. As a result, trustworthiness becomes another important property for emergency messages broadcast by vehicle safety applications. Trustworthiness represents the degree of confidence that recipients place in the emergency messages, so that recipients can make proper decisions to avoid potential damage; without this property, drivers are more likely to become victims of aggressive or ill-intended drivers.

In most cases, a VANET performs message propagation via multihop transmission, particularly in suburban areas where fewer RSUs are installed. Therefore, efficient dissemination of emergency messages to the vehicles in a specific area becomes very crucial. The fast propagation of emergency and local warning messages to approaching vehicles will be helpful in preventing secondary accidents. Many previously reported

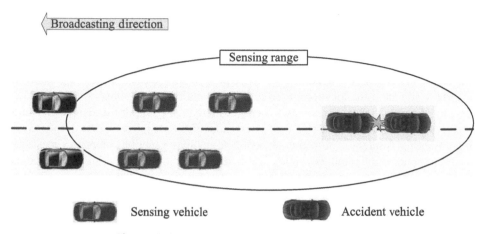

Figure 8.3. Emergency event sensing in VANETs.

studies have focused on data dissemination in VANETs [4, 5]. However, the security issues, especially regarding how to ensure the authenticity and trustworthiness of emergency messages in a VANET, are still subject to great challenges. First, since most of the life-critical applications in VANETs rely on multihop transmission to disseminate data packets to the surrounding geographic area, adversaries may intentionally modify (or even forge) an invalid emergency event, which may pose a serious threat to road safety. Second, in such a highly dynamic network environment with potential vehicle nodes, the conventional security mechanisms, such as public key certificate and digital signature, are not sufficient to ensure the security of VANETs since the adversaries can still launch the attack by compromising one or several nodes and disseminate false emergency messages with the credentials of the other users. On the other hand, for any given emergency event, it is expected that multiple sensing vehicles would be able to detect the common event. As shown in Fig. 8.3, the sensing vehicles include not only the current witness vehicles (the yellow vehicles) but also potential witness vehicles (the white vehicles), which are approaching the emergency event promptly. As a result, they can work together collaboratively to prove that an emergency is indeed happening.

It is worth noting that sensing an emergency can be done either manually or automatically. Sensors in cars today can detect car accidents automatically, alerting anyone who is approaching the scenes. Taking advantage of the common view of these sensing vehicles allows cross-validation of the emergency messages, and could possibly serve as a promising approach to enhance the overall security level in VANETs, these methods have been employed successfully in other fields, such as rating the trustworthiness of web pages. Such a method of cross-checking the emergency event by collecting the feedback of witnesses is defined as a voting mechanism, which was originally used to detect the misbehaving nodes in a distributed ad hoc network, without any centralized security authority [6]. The mechanism can be migrated to VANETs to enhance the overall security of emergency event authentication [7, 8]. This type of approach is also known collectively as *a priori countermeasures*. Raya et al. [7] implemented a voting scheme on location-based groups, where vehicles are grouped according to their location. Within each group, a group leader will be elected to take the responsibility of collecting more than a threshold of k proofs from k distinct witnesses to prove the validity of an emergency event. However, such a group-based voting mechanism certainly faces the challenge of a highly dynamic network topology in VANETs, which requires extra efforts to maintain the location-based groups. In addition, in an area with low vehicle density, the group leader cannot always collect more than k supporting signatures within the group. Ostermaier et al. [8], further extended the concept of voting to the "destination voting" strategy. The witnesses will continuously generate emergency messages and send them to the remote vehicles, who will then decide, by checking, whether most of these messages are consistent. Existing voting mechanisms depend on a predefined threshold, but it may not be feasible to collect more than k supporting signatures under certain circumstances. Daza et al. [3] proposed a flexible threshold authentication protocol such that a vehicle can verify the trustworthiness of a received message. This is done by determining whether a received message has been endorsed by at least t vehicles; the threshold t can dynamically change, according to the surrounding context (e.g., it will be higher if there are 100 cars around instead of 10).

Nevertheless, existing voting mechanisms treat all voters equally, and don't work well if directly applied in VANETs, since they don't take the different levels of credibility of emergency event witnesses into consideration. In reality, there are many types of vehicles on the road. For example, a warning from emergency vehicles (fire truck, ambulance, police car) is much more trustworthy than any other vehicles, and should automatically be trusted by the public. This must be taken into consideration when implementing the system.

Furthermore, the voting mechanism can effectively improve the security of VANETs, at the expense of increased computation and transmission overhead. For both approaches in Ref. 7 and 8, only distinct messages from distinct vehicles are considered, to prevent the attackers from sending duplicate emergency messages; that is, if messages are not confirmed to be from the vehicle they claim to be sent from (possibly spoofed), they are not considered trustworthy. To accommodate this requirement, every emergency message will be signed by the sender in order for the receivers to authenticate; unfortunately, this creates another problem. The size of digital signatures is typically very large, in order of tens (using elliptic curve cryptography) to hundreds (RSA) of bytes, which will still incur more transmission overhead.

Generating and verifying a digital signature and its corresponding certificate will also incur additional computational costs. Such costs will be scaled up even further with the number of active sensor vehicles, as each additional vehicle creates, signs, and sends an additional emergency message. When all these vehicles transmit the information by way of flooding or geocasting, the transmission and computation overhead can easily overload the entire network. To combat this problem, aggregating the relevant emergency messages is of high importance, as well as providing message authentication, but these processes must also maintain the guarantee of message trustworthiness.

In this chapter, we study context-aware ways to protect some specific types of messages in VANETs while considering their unique requirements. The concept of "awareness in context" would consider situational information [such as type of message, credibility of emergency event sources, emergency event witness validation, geolocation, affected physical area(s), roadway maintenance history, message broadcasting direction, and other potential factors]. This information would be further used to establish credibility for message sources; each of the contextual factors mentioned here can serve as a trustworthiness cue [9, 10], and multiple trustworthiness cues can be aggregated into a trustworthiness coefficient. For example, as weather starts to warm up (weather conditions) in winter (season information) along with constant rain fall (weather conditions), it is very easy for weak roads (roadway maintenance history) to develop potholes (road emergency); understanding this information, a "pothole ahead" warning during certain seasons in some areas is more trustworthy than that in other scenarios. A context-aware approach would enable these different scenarios to be handled differently, and more appropriately. In particular, we are focusing on one specific type of message (i.e., emergency message), and propose a novel aggregated emergency message authentication and trustworthiness (AEMAT) scheme to efficiently validate the emergency messages in VANETs [11]. It not only meets the unique requirements of the emergency messages but also minimizes costs of computation and communication by using aggregation and batch verification techniques. To summarize, during the emergency message opportunistic data forwarding process, a vehicle can hold multiple messages, which can be aggregated into a single one before the vehicle sends any data. The proposed AEMAT scheme takes advantage of syntactic and cryptographic aggregation techniques to reduce the transmission cost, and adopts a batch verification technique to reduce the computation cost [12]. Also, we aggregate multiple trustworthiness cues to provide drivers with robust and reliable ways to evaluate the trustworthiness of emergency messages they received, so as to enhance their decisionmaking. We will demonstrate that the proposed scheme can dramatically reduce both computation and transmission overhead in achieving efficient and effective authentication of emergency messages.

8.3 SYSTEM MODEL AND DESIGN GOAL

This section describes our system model, attack model and design goals.

8.3.1 Network Model

We consider IVC in a VANET without any presence of fixed infrastructure (such as access points, RSUs, and satellite communication) for assisting data propagation. There are two types of entities in AEMAT, namely, the *offline security manager* (OSM) and the vehicles. Before joining the network, every vehicle should register to the OSM and obtain its corresponding public key certificate. We assume that an opportunistic data forwarding mechanism is adopted [4, 5], in order to achieve the globally routing objective.

8.3.2 Attack Model

In this study, we consider mainly *false data injection attacks*, where the attacker tries to make the receiving vehicles accept false emergency reports. To maximize the effectiveness of the attacks, multiple adversaries could collude to launch an attack by cooperatively injecting false messages, which is also known as a *collusion attack*; doing so increases the trustworthiness coefficient of the offending messages. Similar to other distributed trust mechanisms, the number of adversaries in the system during a given time period; e.g., the public key revocation period, is less than a threshold denoted as k. Therefore, unless explicitly specified, an emergency event can be considered to be true at the receiver if and only if more than k signatures from k distinct witnesses are collected. For simplicity, we assume that each vehicle reports the same emergency only once and outputs one signature on the emergency.

8.3.3 Design Goals

The proposed AEMAT scheme has the following security and efficiency design goals:

- *Collusion Freedom*. No subset of k or less vehicles can forge an emergency event.
- *Efficient Authentication*. The proposed emergency message authentication and trustworthiness scheme should be performed in an efficient way to reduce the communication and transmission overhead.
- *Reliable Trustworthiness Evaluation*. The proposed emergency message authentication and trustworthiness scheme should provide drivers with robust and reliable ways to evaluate the trustworthiness of emergency messages they received even under the existence of both external and internal attackers.
- *Generality*. The proposed scheme should be applicable in different network densities, including both networks of high density, and those of low density.

8.4 PRELIMINARIES

8.4.1 Pairing Technique

The proposed AEMAT scheme is based on bilinear pairing, which is briefly introduced below. Let $\mathbb{G}$ be a cyclic additive group and $\mathbb{G}_T$ be a cyclic multiplicative group of the same prime order q, i.e., $|\mathbb{G}| = |\mathbb{G}_T| = q$. Let g be a generator of $\mathbb{G}$ and $e : \mathbb{G} \times \mathbb{G} \rightarrow \mathbb{G}_T$ be an efficient admissible bilinear map with the following properties:

- Bilinear: for $a, b \in \mathbb{Z}_q^*$, $e(g^a, g^b) = e(g, g)^{ab}$.
- Nondegenerate: $e(g, g) \neq 1$.

8.4.2 Aggregate Signature and Batch Verification

The major computational cost for authenticating an emergency message comes from verifying a set of supporting signatures issued by different emergency witnesses. The corresponding public key certificates of the signers also need to be verified together. All of them will incur a significant transmission and verification cost. In this study, we take advantage of aggregate signatures to reduce the transmission cost of supporting signatures and certificates, as well as batch verification to realize efficient signature verification.

An aggregate signature is a digital signature that supports aggregation of n distinct signatures issued by n distinct signers to form a single short signature [13]. This single signature (and the n original messages) will convince the verifier that the n signers indeed sign the n original messages. In addition to enjoying the benefit of the reduced transmission size, the aggregate signature technique supports batch verification, which enables the receivers to quickly verify a set of digital signatures on different messages by different signers. Because the techniques are used in conjunction, the signatures being batch-verified are aggregate signatures, so the compounded benefits are significant. In this study, we adopt the aggregate signature and batch verification due to Camenisch et al. [12] as our basic cryptographic aggregation technique to improve the aggregation performance.

8.5 PROPOSED AEMAT SCHEME

We present the details of the six procedures of our AEMAT protocol.

8.5.1 System Setup

The OSM generates a tuple $(q, g, \mathbb{G}, \mathbb{G}_T, e)$ as the system parameters. The OSM selects a random $sk \in \mathbb{Z}_q^*$ as its secret key and generates its public key $pk = g^{sk}$, by which four hash functions are formed: $H : \{0, 1\}^* \rightarrow \mathbb{G}$, $H_1 : \{0, 1\}^* \rightarrow \mathbb{G}$, $H_2 : \{0, 1\}^* \rightarrow \mathbb{G}$, $H_3 : \{0, 1\}^* \rightarrow \mathbb{Z}_q$. The group public key and secret keys are $(q, g, \mathbb{G}_1, \mathbb{G}_T, e, pk, H, H_1, H_2, H_3)$ and sk, respectively.

An important task of the setup procedure is to determine the format of emergency report message. In our study, the format of a secure emergency report (SER) is defined as follows. For an emergency event $\mathcal{E}_i$, the sensor vehicle $\mathcal{V}_j$ will generate a SER_j^i:

$$SER_j^i = \left(Type_i, Loc_i, ID^j, Time_j^i, Sig_j^i, Cert_j \right) \tag{8.1}$$

where

$Type_i$ = type of emergency event reported in this report
Loc_i = place where emergency event takes place
ID_j = identity of vehicle that generates the claim
$Time_j^i$ = time when vehicle j makes claim on this emergency event i
Sig_j^i = supporting signature generated by vehicle j on emergency event i
$Cert_j$ = certificate held by vehicle j

For a specific event $\mathcal{E}_i$, it is reasonable to assume that the relevant SERs will share the same $Type_i, Loc_i$.

8.5.2 Registration

A vehicle can join the network by performing the following steps:

1. *Public Key Generation.* A vehicle can randomly choose $x_j \in \mathbb{Z}_q^*$ as its secret key and generate its public key $X_j = g^{x_j}$. To keep the identity privacy, the vehicle can also randomly choose $\mathcal{V}_j$ as its pseudonym. Before joining the VANET, $\mathcal{V}_j$ will contact the OSM to obtain its corresponding certificate.

2. *Public Key Certificates Issuing.* After ensuring the legitimacy of this vehicle, the OSM will issue its public key certificate by signing its signature on $(\mathcal{V}_j, X_j)$. Here, the certificate generation process follows a typical Boneh–Lynn–Shacham signature scheme [13]. The OSM computes $h_j \leftarrow H(\mathcal{V}_j || X_j)$ and $\sigma_j \leftarrow h_j^{x_j}$. $Cert_j = (\mathcal{V}_j, X_j, \sigma_j)$ is the public key certificate of $\mathcal{V}_j$.

3. *Certificate Verification.* Given a vehicle's public key certificate $Cert_j$, $h_j \leftarrow H(\mathcal{V}_j || X_j)$ can be computed, and it is accepted if $e(\sigma_j, g) = e(h_j, pk)$.

8.5.3 SER Generation and Broadcasting

Once an emergency event $\mathcal{E}_i$ is sensed by one or multiple vehicles and the observation is $(Type_i, Loc_i, Time_j^i)$, the sensing vehicles $\mathcal{V}_j, j = 1, 2, \ldots$ may independently generate their SERs as follows:

1. *SER Generation.* Given the type and observation time of the emergency message $TL_i = Type_i || Time_j^i$ as well as the location information $\ell_i = Loc_i$, a witness vehicle with its public and private key pairs (X_j, x_j) can compute $w_i \leftarrow H_3(TL_i || \ell_i)$, $a \leftarrow H_1(\ell_i)$, $b \leftarrow H_2(\ell_i)$ and generate the signature $Sig_j^i = a^{x_j} b^{x_j w_i}$. Thus, $(Type_i, Loc_i, \mathcal{V}_j, Time_j^i, Sig_j^i, Cert_j)$ constitutes a SER claim generated by vehicle j toward event i. After that, $\mathcal{V}_j$ will broadcast this SER_j^i to its neighbors.

2. *SER Verification.* A single SER verification can be performed as follows: given $SER_j^i = (Type_i, Loc_i, \mathcal{V}_j, Time_j^i, Sig_j^i, Cert_j)$, the verifier will first check the validity of certificate included in this SER. After that, it can check the validity of supporting signature by computing $w_i \leftarrow H_3(TL_i || \ell_i)$, $a \leftarrow H_1(\ell_i)$, $b \leftarrow H_2(\ell_i)$. It is accepted if $Sig_j^i = a^{x_j} b^{x_j w_i}$.

8.5.4 SER Opportunistic Forwarding

In VANETs, the network topology could be very dynamic and diversified in shape from time to time, sometimes even sparse, and frequently partitioned. Communication between vehicles is expected to be performed in an opportunistic manner, where nodes carry packets when routes do not exist, and forward the packets to the new receiver that moves into its vicinity [4]. To enable opportunistic data propagation, vehicles that are within a range r and maintain connectivity for a minimum time t with each other, can be arranged to form a cluster. The detailed discussion on cluster creation and maintenance can be found in Ref. 4. We refer to the node at the head of every cluster as the *header* which, in a typical opportunistic data-forwarding algorithm [4, 5], is responsible for forwarding the data to the next cluster. The messages will be buffered at the header until they are forwarded to the next cluster; this is also referred to as the *carry and forward* strategy. In this study, it is considered that the header can also play the role of emergency message aggregator because of the following two reasons:

1. If taking the header of a cluster as the aggregator, the aggregation process will be merged into a part of the data forwarding process; therefore, there is no need to elect an additional cluster head to perform the data aggregation operations.
2. The process of message propagation between two clusters is referred to as a *catchup process*, where a message traverses along with its carrying vehicles until it is within the radio range of the vehicle at the end of another cluster. This obviously presents a considerable propagation interval, depending on the relative speeds of vehicles, and the gap between clusters. Therefore, we can use such an interval to aggregate the related emergency messages and minimize the aggregation latency.

In the following sections, a cluster head will be taken as the aggregator, who will perform the following SER aggregated authentication algorithm.

8.5.5 SER Aggregated Authentication

For any specific emergency event $\mathcal{E}_i$, each aggregator maintains two local message lists, which keep the forwarded SERs and ReadytoForward SERs, respectively. The forwarded message list, denoted as $\mathcal{F}$, contains all the SERs that have been forwarded by this vehicle before, while the ReadytoForward message list, denoted as $\mathcal{R}$, stores messages which have not been transmitted but can be forwarded some time later. The *SERs* set $\mathcal{F} \bigcup \mathcal{R}$ includes all the *SERs* related to event i. Whenever receiving an SER, the aggregator should check if this SER is a duplicate. If yes, such an SER will be dropped; otherwise it will be put into the message list $\mathcal{R}$. Before the forwarded propagation, the aggregator will perform the SER aggregation (or *Aggregate_SER*) and SER batch verification (*BatchVerify_SER*) operations as follows.

8.5.5.1 SER Aggregation. *Aggregate_SER* is used to aggregate multiple SERs into a single SER, which includes two steps: *syntactic aggregation* and *cryptographic aggregation*.

1. *Syntactic Aggregation.* For emergency event i, given n SERs $SER_j^i = (Type_i, Loc_i, \mathcal{V}_j, Time_j^i, Sig_j^i, Cert_j)$ by vehicles $\mathcal{V}_j, j = 1, \dots, n$, we can obtain syntactically aggregated SER as $SER_{agg} = (Type_i, Loc_i, \mathcal{V}_1, \dots, \mathcal{V}_n, Time_1^i, \dots, Time_n^i, Sig_1^i, \dots, Sig_n^i, Cert_1, \dots, Cert_n)$.

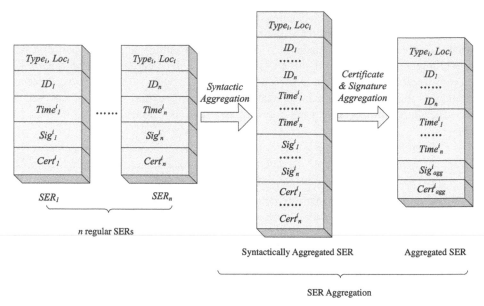

Figure 8.4. SER aggregation: syntactic aggregation and cryptographic aggregation.

2. *Cryptographic Aggregation.* This is used to aggregate multiple signatures and certificates into a single signature and certificate, which includes the following two steps:

 a) Certificate aggregation: $Cert_{agg} \leftarrow (\mathcal{V}_j, X_j, \sigma_{agg})$, where $\sigma_{agg} \leftarrow \prod_{j=1}^{n} Cert_j$.

 b) Signature aggregation: $Sig_{agg} \leftarrow \prod_{j=1}^{n} Sig_j^i$.

This aggregation procedure is illustrated in Fig. 8.4. After syntactic aggregation and cryptographic aggregation, we can obtain the aggregated SER as $SER_{agg} = (Type_i, Loc_i, \mathcal{V}_1, \dots, \mathcal{V}_n, Time_1^i, \dots, Time_n^i, Sig_{agg}, Cert_{agg})$.

8.5.5.2 SER Batch Verification. *BatchVerify_SER* includes batch signature and certificate verification which are given as follows:

1. *Certificate Batch Verification.* Given an aggregated certificate $Cert_{agg} \leftarrow (\mathcal{V}_j, X_j, \sigma_{agg})$, the verifier accepts, if $e(\prod_{j=1}^{n} \sigma_j, g) = e(\prod_{j=1}^{n} h_j, pk)$ holds.

2. *Signature Batch Verification.* Given the aggregate signature Sig_{agg}, the message set $SER_i^j| \leq i \leq n$ and public keys $X_i| \leq i \leq n$ for all the vehicles in set $\mathcal{V}$, accept if $e(Sig_{agg}, g) = e(a, \prod_{i=1}^{n} X_i) \times e(b, \prod_{i=1}^{n} X_i^{w_i})$.

If the batch verification holds, the aggregator will accept SERs in list $\mathcal{R}$ as valid SERs. Then the aggregated SER in $\mathcal{R}$ will be forward-propagated. Meanwhile, the aggregator will put all the SERs in $\mathcal{R}$ to message list $\mathcal{F}$. Once the total number of $\mathcal{F}$

exceeds k, this emergency event $\mathcal{E}_i$ will be accepted as a valid emergency event. The above algorithm is summarized in Algorithm 4.

Algorithm 4: SER Aggregated Authentication

Data: **Input** $(\mathcal{F}, \mathcal{R}, SER')$
Result: **Output** valid or invalid
begin
    if $|\mathcal{F}|+|\mathcal{R}| < k$ **then**
        for *any newly received SER'* **do**
            if *SER'* $\notin \mathcal{F} \cup \mathcal{R}$ **then**
                | *Add_List($\mathcal{R}$, SER')*
            end
            else Drop *SER'*

        end
        SER_agg $\leftarrow$ *Aggregate_SER($\mathcal{R}$)*
        if *BatchVerify_SER($\mathcal{R}$)* **then**
            ForwardPropagation($\mathcal{R}$)
            Add_List($\mathcal{F}$, $\mathcal{R}$)
        else
            return *invalid*
        end
    end
    else Accept emergency event as True

    return valid
end

8.5.6   SER Aggregated Trustworthiness

Traditional schemes for establishing message trustworthiness depend mainly on the number of witnesses to emergencies, and are implemented through social validation (the actions of many reflect the "correct" behavior), or voting mechanisms using digital signature techniques. Instead, the proposed scheme considers many different factors that can determine the trustworthiness of the emergency messages. These contextual factors can be aggregated into a single coefficient called *aggregated trustworthiness*. As shown in Fig. 8.5, aggregated trustworthiness can include, but is not limited to, witnesses, authority and credibility of source, message broadcasting direction, geolocation (including the location of the witness vehicle, and the location of the accident), roadway maintenance history, weather conditions, and road conditions. We can use suitable contextual information to judge whether an emergency message is trustworthy, according to the types of emergencies expected on the road.

Regarding our proposed aggregated message trustworthiness scheme, the receiver collects more input (elements from aggregated trustworthiness) than existing schemes.

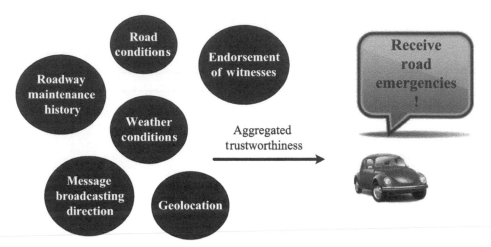

Figure 8.5. Aggregated trustworthiness of emergency messages in VANETs.

Thus, his/her judgment on the emergency message becomes more accurate and reliable. For instance, "situational information" such as "witness" is based on the number of witnesses who observe the emergency. The witnesses can cross-validate the emergency event. Typically, the more witnesses to an emergency, the higher degree of confidence recipients place in the emergency message. In other words, the emergency with more witnesses is more likely to be trusted by the recipients. In particular, an emergency message is considered trustworthy if it attains a predefined certain threshold. Also, situational information such as weather conditions and road conditions can also assist the receivers in accurately determining the trustworthy of the emergency message, particularly those related to weather. Additionally, the designated authority vehicles that have established trust with the public would be classified under "authority and credibility of sources." People are more likely to trust emergency messages originating from emergency vehicles. These emergency vehicles would include fire trucks, ambulance, and police cars. Combined with knowledge of the routing path that an emergency message travels through, we can discern the message's origin. People tend to trust messages that are sent from an affected area as opposed to ones that are secondhand accounts who haven't witnessed the accident firsthand, as shown in Fig. 8.6.

There are many types of emergency messages for each different information input, so we will illustrate our proposed methodology by discussing three typical scenarios that we observe very often on the road. In all scenarios, it is assumed that the emergency message is already authenticated to ensure the integrity and origin of message, preventing external attacks on emergency messages, before going through the following trustworthiness evaluation. To be clear, authenticity, confidentiality, and integrity posttransmission have already been established in these examples; the following is solely about establishing trustworthiness of the message contents.

The first scenario considers a car accident (and note that the following procedure can be abstracted to other warning-worthy scenarios, such as landslides, severe potholes,

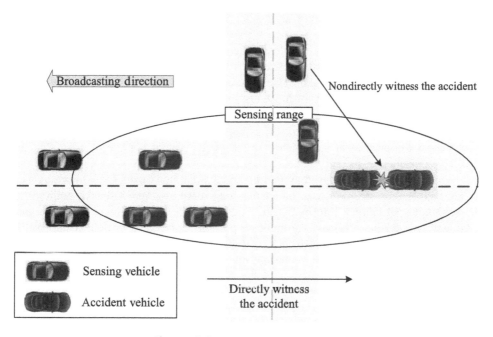

Figure 8.6. Scenario of route path.

traffic jams, etc.). First, the receiver checks to see if any witness to the emergency is an emergency vehicle; in other words, the receiver checks whether the emergency message received is signed by authority vehicle(s), and then the message is trusted by the receiver. (It is worth noting that authority vehicles are not subject to the identity privacy requirement, and their identities can be revealed to the public.) If this is not the case, the receiver relies on the witness' accounts of the accident as shown in Fig. 8.6. The broadcast message that is carried over multiple hops, from car to car, originates from the affected area (car accident scene); the broadcast path from the affected area to the receiver matches the roadmap in which is it propagated. This means that the witness is considered genuine (the witness is trustworthy) because it is from a reliable source who directly witnessed the accident, and the message has been passed along in a consistence manner.

Suppose that the message came from an area that is out of range; we cannot guarantee that the vehicle has directly witnessed the accident, based on the vehicle location reported at the time of sending. As long as the number of trustworthy witnesses reaches the previously mentioned threshold of k trusted signatures, the message is still distributed trusted. Unfortunately, in many cases, we may not have sufficient witnesses to make a decision that has a high probability of being correct; in these cases, some other situational information comes into play. For example, difficult road conditions like heavy snowfall or rainfall are challenging to drive through, causing traffic accidents and delays. Drivers are more likely to trust a message about car accidents when faced with treacherous road conditions and bad weather, or they witness traffic suddenly slowing to a crawl.

The second scenario is a road closure due to the bad weather. Drivers will receive many different emergency messages about road closures and detours due to various reasons, for example, bad weather. The receiver will filter them through weather reports that coincide with the validity of those testaments. For instance, a message issuing a blowing snow advisory on the roads when there is an accumulation amount of snowfall will be seen as being more trustworthy, as opposed to the same message sent on a day when the weather is clear, in which case the good weather conditions contradict the message contents.

The third scenario revolved around harsh cold and hot weather conditions as well other factors that are known to affect the road regularly. We will take potholes as our example. Situational information like the weather condition, road condition, and roadway maintenances history can indicate possible pothole formation. If the road is notorious for containing potholes because that area is known for its seasonal cooldown and warmup, recognized as a popular roadside used by many vehicles, and known to be infrequently maintained, we can assume that there is a high probability of potholes. As a result, a pothole warning from a vehicle in this area would be perceived as being more trustworthy than average, based on the situational arguments aligning with the message contents.

8.6 SECURITY DISCUSSION

8.6.1 Collusion Attacks

The effectiveness of AEMAT for defending against a collusion attack is based on the combination of the traceability property and the distributed trust mechanism. The traceability property ensures that any adversary sending multiple claims against a common event will be detected. As a result, an adversary can send only one SER per event. Moreover, the existence of the distributed trust mechanism guarantees that the number of adversaries in the VANET system is less than k. Consequently, even if all the adversaries collude with each other, they cannot generate k or more SERs to convince the other vehicles of the existence of a nonexistent emergency event.

8.6.2 Privacy Protection of Witnesses

In AEMAT, we propose to use randomly generated pseudonyms, as well as corresponding public key certificates to preserve the privacy of witness vehicles. To further enhance the privacy-preserving functionality of the AEMAT scheme, before joining the VANET, a vehicle can request multiple pseudonyms and corresponding public keys from the OSM. To avoid Sybil attacks, which are defined as a malicious vehicle impersonating multiple identities, we should carefully define the expiration date of public key certificates to ensure that only one pseudonym and public key certificate is valid for any time slot.

8.7 PERFORMANCE EVALUATION

In this section, we evaluate the performance of the proposed AEMAT scheme in terms of the resultant communication cost and computation overhead. To demonstrate the superiority of AEMAT, we also compare AEMAT with the existing approach in Ref. 7, which adopts the nonaggregated ECDSA signature scheme as building blocks.

8.7.1 Transmission Cost

One of the major advantages of AEMAT is the reduction of transmission cost. The communication cost is determined by the size of aggregated SERs, which is due mainly to the supporting signatures and corresponding public key certificates. To ensure the security of the protocol, the elements in G could be up to 160 bits for achieving a security level compared with ECC-160. Since the signature and certificate in AEMAT require only one element in G, respectively, the whole supporting signature plus the certificate could be represented in three G elements, or 480 bits. The approximated length of components of an SER in AEMAT is shown in Table 8.1. If we take multiple SERs into consideration and the total number of the collected SERs is n, the total size of the SERs without aggregation should be $92n$. However, in our AEMAT scheme, the total size can be reduced to $36n + 56$ by taking advantage of aggregation signature, which is also shown in Table 8.1. Under the same parameter assumption, the total size of concatenated ECDSA signatures scheme is $116n+36$ in [7], which is much longer than that of the AEMAT scheme.

8.7.2 Computational Cost

The computational costs are measured by the most expensive pairing (Pair) and point multiplication (Pmul) operation. Because of the cryptographic aggregation technique, the aggregate verification cost on n distinct signatures and certificates costs about 5 pairings, which is a significant improvement over the $3n$ pairings required by individual verification. As a comparison, ECDSA signature scheme requires $2n$ Pmul operations. By adopting the pairing technique in Ref. 14, we can obtain the approximate time costs for Pair and Pmul to be 2.82 ms and 0.78 ms, respectively. From Fig. 8.7, we can observe that the computational cost of the AEMAT scheme is constant, even if the number of SERs increases; comparatively, the computational cost of ECDSA increases with the increase of SERs until it significantly exceeds the computational costs of AEMAT.

TABLE 8.1. Size of Each Component of SER (bytes)

Component	T & L	ID	Time	Sig	Cert	Total
Size	16	8	8	20	20+20	92
Aggregated	T & L	nID	nTime	Sig_{agg}	$Cert_{agg}$	Total
Size	16	$8n$	$8n$	20	$20n+20$	$36n+56$

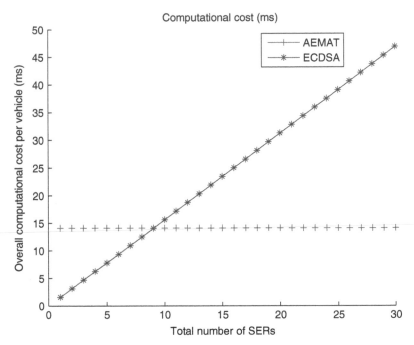

Figure 8.7. Comparing AEMAT with ECDSA-based authentication scheme with different number of SERs.

8.8　CONCLUDING REMARKS

In this chapter, we have proposed an efficient aggregated emergency message authentication and trustworthiness scheme, which can effectively address both efficiency and security issues in VANETs. Also, we aggregate multiple trustworthiness cues to provide drivers with robust and reliable ways to evaluate the trustworthiness of emergency messages they received, so as to enhance the efficiency and effectiveness of decisionmaking.

REFERENCES

1. "East coast braces for monday morning commute from hell: Winter storm threatens to bring freezing rain and has already caused 50 car pile-up in Pennsylvania," Jan. 18, 2014. (Available online at http://www.dailymail.co.uk/news/article-2520578/Winter-storm-threatens-bring-freezing-rain-car-pile-Pennsylvania.html.)

2. Kenyon Wallace, "Moose-vehicle collisions in Newfoundland at issue as computerized animal detection systems fail," Jan. 18, 2014. (Available online at http://www.thestar.com/news/canada/2012/04/19/moosevehicle_collisions_in_newfoundland_at_issue_as_computerized_animal_detection_systems_fail.html.)

3. V. Daza, J. Domingo-Ferrer, F. Sebé, and A. Viejo, "Trustworthy privacy-preserving car-generated announcements in vehicular ad hoc networks," *IEEE Transactions on Vehicular*

Technology, vol. 58, no. 4, pp. 1876–1886, 2009. (Available online at http://dx.doi.org/10.1109/TVT.2008.2002581.)

4. T. D. Little and A. Agarwal, "An information propagation scheme for VANETs," *Proc. IEEE Intelligent Transportation Systems, 2005*. IEEE, 2005, pp. 155–160.

5. H. Wu, R. Fujimoto, R. Guensler, and M. Hunter, "MDDV: a mobility-centric data dissemination algorithm for vehicular networks," *Proc. 1st ACM International Workshop on Vehicular ad hoc networks*. ACM, 2004, pp. 47–56.

6. X. Lin, H. Zhu, B. Lin, P.-H. Ho, and X. Shen, "Nis01-5: A novel voting mechanism for compromised node revocation in wireless ad hoc networks," *Proc. IEEE Global Telecommunications Conference, 2006 (GLOBECOM'06)*. IEEE, 2006, pp. 1–6.

7. M. Raya, A. Aziz, and J.-P. Hubaux, "Efficient secure aggregation in vanets," *Proc. 3rd International Workshop on Vehicular Ad Hoc Networks*. ACM, 2006, pp. 67–75.

8. B. Ostermaier, F. Dotzer, and M. Strassberger, "Enhancing the security of local danger-warnings in VANETs—a simulative analysis of voting schemes," *Proc. 2nd International IEEE Conference on Availability, Reliability and Security, 2007 (ARES 2007)*. IEEE, 2007, pp. 422–431.

9. E. A. Harvey, *Cues of Observation on Trusting and Trustworthy Behaviours*, master's thesis, McMaster University, Aug. 2011.

10. J. Jessen and A. H. Jrgensen, "Aggregated trustworthiness: Redefining online credibility through social validation," *First Monday*, vol. 17, no. 1, 2011.

11. H. Zhu, X. Lin, R. Lu, P. Ho, and X. Shen, "AEMA: An aggregated emergency message authentication scheme for enhancing the security of vehicular ad hoc networks," *Proc. IEEE International Conference on Communications, 2008 (ICC'08), Beijing: IEEE, May 19–23*, 2008, pp. 1436–1440. Available online at http://dx.doi.org/10.1109/ICC.2008.278.

12. J. Camenisch, S. Hohenberger, and M. Ø. Pedersen, "Batch verification of short signatures," *Proc. Advances in Cryptology—EUROCRYPT 2007*. Springer, 2007, pp. 246–263.

13. D. Boneh, B. Lynn, and H. Shacham, "Short signatures from the weil pairing," *Proc. Advances in Cryptology—ASIACRYPT 2001*. Springer, 2001, pp. 514–532.

14. P. S. Barreto, B. Libert, N. McCullagh, and J.-J. Quisquater, "Efficient and provably-secure identity-based signatures and signcryption from bilinear maps," *Proc. Advances in Cryptology—ASIACRYPT 2005*. Springer, 2005, pp. 515–532.

FAST HANDOVER AUTHENTICATION BASED ON MOBILITY PREDICTION

9.1 INTRODUCTION

In VANETs, a variety of vehicle applications are enabled by communication between vehicles and RSUs. One promising advantage of these applications is that they can efficiently enhance the safety of transportation. This is a promising solution for metropolitan areas, as the growing number of dangerous driving incidents could be prevented with this technology. Furthermore, with widespread vehicular networks, connecting vehicles to the Internet becomes a desirable driver requirement. Obviously, this promising application can bring not only entertainment to passengers but also economic benefits to the Internet service provider (ISP) as they would provide the network services. Nevertheless, the application may require users (driver or passengers) to register and pay for the services. Therefore, users are required to authenticate themselves before using the services.

From the technological point of view, an application that allows vehicles to gain access to the Internet is feasible, since there exist a number of routing protocols [1, 2] to achieve this. However, these protocols, for either safety-related applications or online entertainment, do not take security issues into consideration, and this drawback can cause tremendous commercial loss and potentially unsafe driving when vehicles are under malignant attack. For example, once an adversary obtains a legitimate user's identity

Vehicular Ad Hoc Network Security and Privacy, First Edition. Xiaodong Lin and Rongxing Lu.
© 2015 The Institute of Electrical and Electronics Engineers, Inc. Published 2015 by John Wiley & Sons, Inc.

and password under an insecure vehicular network without a robust authentication scheme, the adversary can arbitrarily use the user's valuable online service or even distribute the user's personal information to others. In another case, a malicious adversary impersonating a legitimate user could send a fake message to the RSU and make the RSU broadcast this fake message to other users. If the fake message is fatal, then the total loss to the whole network could be devastating. Therefore, exploiting a promising authentication scheme is a necessary and urgent issue to address. Furthermore, to avoid interrruption of the Internet service connection and achieve the seamless handoff, especially for a vehicle traveling at high speeds, a promising fast authentication scheme is preferred. Preauthentication is an efficient method of achieving fast authentication. It is often used to perform an authentication task for a mobile user in advance, thus efficiently reducing authentication delay.

Intuitively, we could consider employing the existing preauthentication approaches for mobile ad hoc networks (MANETs) [3–5] to vehicular networks because of their similar properties, for instance, nodes moving in both network paradigms. However, vehicular networks have their intrinsic features that make it unsuitable to apply the existing preauthentication schemes of MANET onto VANET. For instance, the density of nodes in a MANET is much lower than the density of vehicular networks because the roaming speed of a vehicle is much higher than the speed of a mobile station. Furthermore, the schemes in MANETs do not take advantage of the unique characteristics of vehicular networks, making them ineffective when applied into VANETs. First, the movement pattern of the mobile stations in MANETs usually has no regular mobility patterns, and the position of a mobile station in some timestamp is unpredictable. However, in a vehicular network, the route of vehicles is more regular and steady because vehicles are restricted to traveling one road and in only one direction. Second, as mentioned before, vehicles travel much faster than mobile stations in MANETs. However, a vehicles can keep a nearly constant velocity for most of their driving time except approaching intersections. Thus, these unique characteristics in VANETs are prompting researchers to explore a more efficient protocol to deal with fast handoff and fast preauthentication issues in VANETs. This chapter takes a look at the characteristics of VANETs and how vehicles are moving on the road. It presents a fast handover authentication scheme based on a vehicle's mobility prediction. According to traffic information broadcast by vehicles, the RSU is able to obtain the driving conditions of a vehicle, such as direction, acceleration/deceleration, speed, and position. We then use such information as training data, and design a mobility prediction scheme based on a multilayer perceptron (MLP) network, which has the ability to predict the possible future direction in which a vehicle will travel in. With the help of this information, we can predict with a high probability on which RSU the vehicle will hand over. As the first effort to fast handover authentication that utilizes the vehicle's movement features for predictions in VANETs, the proposed authentication scheme does not need to broadcast preauthentication profiles to all neighbor wireless access points (APs), so it dramatically reduces the Internet traffic overhead, particularly when the number of vehicles on the road is large.

The rest of the chapter is organized as follows: Section 9.2 illustrates the architecture of vehicular networks for preauthentication. Section 9.3 designs a fast handover authentication scheme based on mobility prediction in VANETs. Sections 9.4 and 9.5

analyze the security and performance of the proposed scheme, respectively. Finally, Section 9.6 draws conclusions.

9.2 VEHICULAR NETWORK ARCHITECTURE

In this section, we introduce a two-layer network architecture based on WiMax and 802.11p [6] as shown in Fig. 9.1, in which broadband wireless Internet access supports both vehicles' safety-related applications and general mobile users' entertainment-related applications.

The top layer is composed of WiMax base stations, which are interconnected through peer-to-peer wireless communication or through wired Internet connection if the base station acted as a gateway. The second layer is composed of roadside access points (APs), vehicles, and RSU. Vehicles communicate with each other with 802.11p protocol. Roadside APs work as a gateway, which transform the 802.11p packet sent by vehicles into IP packets and forward them to the upper-layer base stations. IP packets sent by the users' terminals are directly forwarded by APs. Note that RSU and AP can be integrated into a single hardware, which are current technology trends. For the purpose of the presentation, we distinguish them hereafter because they have different functions for different areas, AP for Internet access and RSU for traffic management. Through

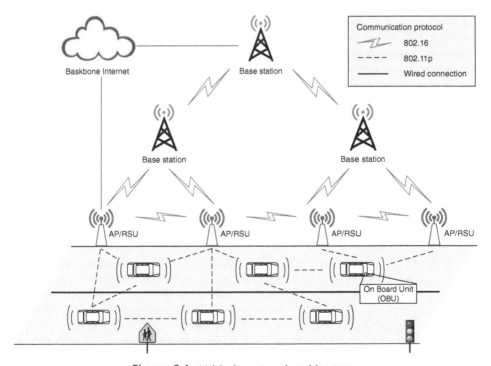

Figure 9.1. Vehicular network architecture.

this scheme, vehicles can get access to the Internet when passing through any of the roadside APs.

The transition time from one AP to another is short; thus, APs should be able support Internet services such as emails and TCP applications using fast authentication. Since onboard units (OBUs) (the communication devices on the vehicles) frequently broadcast routine traffic-related messages with information on the vehicle's position, direction, speed, acceleration/deceleration and the current time, traffic events, etc., the moving pattern of the vehicle can be tracked through these collected data by APs. Therefore, the fast authentication can be achieved using our proposed scheme of mobility prediction.

9.3 PROPOSED FAST HANDOVER AUTHENTICATION SCHEME BASED ON MOBILITY PREDICTION

9.3.1 Multilayer Perceptron Classifier

As a fundamental enabling technique of the proposed system, the preliminary knowledge about multilayer perceptron classifier is briefly introduced in this subsection.

The *multilayer perceptron* (MLP) network is a popular neural network that is based on the human brain's ability to correlate functions and classify patterns. Each neuron acts much like nodes in a large network, processing and transmitting information through signals. However, the link between neurons are given certain priority (or weight) depending on their defined pathways and proximaity of their neighboring neurons, meaning that certain neurons transfer and receive signals at a specific route that is defined (or this case, trained) for them. Thus, a neural network in which neurons are appropriately interconnected by its connection that is defined for them can achieve an "intelligent" mission such as pattern classification, clustering/categorization, function approximation, prediction/forecasting, optimization, content-addressable memory [7].

As the name implies, the MLP network consists of multiple layers, including the input layer, hidden layer (one or more sublayers), and an output layer, as shown in Fig. 9.2. It is often used for pattern classification that can find arbitrarily complex decision boundaries and represent Boolean functions [8]. The success of this design is its efficiency in approximating any desired function and achieving great accuracy given that enough neurons and layers are known. The number of neurons of an input layer is determined by the number of dimensions of input data space, while the number of sublayers of a hidden layer and neurons in each sublayer depends on the complexity of classification. Roughly speaking, the more sublayers and neurons the hidden layer has, the more accurate the result of the classifications is. However, as the number of neurons increases, the time consumed on training the network increases as well. Thus, in most cases, a tradeoff is required. For classification purpose, the number of neurons of an output layer is equal to the number of classes, and each neuron stands for each class. As a MLP classifier, there is two phases: classification phase and training phase.

In the *classification phase*, from the input layer to the output layer, each neuron sums up all data coming from the neuron of the previous intermediate neighbor layer. Before summation, each dataset is multiplied by a weight, which is obtained from a

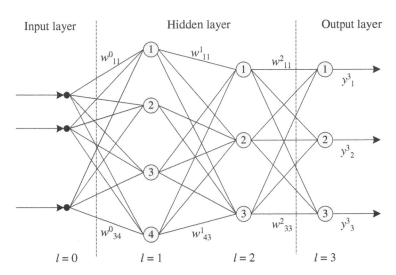

Figure 9.2. A three-layer perceptron network.

training process. At the output layer, the neuron having the largest summation value indicates that the input data belongs to the neuron (the class).

With L representing the number of the layer, the input layer l is equal to 0 (as shown in Fig. 9.2), and the next layer connecting with the input layer l is equal to 1, etc. Let w_{ij}^l represent the weight of a link that connects the ith unit of the layer l with the jth unit of the layer $l + 1$. Furthermore, the notation y_i^l represents the output of the ith unit of the layer l, $g(.)$ represents an activation function such as sigmoid function, and x_i represents the ith element of an input vector. Therefore, the classification algorithm is presented as follows:

1. Compute $y_i^0 = g(\sum_{i=1}^u x_i \times w_{ij}^l)$ for the input layer.
2. Compute $y_i^l = g(\sum_{i=1}^u y_i^{l-1} \times w_{ij}^l)$ for the hidden or output layer, where $l = 1, 2, \ldots, L - 1$.
3. Return i such that $\arg \max_i \{y_i^{L-1}\}$.

In the *training phase*, the objective is to find a suitable weight for each link based on a large number of training samples and their corresponding desired output, so that these weights can properly classify the result. Compared with the classification phase, the training phase is relatively complicated. The typical training algorithm is the backpropagation algorithm [9] that calculates the gradient of the error of the network. Through the learning process, the errors propagate backward from output layer to input layer, and the weights of the network are modified to minimize any error that might happen next time. Generally, the backpropagation algorithm follows these steps [7]:

1. Initialize the weights w_{ij}^l to small random values.
2. Randomly choose an input pattern X^u, and propagate the signal forward through the networks.

3. Compute δ_i^L in the output layer; $\delta_i^L = g'(h_i^L)(d_i^u - y_i^L)$, where h_i^L represents the net input to the ith unit in the Lth layer, d_i^u represents X^u's desired output, and $g'(.)$ is the derivative of the function $g(.)$.

4. Compute the deltas for the preceding layers by propagating the errors backward:

$$\delta_i^l = g'(h_i^l) \sum_j w_{ij}^{l+1} \delta_j^{l+1} \ for \ l = 1, 2, \dots, L - 1.$$

5. Update w_{ij}^l using $\Delta w_{ij}^l = \eta \delta_i^l y_j^{l-1}$.

6. Go to step 2 and repeat for the next pattern until the error in the output layer is below a threshold or a maximum number of iterations is reached.

9.3.2 Proposed Authentication Scheme

Our proposed seamless authentication scheme is composed of the following four phases: initial vehicle authentication phase, movement prediction phase, preauthentication phase, and handover phase.

9.3.2.1 Phase I: Initial Vehicle Authentication.
Before a vehicle (denoted by V) can gain access to the Internet service, it has to process a mutual authentication with an authentication–authorization–accounting (AAA) server. Since the current protocol standard by which devices or applications communicate with an AAA server is the remote authentication dial-in user service (RADIUS) [10], it is also known as RADIUS server. As shown in Fig. 9.3, V first initiates an association request to its nearest AP,

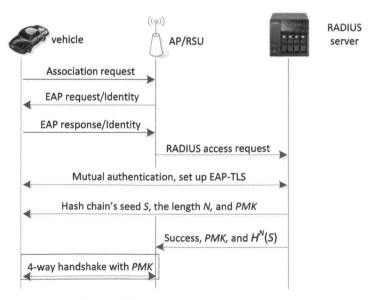

Figure 9.3. Initial vehicle authentication.

and then the same AP sends an Extensible Authentication Protocol (EAP) request back to ask for V's identity. On receiving the identity of V, the AP sends an RADIUS access request along with V's identity to the AAA server. Afterward, the AAA server and V establishes a mutual authentication based on the public key infrastructure. Once they verify each other, a secure channel like transport layer security (TLS) can be set up. Note that the AP here is transparent between V and the AAA server; it just forwards messages for both of parties.

In order for V to gain access to the AP, the AAA server generates a pairwise master key (PMK) for them. In addition, the AAA server creates a seed S and length N, which are used to generate a one-way hash chain, and sends them to V. The length N indicates that V can go through at most N APs before it disconnects with the Internet service; thus, N should be large enough to maintain a steady connection. At the same time, $H^N(S)$ is also created by the AAA server, and is sent together with the PMK to the AP. In order to enhance the speed of generating $H^N(S)$, the AAA server can create a set of tuples, $< S, N, H^N(S) >$ offline. Finally, V and the AP (having received the PMK) begin a four-way handshake to negotiate security parameters for the 802.11 protocol.

After V has gained access to the Internet, it can use the seed S and the length N, which are obtained from the AAA server, to generate a hash chain for future authentications. Since generating the hash chain is done after the initial authentication and before V's first handover to the next AP, it does not increase the authentication delay to the next AP. Also, it is worth pointing out that the AP has knowledge of only one hash chain element, $H^N(S)$, but not other hash chain elements.

9.3.2.2 Phase II: Movement Prediction.

In this phase, the AP that a vehicle is currently associated with does a movement prediction to judge which AP the vehicle should hand over in the near future. This phase is a preparation for phase III. The vehicle's movement prediction comprises two scenarios: along a road and at an intersection. There are only two directions in which a vehicle would go in the first scenario, either frontward or backward. In this scenario, we define a R^3 space, where a sample in the space is a three-dimensional vector that is presented as follows:

$$\langle Direction, \ Speed, \ Acceleration \rangle \tag{9.1}$$

Here, *Direction* denotes the direction that a vehicle is going in, such as east or west; *Speed* denotes the velocity of a driving vehicle; and *Acceleration* denotes whether a driving vehicle accelerates or decelerates. If the value of the field *Acceleration* is positive, then the vehicle is accelerating. Otherwise, the vehicle is decelerating.

The vectors (X) in the R^3 space are regarded as a feature of the vehicle that can be extracted from an RSU in an offline manner. Then, these vectors as training samples are input into the multilayer perceptron classifier as represented in Section 9.3.1. The backpropagation algorithm is employed to train the weights of our classifier. In this scenario, the number of neurons in an output layer is equal to two because there are only two possible outputs, going frontward or backward. To make a decision, the larger output of the two neurons is treated as a correct result. For instance, the first neuron denotes going frontward, and the second neuron denotes going backward. If the result

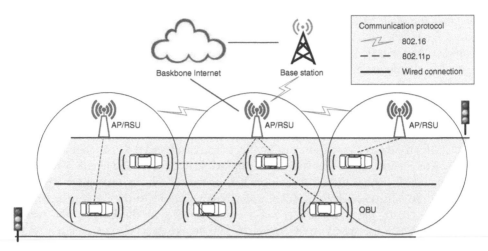

Figure 9.4. Movement direction prediction along a road.

of the output layer is that the first neuron is larger than the second, this means that the vehicle will go frontward in the near future.

In a VANET, in most cases of the first scenario, a vehicle will go forward as shown in Fig. 9.4 unless some accidents occur. However, when we take the second scenario into account, in which a vehicle is going through an intersection, the direction prediction of a vehicle will become much more complicated. Generally speaking, when a vehicle arrives at an intersection, as shown in Fig. 9.5, a vehicle can choose among four different directions. For example, a vehicle might turn left, turn right, go ahead, or perform a U-turn. Similar to the first scenario, we define a R^5 space, and a sample in the space is a five-dimensional vector as:

$$\langle Direction,\ Speed,\ Acceleration, Turn\text{-}Light,\ Traffic\text{-}Light \rangle \qquad (9.2)$$

where the first three fields have the same meaning as presented in the first scenario. The fourth field, *Turn-Light*, denotes signals of the turn light of a vehicle, particularly when a vehicle is going to turn at an intersection. As we define it, this field has five possible values, 0.2, 0.4, 0.6, 0.8, and 1, which denotes the flashing of a left-turn light, the flashing of a right-turn light, the flashing of a brake light, the flashing of both a left-turn light and a brake light, and the flashing of both a right-turn light and a brake light of the vehicle, respectively. The last field, *Traffic-Light*, indicates the color of the current traffic light: red, green, or yellow.

Similar to the first scenario, vectors (X) in the R^5 space are regarded as training samples that are also obtained from an RSU. The number of neurons of the output layers depends on how many possible directions an intersection has, and the value is equal to four in Fig. 9.5, for example. Each neuron denotes the direction that a vehicle is going to turn to, and the neuron in the output layer that has the largest value indicates the predication result.

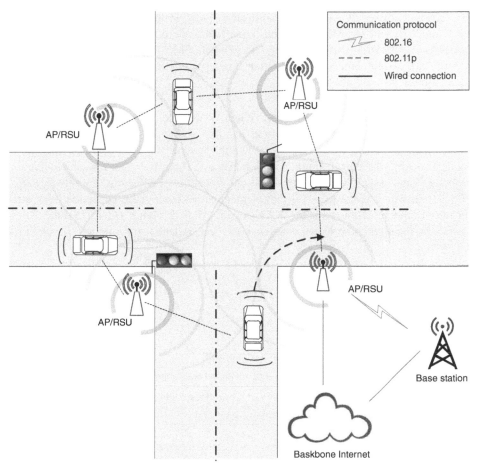

Figure 9.5. Movement direction prediction at an intersection.

With the current AP associated with the vehicle predicting its movements, the AP is able to preestablish an authentication credentials between the vehicle and the next AP that the vehicle is going to associate with in the future.

9.3.2.3 Phase III: Preauthentication.
Based on the prediction result in phase II, the AP_i (let AP_i represent the ith AP that a vehicle V is currently associated with since V's initial authentication with the AAA server) can predict which AP_i's neighbor AP will be AP_{i+1}. Before V disassociates with AP_i and hands over to AP_{i+1}, AP_i is responsible to send V's identity and corresponding authentication credentials to AP_{i+1}. Note that the communication channel between AP_i and AP_{i+1} is assumed to be secure. In particular, in our scheme, AP_i sends $H^{N-i}(S)$, $H(PMK_i)$ and V's identity to AP_{i+1}. $H^{N-i}(S)$ is the $(N-i)$th element of the hash chain given by the AP_{i-1}, and S is the hash chain's seed that is sent by the AAA server to V during the initial authentication process.

$H^{N-i}(S)$ will be used by AP_{i+1} to authenticate V. PMK_i is the pairwise master key shared by V and AP_i, and $H(PMK_i)$ is the hash of PMK_i, where $H(.)$ is a hash function such as SHA-1. $H(PMK_i)$ is used for AP_{i+1} to generate PMK_{i+1}. After AP_{i+1} receives V's identity and its authentication credentials, AP_{i+1} stores these information to its local data base for the next phase use.

9.3.2.4 Phase IV: Handover. When V detects that the signal strength of AP_{i+1} is stronger than AP_i's, V will start handing over itself to AP_{i+1} and perform an authentication process with AP_{i+1} as shown in Fig. 9.6. V first initiates an association request to AP_{i+1} to start the authentication process. Then, AP_{i+1} returns an association response, and asks for its authentication credentials. Afterward, V gives AP_{i+1} $H^{N-i-1}(S)$, which is the $(N-i-1)$th element of the hash chain generated by V after its initial authentication with the AAA server. After receiving $H^{N-i-1}(S)$, the AP_{i+1} checks its local database to see whether it has V's credential information. If so, AP_{i+1}

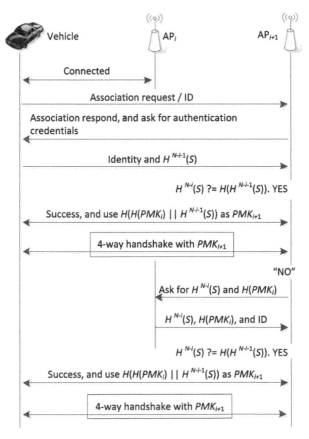

Figure 9.6. Vehicle preauthentication.

verifies whether $H^{N-i}(S)$ is equal to $H(H^{N-i-1}(S))$. If equal, AP_{i+1} notifies V that the authentication is approved. Since both V and AP_{i+1} have the same $H(PMK_i)$ and $H^{N-i-1}(S)$, they can generate $H(H(PMK_i)||H^{N-i-1}(S))$ as their pairwise master key, and a separate process creates PMK_{i+1}.

If AP_{i+1}'s local database does not have V's credential information, this means that the result of V's movement predicted by AP_i is wrong (in Section 9.5, the performance result shows that the probability of the wrong prediction is very small). In this case, AP_{i+1} immediately asks AP_i for $H^{N-i}(S)$ and $H(PMK_i)$ associated with V's identity. After receiving these information, AP_{i+1} checks again whether $H^{N-i}(S)$ is equal to $H(H^{N-i-1}(S))$. Similar to the abovementioned content, if the two items are equal, V is authenticated; otherwise, V is denied. The last step of the scheme is to perform a four-way handshake.

After AP_{i+1} has successfully authenticated V, it deletes V's credential information from its local database. AP_{i+1} collects V's movement feature information to form a five- or three-dimensional vector as was defined in phase II, and predicts which of its AP neighbors is AP_{i+2} for V to hand over in a near future. Then, AP_{i+1} repeats the phase II process.

9.4 SECURITY ANALYSIS

In this section, we analyze the security properties of our proposed scheme. In particular, we will show how the scheme can effectively resist replay attack and provide forward secrecy.

9.4.1 Replay Attack

Suppose that an adversary is attempting to launch a replay attack, and replays the authentication credentials from a previous session in order to impersonate a legitimate vehicle. This impersonation cannot work in our proposed scheme because of the adoption of a one-way hash chain, which is generated after V initializes a full authentication with the AAA server. Because of the property of the one-way hash chain, the adversary holding $H^{N-i}(S)$ cannot calculate $H^{N-i-1}(S)$ unless s/he can obtain the seed of the hash chain S. Since a secure channel, EAP-TLS, is used by the AAA server and V to transmit the seed S, it is infeasible for the adversary to eavesdrop the seed S.

9.4.2 Forward Secrecy

Forward secrecy should satisfy the requirement that the pairwise master key, PMK_i shared by V and AP_i for example, cannot be recovered by AP_{i+1}. In our scheme, AP_i only gives $H(PMK_i)$ to AP_{i+1}, which uses it to generate the pairwise master key PMK_{i+1}, so AP_{i+1} holding $H(PMK_i)$ cannot calculate PMK_i again, due to the property of the one-way hash function. Therefore, the proposed fast handover authentication scheme can provide forward secrecy.

9.5 PERFORMANCE EVALUATION

In an effort to evaluate the performance of the proposed preauthentication scheme, the accuracy rate of the direction prediction of a vehicle's movement plays an important role. Hence, the primary issue is to calculate the accuracy rate of the direction prediction of a vehicle's movement. There are two possible driving scenarios to study: (1) where a car drives into an intersection and (2) where a car drives alongside a road. Since scenario 1 is much more complicated than scenario 2, without loss of generality, we take the first one as a test environment. Specifically, the physical location, 398 Westmount Rd. N, Waterloo, Ontario, Canada, is taken as our test intersection, which is shown in Fig. 9.7 [11]. Eight hundred samples are collected, and each sample is a five-dimensional vector, where each element of the vector is the same as presented before. In our dataset, *Direction* is toward the west, and *Speed* records the instant velocity of a vehicle. In addition, the *Addition* field provides the information about traffic light, such as red, yellow, green, and left-arrow green. Since it is forbidden for a vehicle to U-turn at that intersection, the desired output of a vehicle's movement is turning left, turning right, and going straight ahead.

A three-layer perceptron is employed, and the number of neurons of the input layer is equal to five, where each presents a feature. The number of neurons of the hidden layer is equal to 10, and the number of neurons of the output layer is equal to three, where the biggest associated output on the neuron denotes the responding decision. The dataset is divided into two parts, a training set with 600 samples and a testing set with 200 samples.

Table 9.1 presents data on the accuracy of the prediction. There are a total of 200 samples for testing. In this study, 71 out of 200 vehicles turned left at the intersection, and

Intersection of Westmount Road and
Columbia Street, Waterloo, ON, Canada

Figure 9.7. Intersection of the data collection.

TABLE 9.1. Performance of Movement Prediction

	Turn Left	Turn Right	Go Straigth	Total
Total number	71	65	64	200
Accurate number	68	64	64	196
Accurate rate	95.7	98.4	100	98.0

68 samples are classified correctly; 65 out of 200 vehicles turned right at the intersection, and 64 samples are classified correctly; 64 out of 200 vehicles went straight ahead at the intersection, and 64 is classified correctly. Thus the total accuracy rate is 98.0%. The key reason why the wrong prediction occurs is traffic violations. For example, some vehicles do not show their left-turn (right-turn) light when they turn left (right), or even indicate the wrong turn light.

Based on the prediction accuracy rate, the expected authentication delay T can be formulated as follows:

$$
\begin{aligned}
T &= T_1 \times p + (T_1 + T_2) \times q \\
  &= T_1 \times p + (T_1 + T_2) \times (1 - p) \\
  &= T_1 + T_2 \times q
\end{aligned}
\tag{9.3}
$$

where p denotes the probability of the correct prediction, and q is the probability of a wrong prediction. The notation q is also equal to $1 - p$. T_1 denotes the authentication delay when the prediction is accurate. In this case, T_1 is equal to the time used for verifying whether $H^{N-i}(S)$ is equal to $H(H^{N-i-1}(S))$ as presented in Section 9.3.2.4. $T_1 + T_2$ denotes the authentication delay when the prediction is not accurate. This delay is composed of two parties, T_1 and T_2. T_2 is equal to a two-message transmission delay. As presented in Section 9.3.2.4, the two messages are composed of a request message sent by AP_{i+1} to AP_i and a response message containing $H^{N-i}(S)$ associating V's identity. The final result of Eq. (9.3) shows that the expected authentication delay is linearly dependent on the accuracy of the prediction rate. The maximum is equal to $T_1 + T_2$, and the minimum is equal to T_1.

From the performance result in Table 9.1, our proposed movement prediction scheme based on a MLP classifier can achieve very high accuracy; thus, the expected authentication delay is tightly closed to the minimum delay T_1. Obviously, T_1 is the time spent on doing a hash function operation and, therefore, shows that the time is rather small.

9.6 CONCLUDING REMARKS

To address the fast authentication issue in VANETs, a novel and seamless authentication scheme based on the combination of mobility prediction with a MLP and a one-way hash chain is proposed in this chapter. This scheme takes advantage of unique features of VANETs. It can achieve a high accuracy rate of vehicles' movement predication, as our experiment and theoretical analysis have concluded. We have determined that with the help of movement prediction authentication in VANETs, the scheme can effectively reduce the authentication delay.

REFERENCES

1. E. H. H. Alshaer, "An optimized adaptive broadcast scheme for inter-vehicle communication," *Proc. 61th IEEE Vehicular Technology Conference*, IEEE, 2005, pp. 2840–2844.

2. Z. A. Y. Peng and J. M. Chang, "Roadside-aided routing (rar) in vehicular networks," *Proc. IEEE International Conference on Communication*, IEEE, 2006, pp. 3602–3607.

3. S. Pack and Y. Choi, "Fast handoff scheme based on mobility prediction in public wireless LAN systems," *IEE Proceedings Communications*, vol. 10, no. 5, 2004.

4. N. P. T. C. C. A. Mishra, M. Shin, and W. A. Arbauch, "Proactive key distribution using neighbor graphs," *IEEE Wireless Communication*, vol. 11, no. 1, pp. 26–36, 2004.

5. H. Z. P.-H. H. X. S. Xiaodong Lin, and Xinhua Ling, "A novel localised authentication scheme in IEEE 802.11 based wireless mesh networks," *International Journal of Security and Networks*, vol. 3, no. 2, pp. 122–132, 2008.

6. "IEEE 802.11, standard specification for wireless local area networks," http://standards.ieee.org/wireless/.

7. K. M. M. K. Jain and J. Mao, Artificial neural networks: A tutorial, *Computer*, vol. 29, no. 3, pp. 31–44, 1996.

8. M. Minsky and S. Papert, *Perceptrons: An Introduction to Computational Geometry*, MIT Press, Cambridge, MA, 1969.

9. D. E. Rumelhart and J. L. McClelland, *Parallel Distributed Processing: Exploration in the Microstructure of Cognition*, MIT Press, Cambridge, MA, 1986.

10. A. R. W. S. C. Rigney and S. Willens, *Remote Authentication Dial in User Service (Radius)*, IETF RFC 2865, 2000.

11. "Google maps," http://maps.google.ca/.

INDEX

Vehicular Ad Hoc Network Security and Privacy, First Edition. Xiaodong Lin and Rongxing Lu.
© 2015 The Institute of Electrical and Electronics Engineers, Inc. Published 2015 by John Wiley & Sons, Inc.

IEEE Press Series on
Information and Communication Networks Security (ICNS)

Series Editor, **Stamatios Kartalopoulos, PhD**

Mission Statement:
This series provides high quality technical books on Information and Communication Networks Security Theory and Technology. The series is interested in the security aspects of all types of communication networks (wireless, wired, optical, quantum, chaotic, hierarchical, non-hierarchical, IP, ad-hoc, cloud, and so on), and in the security of information transported through their nodes and across them. Our security interests are on all levels of the OSI model, from the network physical layer to the application layer, on the node level and end-to-end, and on all levels of mathematical and technical complexity. Books are intended for professionals, researchers, and students, as well as for private, academic and government organizations.

1. *Security of Information and Communication Networks*
   Stamatios V. Kartalopoulos

2. *Engineering Information Security: The Application of Systems Engineering Concepts to Achieve Information Assurance w/CD*
   Stuart Jacobs

3. *Public Key Cryptography: Applications and Attacks*
   Lynn Margaret Batten

4. *Quality of Service in Optical Packet Switched Networks*
   Akbar Ghaffarpour Rahbar

5. *Vehicular Ad Hoc Network Security and Privacy*
   Xiaodong Lin and Rongxing Lu